The Women's Khutbah Book

Ə𝖜Ə

The Women's Khutbah Book

Contemporary Sermons on Spirituality and Justice from around the World

Sa'diyya Shaikh and Fatima Seedat

With an Edited Collection of New Khutbahs

Yale

UNIVERSITY PRESS

NEW HAVEN AND LONDON

Yale University Press books may be purchased in quantity for educational, business, or promotional use. For information, please e-mail sales.press@yale.edu (U.S. office) or sales@yaleup.co.uk (U.K. office).

"The Subject Tonight Is Love," from the Penguin publication *The Subject Tonight Is Love: 60 Wild and Sweet Poems of Hafiz* by Daniel Ladinsky, copyright 2003, is used with permission.

Designed by Sonia L. Shannon.
Set in Fournier type by Integrated Publishing Solutions.
Printed in the United States of America.

Library of Congress Control Number: 2021948035
ISBN 978-0-300-24416-8 (hardcover : alk. paper)

A catalogue record for this book is available from the British Library.

This paper meets the requirements of ANSI/NISO Z39.48–1992 (Permanence of Paper).

10 9 8 7 6 5 4 3 2 1

To courageous Muslim futures
All around the world Muslim feminists have planted
the seeds for change: we await the blossoming.

Contents

Introduction   1

1. FROM THE *MUSALLAH* TO THE MINBAR:
   Tracing Women's Presence in the Mosque   7

2. A *TAFSIR* OF EXPERIENCE: *Spirituality,
   Embodiment, and Knowledge*   19

   Engaged Surrender, *by amina wadud*   20

   Feminist Ontologies: *Rahmah* and *'Adl*   29

   An-Nur (Divine Light), *by Shaykha Oumou Malik Gueye*   31

   Khutbah al-Muwaddah lil Ghuraba—For the Love of the
        Queer Strangers, *by Ghazala Anwar*   38

   Ethics of Gender Justice, *by Omaima Abou Bakr*   46

   Resisting the Satanic Principle, Recovering *Maslahah*,
        by Rabeya Müller   52

   This Speaking Earth, *by Rabia Terri Harris*   59

   Subjectivity and Consciousness: *Ihsan*   67

   The Gift of Four Human Births, *by Nur Rofiah*   69

   Spirituality of the Ordinary, *by Sa'diyya Shaikh*   74

   The Overview Effect, *by Sheena Baharudin*   81

   Darkness to Dawn and the Spiritual Journey In Between,
        by Amira Quraishi   87

   Ramadan: The Divine Treatment, *by Shaykha Amina Teslima
        al-Jerrahi (Edlín Ortiz Graham)*   94

   Sociality and Difference: *Maslahah*   103

   Knowing in and through Difference, *by Fatima Seedat*   105

God's Command for Justice in the Qur'an, *by Gwendolyn*
Zoharah Simmons   111

Rethinking Shari'ah—A Guidance and a Mercy,
by Sherin Khankan   119

No Justice, No Peace: Social Justice as an Islamic Imperative,
by Tamsila Tauqir   126

Resisting Injustice: *Ummah* and *Ubuntu*   135

Our People First: Reclaiming the Spirit of June 16, 1976,
by Tshegofatso Masibi   137

Black Consciousness and Intersectionality: Toward Social
Justice and Spiritual Growth, *by Leila Khan*   143

A Self-Reflexive Response to Gender-Based Violence in Our
Communities, *by Nafisa Patel*   150

Black Muslim Women Preserving Islam in Women-Headed
Households, *by Sindile Amina Ngubane*   157

Knowing God, Seeking Justice, *by Zainah Anwar*   165

Knowing God, Opening the Heart, *by Farah Zeb*   171

Marriage: *Mawaddah* and *Mithaq*   179

Marriage: Foundation for a Peaceful Society, *by Musdah Mulia*   181

Two Wedding Khutbahs, *by Seemi Ghazi*   187

Divine Love, Human Love: Marriage as Heart-Cultivation,
by Sa'diyya Shaikh   195

Not a *Nikah* Khutbah, *by Fatima Seedat*   198

3. CONCEPTUALIZING A *TAFSIR* OF
   EXPERIENCE   201

4. A PRACTICAL GUIDE TO WRITING
   KHUTBAHS   213

Glossary of Arabic Terms   221
Notes   225
Acknowledgments   237
General Index   239
Index of Qur'anic Verses   246
Index of Hadiths   248

The Women's Khutbah Book

Introduction

If only Sakina were not such a perfectionist. Third daughter of Umm Fu'ad, connoisseur of Syrian dates, ardent camel-rider, and markswoman extraordinaire, she had spent hours making arrows for the archery competition to be held the next day. And she had to get each one exactly right—the balance, the weight, the sharpness of the point; meticulous precision was required to find their target at the tournament. She'd trained for months—she had to win this year. Now she might be late for the *tarawih* prayer!

Tonight she was spoiled for choice. She could accompany her parents on the long journey to the mosque of the Prophet. Who would not want to bask in the incandescent presence of the Messenger of God, the emissary of divine words? Or she could attend the local congregation led by Umm Waraqa, protégé of the Messenger himself and the only person invited to lead another congregation, on this far side of the city. In a split second, she decided on the latter, not only because Umm Waraqa was a sage of some distinction, known for her uplifting *nasiha* (spiritual teachings) and her melodic Qur'an recitation when leading prayers, but also because a woman leading congregational prayer, an *imamah*, nourished Sakina's ardent heart.

It was said that the Messenger had deliberately chosen Umm Waraqa to lead this mixed congregation to establish a sunnah of women's *imamah*, even when Umm Waraqa preferred to go to battle.[1] But sustained by her deep love for the Prophet, Umm Waraqa stayed and weaved her own personal experiences into her spiritual teachings so that they contained both the prophetic wisdom and her unique perspective of the world. So Sakina decided to take the Prophet's prudent intentions of inclusivity to heart. She hastened to the *musallah* (prayer space) in the courtyard of Umm Waraqa. Men and women of the neighborhood were performing their sunnah prayers. Sakina spotted a place in the first row, just before the minbar (pulpit). Did the Messenger not say that the first row in the mosque, fragrant with angelic presence, was the best of all rows for worshippers? She determinedly made her way to the front and sat down, just as the powerful Umm Waraqa began to speak.

Sakina was captivated by Umm Waraqa's ability to traverse an array of social and spiritual concerns. Her profound existential insights were rivaled only by her sharp analyses of the political challenges within the community. Sakina experienced a shimmer of loving inspiration; Umm Waraqa made obvious that she, Sakina, just like every Muslim in that congregation, was directly responsible for their collective well-being. The integrity of the community depended on all of them, each one the subject of divine teaching. Echoing quietly to herself the poetic insistence of Umm Salamah, wise wife of the Prophet, Sakina thought, "Indeed, I too am one of the people."[2]

This creative portrait of a fictional young woman, Sakina, imagines an encounter with the historical Umm Waraqa in an effort to retrieve marginalized traces of women's power in the early Muslim community, traces that have been buried for much of Muslim history. From the inception of the prophetic message of Muhammad, peace be upon him, the gender-egalitarian imperatives of that message vied with dominant patriarchal forces and were attacked and diminished, but not eliminated. Social forces reflect a trajectory that shifts from women's early inclusion to increasing marginalization and exclusion, and finally to a return to the minbar. Through time, the resistant spirit of powerful female ancestors has persisted, and that spirit continues to inspire an Islam of prophetic, revolutionary justice, capturing for future communities the historical reality that the Prophet Muhammad appointed a woman to lead congregational prayer. Exciting social changes are unfolding in the contemporary period, supported by engaged, critical rereadings of historical sources; communities in diverse contexts have begun to embrace gender-inclusive ideas of religious community and authority.

Today, women no longer are only congregants in the mosque but also are leading communal prayers, officiating at public ceremonies, and participating in mosque governance. In other contexts, entirely new and inclusive congregations that challenge fixed notions of gender and sexual diversity have emerged. Most recent is the development of mosques in the United States and Europe that are exclusively led by and for women. While the precedent for exclusively women-led mosques has existed in China for hundreds of years, the appeal of women-only mosques in the present historical moment has created transnational conversations that signify a meaningful shift in contemporary debates about gender and religious authority.

Khutbahs, or sermons, produced by women entering into spaces of religious authority reveal an innovative body of religious knowledge and literature. This book gathers women-produced khutbahs to constitute an incipient archive of knowledge production and wisdom rooted in women's lived social, religious, and spiritual experiences. It offers a pioneering primary source text of contemporary Muslim women's voices at the minbar, some of whom had not previously presented a khutbah. The first aim of this book is to present their ideas as a source of feminist Muslim theology. Each khutbah appears alongside a biographical essay by its author that conveys insights into her life experience and the sociohistorical context for her khutbah. The combination of sermon and reflective essay illustrates that the journey to the minbar is integral to the knowledge presented in the khutbah.

Mediating belief and conscience through personal experiences, the women who present these khutbahs, the *khatibahs,* produce a theology drawn from their own experiences and understandings of the Qur'an and tradition. Critical interpretations of the Qur'an, or exegesis (*tafsir*), rely on the knowledge and worldview of the exegete, traditionally the male *mufassir* (author of the *tafsir*). Given the historical marginalization of women in the field of formal Qur'anic interpretation and ethics, Sa'diyya Shaikh conceptualizes the "*tafsir* of praxis," focusing on how women use their lived experiences to give meaning to Qur'anic ethics.[3] Building upon this, in our reading of the *khatibah*'s practices we find a *tafsir* of women's experience projected into Muslim publics that constitutes authoritative meaning-making beyond the personal and into the realm of public authority. Their khutbahs signify a development from the authority of women's experience, as initially conceptualized by Shaikh, to the experience of authority represented when women enter and shape the minbar as *khatibahs*.

Coming to the minbar, women move from being positioned as secondary, marginalized subjects in a public conversation among men to interlocutors themselves producing public knowledge. This movement shifts the locus of knowledge production away from the illusion of a disembodied male universal toward the realities of embodied gendered subjectivity that inform all ways of knowing.

Building upon the *tafsir* of praxis with the intention to expand our horizons for communal leadership requires what we call a *tafsir* of possibility. Ascending the minbar requires women moving from lived experiences of marginalization to imaginaries of inclusion. Such pioneers reconfigure Muslim social repertoires and bring new epistemological, ethical, and political possibilities out of the realm of the "unthinkable" into manifest reality. In other words, once women and other marginalized individuals arrive at the minbar, the authority of their experience also translates into new imaginaries of being and generative modes for becoming for the entire community. Similarly, feminist approaches to authority shift us from hierarchical power to diffuse power produced through lateral networks, exemplified by the *khatibahs*. Thus the presentation of the *khatibahs* through their autobiographies serves the second aim of this book, namely, to foster an epistemological inclusivity that we suggest enables a *tafsir* of possibility.

The third aim of this book is to constitute a virtual minbar providing resources for communities seeking to develop egalitarian khutbah practices. The book is a Muslim feminist project, articulated sometimes as Islamic feminism and more broadly as Muslim feminist engagements with tradition, drawing on a genealogy of Islamic teachings originating in the revolutionary prophetic impulse toward social and spiritual equality of all people. It is an intentionally disruptive engagement with the traditional khutbah genre.

The first Friday khutbah delivered by the Prophet is said to have taken place in a valley outside Madinah.[4] Technically, the word *khutbah* refers to a formal talk or sermon that forms part of three congregational gatherings: the Friday prayer, the two Eid prayers, and marriage ceremonies. The Friday khutbah functions as the locus of political and communal authority, an area of male preserve. Within Muslim culture a traditional genre of khutbah compilations already exists from which imams and leaders often draw their sermons. This book is an intervention into that genre, enriching and expanding it with innovative gendered transformations, offering guidance to those regularly or newly arriving at the minbar.

Beginning with the groundbreaking khutbah of Professor amina wadud offered in Cape Town, South Africa, in 1994, the collection gathers the sermons into the following five thematic clusters:

1. *Feminist Ontologies: Rahmah and 'Adl.* The contribution from Shaykha Oumou Malik Gueye presents an encompassing ontological and cosmological perspective of the unitary origin and journey of human beings. Ghazala Anwar presents a model for the living journey of faith based on the four-arched portal of *Rahmah*, loving compassion and mercy. Omaima Abou Bakr elaborates the central moral vision for humanity in the Qur'an with justice as the seed of ethical values. Rabeya Müller presents a critique of the patriarchal interpretations of the Qur'an as reflective of a Satanic logic, positing instead a restorative approach based on the common public good (*maslahah*). Rabia Terri Harris provides reflections on the spiritual roots of our ecological crisis.

2. *Subjectivity and Consciousness: Ihsan.* Nur Rofiah presents a comprehensive reflection on the nature of human subjectivity through "four births" toward the full realization of human ontological and ethical potential. Sa'diyya Shaikh reflects on the refinement of character and the cultivation of virtue in the crucible of everyday, ordinary relationships. Sheena Baharudin presents a luminous spoken-word poem on the profound intimacy and inner knowledge that human beings have of God. Amira Quraishi reflects evocatively on embracing unknowing in our spiritual journeys. Shaykha Amina al-Jerrahi elaborates on Ramadan as a time of subtle unfolding and receptivity to the Divine.

3. *Sociality and Difference: Maslahah.* Fatima Seedat's khutbah takes up issues

of ontological, social, and legal difference, holding up the Qur'anic figure of the *mujadila* ("the woman who argues") as a model of dissent that does not conclude in disbelief. Gwendolyn Zoharah Simmons demonstrates the need for interpretation beyond historically patriarchal exegesis that is aligned with justice. Sherin Khankan delves into our ideas of shari'ah to suggest important reframings of interfaith marriage and divorce. Tamsila Tauqir elicits lessons gleaned from the fallibility of the prophets and illustrates the intimate connections between our social and spiritual selves.

4. *Resisting Injustice: Ummah and Ubuntu.* Tshegofatso Masibi highlights the spirit of community and the politics of Black consciousness as they relate to the spirit of Ramadan, struggle, and sacrifice. Leila Khan's work makes further connections between contemporary social movements and the spiritual struggles for justice and equality. Nafisa Patel focuses on gender-based violence and toxic masculinities that produce endemic levels of suffering in our communities. Sindile Amina Ngubane weighs in on challenges faced by single Black mothers who are marginalized from collective and community spaces. Zainah Anwar argues that the struggle of faith and justice demands prioritization of the lives of those forced to the margins of society. Reviving an inner awareness of how to engage within a community, Farah Zeb reminds us to speak in a language that can embrace rather than alienate others.

5. *Marriage: Mawaddah and Mithaq.* In this collection of marriage khutbahs, Musdah Mulia outlines five crucial principles of marriage. Seemi Ghazi delights us with evocations of mystical love. Sa'diyya Shaikh invites us to practical ways of embodying divine qualities in our intimate relationships. Fatima Seedat's "Not a *Nikah* Khutbah" is aptly titled as content that we never hear at weddings, however much it might help us develop more enduring marital relationships.

The khutbahs are followed by the authors' reflections on the theological perspectives emerging through them, as well as practical guides for preparing a khutbah. The authors offer this book as a means of conceptualizing a new archive of feminist theology that emerges in the triangular relationship of the khutbahs, the lived experience of the *khatibahs,* and a critical analysis that identifies feminist concerns for divinity, spirituality, and the fullness of human experience.

1. From the *Musallah* to the Minbar

Tracing Women's Presence in the Mosque

Debates on women's religious authority engage with the tradition in a variety of ways as women move from the traditional location on the *musallah*, or general prayer space, toward the minbar, a space of religious authority. Muslim history possesses mixed legacies of gender, characterized by tensions and contradictions between patriarchal norms and egalitarian impulses. Recognizing a complex and diverse history of gender relations within the tradition, Islamic feminist scholarship critically engages with its patriarchal history while retrieving legacies of gender inclusivity that have emerged within that same history, arguing that the latter are more foundational to the spiritual, ethical core of Islam.[1] Those in support of women's full presence and leadership in mosque spaces call attention to historical source texts recording the inclusivity of the religious subject ushered in by Prophet Muhammad, who asserted women's personhood and agency to participate fully at all levels of the community.[2]

Through this chapter we selectively trace the debates on women's mosque presence and argue for four key conceptual moments: (1) the originary prophetic impetus of radical social change allowing for openness and gender inclusivity; (2) an interest in limiting women's mosque presence that sometimes led to almost complete exclusion (characteristic of the premodern period and entrenched in the colonial period); (3) attempts to correct women's pietistic practices and realign their mosque presence to counter popular narratives of Muslim stagnation (particularly in the postcolonial period); and

(4) radical approaches toward full gender inclusivity at the minbar. Although we trace these moments chronologically, they do not in reality function progressively but synchronously in various periods and locations. The broad strokes of women's mosque presence reflect varying instances of openness and inclusion, as well as limitation, discipline, and exclusion, maintained by enduring debate.

Radical Social Change

Muslims characteristically invest reverence, power, and authority in the early prophetic community as a model to emulate in various areas of Muslim personal and public ethics. Within the first established Muslim community in Madinah, the mosque accommodated the homestead of the Prophet Muhammad and his wives and was the spiritual and social nucleus of the emerging early Muslim community.[3] Given that the Prophet was both a religious and a political leader, the mosque was not simply a place for worship but also constituted a vibrant public square. The masjid was the space where members of the community received religious teachings, social disputes and disagreements were mediated, festivities were celebrated, communal gatherings and natterings ensued, and political decisions were deliberated; to be an early Muslim woman or man was to access, inhabit, pray, and engage with one's Prophet and fellow Muslims in the masjid.

The available sources show no evidence of physical barriers, walls, or gender-segregating partitioning between male and female believers in the Prophet's masjid in Madinah. On the contrary, they suggest that men and women within this early community had similar access to and participation in the mosque-cum-public square. The Prophet was buried in the bedroom of his wife A'ishah, within this archetypal mosque in Madinah. Similarly in Makkah, in continuity with pre-Islamic practices, women had full access to the Ka'bah and surrounding sacred precincts of the *haram* during the prophetic period. More especially, according to some traditions, it is believed that the graves of Hajar (peace be upon her) and her son, Prophet Isma'il (peace be upon him), are nestled alongside the Ka'bah within the inner courtyard of the *haram*.

The Qur'anic text is the primary source that helps us to understand the normative contours of gendered Muslim religious subjectivity and provides historical glimpses into the lived gendered practices of the prophetic period. Given that the hadith compilations (purported reports relating to the life of

Prophet Muhammad) took canonical form only in the ninth century with the nascent development of Islamic legal schools, hadith provide an important historical indicator of debates in that later period during which they were standardized into collections—notwithstanding the fact that they might also represent practices prevailing during the prophetic period. The hadith corpus includes contrary narratives relating to women's presence and leadership of prayers, which subsequently became central to emerging Islamic legal debates on the topic. Contemporary feminist debates engage these histories and source texts in a variety of modes.

Given that the Qur'an is the most reliable historical text regarding the prophetic period, we focus on it to explore original gendered Muslim practice. Nevin Reda provides a compelling overview of the types of Qur'anic evidence supporting women's presence in the mosque during the prophetic period.[4] While the Qur'an is silent on the gender of the one who leads congregational prayer, as it is on most practical matters of ritual, a number of verses support the view that the masjid in the Prophet's lifetime was indeed a public space open to believers, irrespective of gender. The Qur'an explicitly encourages the community of believers to pray in the mosque (Q. 7:29, 7:31) and admonishes those who prevent any believer from celebrating God's name in the mosque (Q. 22:25, 2:114).

Other Qur'anic verses frame core ethical and religious imperatives as explicitly gender-inclusive, including the establishment of communal prayers. For example, Q. 9:71 describes men and women believers as *awliya* (friends, protectors, allies) of one another, with the joint moral mandate to "enjoin good and forbid evil, to *establish prayers* and pay alms, and obey God and the messenger" (Q. 4:43; emphasis added).[5] This verse sets up both personal and public religious agency equally for men and women, including the performance of prayer. The term *awliya* conveys a mutually nourishing form of relations between men and women based on friendship, protection, and allyship, together enjoining virtue and rejecting vice as part of the communal Islamic sociospiritual mandate.

Furthermore, Reda points to Qur'anic verses that place Maryam (peace be upon her) in the heart of mixed congregational prayer, summoning her to prostrate and bow down together "with those that bow down" (*ma'a al-raki'in;* Q. 3:43).[6] The Qur'an's use of the masculine plural for the group of worshippers tells us that Maryam is part of an implicitly gender-inclusive congregation.[7] Yet another verse places Maryam in the *mihrab,* the innermost sanctum of the house of worship, sustained with divine provisions (Q. 3:37).

Reda alerts us that in the Qur'anic context, the *mihrab* refers to the sanctuaries reserved for the great Israelite prophets and elite group of spiritual luminaries; it included the sacred space where the Ark of the Covenant was preserved. The Qur'an presents Maryam, a woman receiving direct, intimate communion with God, in the *mihrab,* which is the sacred center of communal worship, thus rendering communal worship space as integrally gender-inclusive.

Finally, Q. 33:35 not only provides a deliberately gender-inclusive ideal for religious virtue and subjectivity, but its very revelation is prompted by a powerful gender contestation. The verse arrives in response to an explicit question raised by Umm Salamah (peace be upon her) to her husband Prophet Muhammad, asking whether revelation also addresses women. Pointedly, she interrogates the androcentric linguistic conventions of the Arabic language reflected in the Qur'an, which addresses all collectives with masculine nouns and pronouns.[8]

The subsequent revelation responds to her incisive question about the potentially exclusive reading of revelation by unambiguously asserting the full inclusion of all humanity in the address of the Qur'an. The verse, arguably one of the most explicit and purposeful scriptural articulations of spiritual and social equality among the genders, goes further than simply stating inclusion. It also demonstrates it through a shared moral vision of humanity, including deliberations on virtue, ethical conduct, and fundamental existential goals of Islam. The verse reassures believers that men and women are equally able to embody all moral virtues and that each person's value is contingent on virtue, not on gender—nor on any other criterion of human difference. The context of its revelation simultaneously discloses a lineage of critical Muslim women who not only questioned their husbands but fearlessly interrogated the Divine with sincerity and intellectual rigor.

There is thus compelling evidence suggesting that the original prophetic community was beckoned to a gender-inclusive vision of religious subjectivity and moral agency which included full participation of women in communal congregations in the mosque. This radically inclusive moral and spiritual summons of the "Muhammadi revolution"[9] was later counteracted by patriarchal social and cultural forces that sought to diminish the agency and space of women in communal spaces, already starting during the reign of Caliph Umar (634–644).[10] As the law schools developed from the ninth century in an increasingly cosmopolitan and culturally diverse Muslim empire, lively contestations on women's presence were captured in legal debates even as women were increasingly sexualized. The scholarly trend reflects an increasing anxiety about the potential threat and disturbance (*fitnah*) that men experience in the presence of women.

Asma Sayeed observes that in early juridical debates the four following kinds of hadith were invoked: (1) records of women's presence in the mosque during the prophetic era, (2) permission for women to attend mosques, (3) stipulations regarding appropriate conduct for women in mosques, and (4) encouragement of women to pray in their homes rather than attending mosques.[11] Sayeed illustrates that while there were substantially more hadith supporting women's masjid attendance, in formulating early Sunni positions, legal scholars drew on the numerically fewer hadith, with less reliable transmission chains, that deterred women from attending the mosque. This suggests an early juristic interest in limiting or prohibiting women's mosque presence. A hadith gaining increasing currency in these legal debates is one reportedly from A'ishah, who states that if the Prophet had witnessed the undesirable innovations latter-day women introduced into mosque practices, he might well have prohibited them from attendance entirely.[12] Importantly, these legal debates reflect the interests of male scholars and not necessarily the lived social realities that indicate women's continued mosque presence in diverse Muslim contexts.

Limiting Women's Presence in Mosques

The early debates on women's mosque attendance are focused through two threads associated with women praying among men, namely, the "contaminating" effects of women's presence among men and the idea that women's presence induces men to lustful thoughts. Importantly, these discussions begin in prescriptions on the transmission of ritual impurity through water used for ritual purification (*wudu*) but conclude in the prohibition of men and women praying side by side or in proximity to one another.[13] The subsequent separation of mosque spaces into demarcated areas for women's prayer ensured that male-only prayer spaces would safeguard heterosexual men from their lustful thoughts during congregational prayer. These debates, first, assumed heterosexual norms, and second, focused on women's embodied presence, which jurists treated as either transmitting ritual impurity or inciting male lust.

Among the hadith invoked in legal discussions of women's presence at congregational prayer was one that encouraged the presence of young and old women at the *salah* for the two annual festivals of the Eid.[14] It also formed the base of scholarly argument on women's mosque presence over the next five centuries until the twelfth century. By that point, this hadith that promotes women's public presence at Eid prayer was interpreted as exceptional to the time of the early Muslim community and paradoxically came to be used to argue for restrictions against women's public prayer in general. In some Hanafi positions, this hadith is used eventually to argue for excluding women from the mosque entirely.[15]

Benham Sadeghi's model of legal logic shows how early patriarchal interests are fashioned into law using the Qur'an and sunnah but that once these laws are established, they also become static.[16] Even as scholarly engagement challenges the authenticity or import of a specific hadith, as has happened with the hadith about women's congregational prayer above, the associated laws are not simply set aside. Instead, legal inertia sets in, and the law is maintained by various other processes of logic as long as the law remains reasonable to the jurists' interests.

This understanding of law-making allows us to discern how discussions on women's mosque presence preserve an early interest, which first arose in Madinah and Kufa, of male legal scholars in limiting or prohibiting women's congregational prayer.[17] Regardless of how juristic interpretations of the Qur'an and hadith evolved, whether or not local situations changed, or the ways in which women's mosque practices themselves changed, interests in limitation or prohibition remained, as a result of which women's mosque presence became a persistently debated question among some jurists. Importantly, however, the fact of women's congregational prayer at the time of the Prophet means that legal debates may not *begin* with the premise of exclusion; instead, they must argue toward it. The effect of these arguments renders women as specific types of religious subjects in that they are not considered the general or normative subject of the law. Rather, they are always situated in relation to the normative male subject of prayer and congregation.

Through the debates it also becomes clear that the jurists do not address women as a single category. Instead, women's mosque presence is argued through a series of distinctions among women so that the debates focus at different times on different concerns or different women. Therefore, against the backdrop of the hadith of the Eid congregations, early legal discussions argued not whether women could attend congregational prayer as much as which women might attend, distinguished by age and mobility or degrees of seclusion; what time of day they might attend; and how and for what purpose. We explore some of this below.

Marion Katz paints a rich and complex picture of women's mosque presence that is surprising to our ideas of the mosque activities in which women engaged. For example, we do not imagine situations where women use the mosque for work, such as spinning yarn, or for legal matters, such as taking an oath or witnessing in a legal case. We can imagine that women used the mosque to celebrate significant dates in the Muslim calendar and to attend study circles, but we probably do not imagine that they would also lecture and teach in the mosques, or spend an entire month in spiritual seclusion (*i'tikaf*) in a mosque, as they did in Basra in the first century after the Prophet's death.[18]

Equally surprising may be juristic discussions on when women could attend. The preference for either the night or the day seems to have built upon local norms. In some contexts, the prescribed time is counterintuitive to present-day concerns with nighttime safety; the cover of darkness appears then to have been preferred to conceal women from public view, especially for "secluded" women who did not ordinarily go out of their homes. In other regions it was preferred that women attend during the day, for fear that the night would be less safe. Again, the focus of the jurists' discussions was not all women; they focused on secluded, upper-class, or free women, not enslaved or working women, who ordinarily would appear in public without juristic sanction.

Moreover, a rich collection of legal discussions focuses on which women may attend the mosque on the basis of age or life stage; rulings differ for different categories of women—those who are youthful (*shabbah*) or mature (*mutajalla*), or older women (*'ajuz*).[19] By the thirteenth century, discussion shifted further to the conditions under which a woman may leave home to attend the mosque, stipulating appearance and behavior, namely, wearing humble clothing, covering the entire body, avoiding perfume, and walking inconspicuously.[20]

Alongside the distinctions among women, some juristic discussions also derogate the ontological integrity of women believers by reducing women's rewards in the afterlife for prayer. Ibn Taymiyya, for example, used the hadith promising believers a beatific vision of God equivalent to their worship on earth to argue that after death, men exclusively would enjoy this vision on a weekly basis on Fridays.[21] This devolution of women's spiritual integrity occurs as the idea of "woman" becomes tied to the idea of *fitnah*, a term used in the Qur'an to refer primarily to political conflict or strife. However, from the ninth century through to the thirteenth century, *fitnah* also becomes a gendered concept, until it is finally located primarily in women and characterized as disruptive sexuality.[22]

By the thirteenth century, legal discussions on women's mosque attendance largely concur that it is "undesirable for latter day women," almost as a paraphrase of A'ishah's earlier cited hadith.[23] Naturally, different legal schools had various positions, and some jurists resolutely argued for women's continuing mosque presence. For instance, the Hanbali school is the most facilitative of women's mosque presence, the Shafi'i school is less restrictive than the Zahiri and Hanbali, and the Hanafi school is the most restrictive. The Maliki school unusually does not recognize women-led prayer among women but simultaneously holds that women's public prayer in mixed congregations is inherently meritorious.[24]

Katz highlights the spirited defense for women's mosque presence provided by the eleventh-century Andalusian jurist Ibn Hazm. Recognizing women's full religious agency, he offers a number of reasons why women should not be excluded from attending the mosque; namely, that God surely knew what was to come in future times and did not exclude women; that women have not subsequently done anything they didn't do in the time of the Prophet to merit their later exclusion; that men behaved badly during the Prophet's time as well and were not excluded for their behavior; that if some women behaved poorly, it wouldn't make sense to exclude all women; and that women's behavior did not ban them from any other social space, so why should it apply uniquely to the mosque? Finally, responding to A'ishah's hadith suggesting the Prophet might have prevented women from attending the mosque, he argues that irrespective of this hadith, the legal discussion must recognize and follow on the fact that the Prophet did not prevent women's mosque attendance.[25]

Yet none of this prevented the later sixteenth-century Meccan ban prohibiting women from the *haram* of the Ka'bah after *'isha* (night prayer) and until *fajr* (dawn prayer).[26] The ban is said to have been caused by women's "dreadful offenses," namely, dressing beautifully, wearing perfume, and expressing joy in their spiritual practices. It prevented women from socializing, holding birth celebrations, praying late at night, and performing *tawaf* and *dhikr* celebrations in the *haram* precinct. It isn't clear when or how the ban of 1530/1531 was ended—whether simply through women's persistent presence or through scholarly refutation of its validity.[27] As with other attempts at limitation/prohibition, the failure of the ban may reflect the enduring practice of women refusing to abide by restrictions in mosque attendance, despite persistent patriarchal interest in controlling them.

In legal arguments, despite numerous pronouncements, the mosque remained among the potentially legitimate spaces for women's public presence. Legal debates could not presume the exclusion of women from mosques but had to argue for and prove why it should be so. Legal discussions were vehement and vigorous precisely to counteract the active resistance they faced from women's stubborn presence. The social reality of women's mosque presence stood squarely and resolutely in the face of arguments scholars made against it. This therefore was not a settled matter but was open to contestation, engagement, and dynamic change over time; mosque spaces either adapted to women's presence or resisted and curtailed it.

The ongoing battle between scholarly restrictions and women's presence meant that over the course of history, women's mosque attendance varied regionally. For example, three hundred years ago in China, women's mosques emerged in the minority Hui Muslim communities, starting as educational spaces located in the backyards of men's mosques and under their supervision. Although significant as women-exclusive spaces that recognized women's authority to teach and lead women in *salah*, these arrangements were not intended to challenge traditional male authority or share in its influence.

A contrary example from the more recent colonial period in Egypt shows that women's mosque practices were also affected by the gender regimes of imported British and French political, economic, and administrative systems. Here the Muslim jurists' interests in limiting women's mosque presence were bolstered by patriarchal European gender norms. Where women might have been present in public, colonial authorities established their paternalistic role by framing local practices of masculinity as barbaric until they also conformed with colonial norms that excluded women from the public sphere.[28]

Discipline and Return

By the twentieth century it appears that the exclusion of women from mosques through the colonial period, in Egypt, for example, had been sufficient to prompt arguments for the "return" of women to mosques for prayer. Although women's mosque presence for prayer had lessened, women continued attending functions outside of congregational prayer such as listening to preachers, visiting shrines, and holding celebrations, which jurists found inappropriate. The concern now was to reinstitute "appropriate" mosque practices and reestablish prayer as the primary purpose for women's presence. From Marion Katz's analysis we can suggest at least three aspects to this move: (1) women's return to mosques was also a reclamation of local Muslim authority over religious norms vis-à-vis colonial authorities; (2) it was an attempt to reform women's public pietistic practices, such as visiting shrines, toward juristically sanctioned forms of piety; and (3) it was a reaction to the colonial imaginary of Muslim backwardness, stagnation, and rigidity thought to be reflected in Muslim women's seclusion and lack of education.[29] These concerns are reflected in a fatwa of the early twentieth-century Muslim Egyptian reformer Rashid Rida, who argued for women's return to mosques and reasserted the centrality of the mosque to Muslim public life.[30]

These early twentieth-century calls to return women to mosques through normative forms of public piety were still reflected by the 1960s and 1970s in South Africa, where some newly built mosques included balconies or other spaces designated for women. Alongside this was an increasingly urgent political struggle for racial equality. Despite proportionally small numbers nationally, Muslim contributions to the anti-apartheid struggle were significant. Echoing national struggles for equality, some within the Muslim community raised critical questions of gender justice. This translated, among other things, into small groups of Muslim activists agitating for greater women's presence and participation in mosques. While many Cape-based mosques had spaces accommodating women, areas in the north of the country did not. In a convergence of Black consciousness, Islamic revivalism, and a Muslim women's equality paradigm, various attempts were made in 1994, before the first democratic elections, to open mosque spaces to women.[31] The convergence of religious and political struggles was evocatively captured in 1996 when an invitation to President Nelson Mandela to address an Eid event could not continue without also including Muslim women.

Hence through the 1990s, smaller Muslim groups formed part of a critical South African moment deeply invested in social justice, where racial and gender equality were prioritized in Muslim public life. As broader national political debates highlighted quotas for women leaders in parliament, discussion in these smaller community spaces also focused on women's religious authority. The stage was set for radically shifting the terrain of struggle; it was no longer sufficient only to include women as participants but also necessary to recognize women's leadership in mosques.

In August 1994, the year of the first post-apartheid democratic election, congregants of the Claremont Main Road Mosque in Cape Town invited Professor amina wadud, a visiting scholar and author of the pioneering work *Qur'an and Woman* (1992), to deliver what they strategically renamed the Friday "pre-khutbah talk."[32] This occasion was also accompanied by female congregants moving permanently from the balcony reserved for women into the central space of the masjid. With women standing next to, albeit separate from, men, this relocation effectively recuperated women at the Claremont Mosque from the charge of contamination made by historical legal scholarship that had generally prohibited adjacency in mixed congregations.

The address by wadud subsequently opened the minbar to women's presence at the Claremont Mosque. Because the leadership had called wadud's presentation the "pre-khutbah talk," they also had retained the necessity for the Arabic *Khutbah al-Hajah* subsequently recited by the regular imam of the mosque who also led the *Jumu'ah salah* (Friday prayers). However, that transformative moment marking the inclusion of women's voices in the role of *khatib* (despite its politicized renaming) has not translated into further substantial change at the Claremont Mosque minbar. Similarly, in 2004 a Durban-based community group, Taking Islam to the People, began an inclusive Eid congregation giving women direct access to the minbar at least twice each year. Despite women's access to the minbar in both instances, however, those spaces continue to keep male authority over the minbar intact substantively and symbolically, with mosque committee members refusing to allow women to perform the Arabic khutbah or lead the congregation in *salah*.

Inclusion at the Minbar

Following wadud's khutbah at the Claremont Mosque and advancing earlier South African Muslim struggles for gender equality, in 1995 a group of friends in Johannesburg used the offices of the Muslim Youth Movement, a nongovernmental organization, to further their struggle for inclusive leadership. In their *musallah* they developed a process of shared *imamat* (leadership) among men and women during *Jumu'ah* prayers, where women presented both the English and Arabic khutbah and led a mixed congregation in *salah*.

This undocumented revolutionary congregation in South Africa lasted quietly for two years.[33] But in 2005 women's leadership as *imamah* took a more public face in New York when amina wadud presented the khutbah and led the *Jumu'ah* prayers in a mixed-gender congregation. This time international media were present to highlight the milestone nature of the event, which catapulted global debates and contestations on Muslim women's ritual authority. What followed was a series of "first" Muslim women–led prayers in other parts of the world.

While earlier changes brought women to the minbar, they had not yet given women authority over it. As a result of vigorous public debate on power, orthodoxy, tradition, and religious authority in a variety of Muslim communities over the fifteen years since the 2005 New York event, Muslim women's religious authority has expanded. It now includes women-only mosques, women-led congregational spaces, and queer-inclusive mosque spaces, all of which facilitate women and nonconforming individuals to lead prayer and perform the khutbah.[34]

As women have entered khutbah spaces, they have reconfigured the substantive nature of the minbar by incorporating women's experiences. Where the minbar previously had centered on male experiences as universal, women's voices have enabled a more complete integration of the full range of human subjectivities. It has also rendered visible the ways in which religious knowledge is deeply situated and embodied, opening up critical insights on the relationship between experience and epistemology. As a result, women in these inclusive spaces now hold full authority of the minbar. For many contemporary Muslims, women's acquisition of the minbar symbolizes an important spiritual, ethical, and political transformation and a potentially new moment in the alignment of religious authority and gender.

2. A *Tafsir* of Experience

Spirituality, Embodiment, and Knowledge

This chapter presents twenty-five khutbahs written by women from a range of national, social, and political contexts across Muslim-majority and -minority communities. The *khatibahs* are religious and community leaders, activists, and academics hailing from Senegal, Pakistan, South Africa, Germany, the United States, the United Kingdom, Indonesia, Malaysia, Egypt, Mexico, and Denmark. The significant number of South African contributions reflects the longer South African history of women's khutbahs and the coauthors' local context.

Our collection begins with the khutbah presented by Professor amina wadud at the Cape Town Claremont Main Road Mosque in 1994—an iconic moment that heralded a new space at the minbar for women. Her khutbah was not only revolutionary in its political implications but also in introducing a woman-centered theology of "engaged surrender." Similarly, the *khatibahs* here bring the *tafsir* of their own everyday experiences to the minbar and develop an inclusive space of religious authority. We assemble the innovative theological wisdom of their khutbahs into five themes, ranging from cosmological and ontological perspectives to explorations on subjectivity and consciousness to issues of social difference, justice, and communal politics.

Engaged Surrender

AMINA WADUD

(Indonesia and the United States)

As Muslims we know the word *Islam* is the most important part of how we understand who we are. A Muslim or Muslimah is one who surrenders himself or herself to Allah. We often translate this word as "one who submits"; however, the concept is proactive, spiritually ripe, and dynamic and might be better translated as "engaged surrender."

Engaged surrender involves an active consciousness in participation in our social, family, community, economic, and political lives by the heart that is always open to the will of Allah and that always gives precedence to Allah's will. The concept we have been inclined toward—submission—sometimes gives the idea that there is no will. But the one who willfully submits to the will of Allah is engaged in surrender.

I will talk about this from a woman's perspective, starting with an important part of many women's lives: giving birth. A woman carries her child under her heart for nine months. What she eats, the child eats. As she cares for her health, she cares for the child's health. As she breathes fresh air, she breathes for the nourishment of the child. As she takes care of her spiritual and emotional states of mind, she cares for the child's well-being and needs. She carries that child for nine months, and this is an act of surrender. She is following the will of Allah.

This is a marvelous example of engaged surrender. The mother cannot take a day's rest. She cannot lay the child down beside her on the bed and say, "Just for today, I think I will not be pregnant." But even more importantly, after the nine months are over, she may not hold on to that child. She must surrender the child and give in to Allah's will. For just as Allah commanded her to hold on to that child for nine long months, so too must she engage in the act of surrender when it is time to bring the child forth.

She can no longer hold on to it. If she continues to, it will mean death for her and the child. So, she will engage in surrender. Each contraction has a duty. As the stomach pulls tight, the cervix opens so that the child might be brought forth into the world. If she resists the contraction, not only will it be uncomfortable for her, it will also curtail the natural motion of the child's gift of life. So she must engage in surrender in the act of labor. She must focus and not be distracted. Her body engaged with the task at hand, her heart and mind must consciously think of Allah in some form of *dhikr* (a formula of remembrance of God). She must surrender her body into the natural act of the contraction in such a way that the child might be brought into the world without discomfort.

This image of a mother carrying her child under her heart, then bringing forth that child consciously as she participates in labor, is not only a reflection of engaged surrender; it is also not unlike Allah Him/Her/It Self, who describes Himself before every *surah* or verse in the Qur'an (save one) as al-Rahman, al-Rahim (the Merciful and the Mercy-Giver).

He is *rahmah*. He is Mercy. He is the ultimate mercy. Both His names of mercy, Rahman and Rahim, come from the same root word as *rahm:* the womb. Allah thus engages us continually to understand the nature of our surrender. Just as He draws us forth from His spirit, so will He push us out into the world. There is a time when Allah's *rubbubiyyah*, His nurturance and love, will push us out into the world. There is also a time when Allah's *rubbubiyyah* will draw us close (to Him). The best articulation of this image that we have (in this world) is the experience of a woman who carries a child under her heart for nine months and then must let that child go.

In Surah al-Inshirah Allah says:

> Have We not opened up your heart and lifted from you the burden
> which weighed heavily on your back, and raised you high in dignity?
> And behold with every hardship comes ease.
> Indeed with every hardship comes ease.
> Hence, when you are freed from your distress,
> Remain steadfast and turn to your Sustainer in love. (Q. 94:1–8)

Allah gives us the mother in pregnancy and childbirth as a living picture of this idea of engaged surrender. We should know that Allah never repeats something for mere redundancy, but to make a point. Indeed, "with every hardship comes ease" is part of the engaged act of surrender that is everyday life. Sometimes there is difficulty, and sometimes there is ease. As long as we are on this earth, we will experience both difficulty and ease; hence the necessity of engaged surrender. Allah has guaranteed that our lives will be engaged with difficulty and with ease at all times. The nature of one who is truly Muslim is that he or she is constantly engaged in surrender, no matter whether it is difficult or easy.

This *surah* also reminds us not to become complacent when things become easy. We should always be conscious, engaged, and we should always keep our hearts open to the surrender to Allah—so that the act of engaged surrender becomes part of our everyday lives, and so that we never take for granted that the ease will go on and on. If we are successful in our businesses, in our struggles against apartheid, etc., it does not mean the battle is over. The battle forever wages on.

Another important part of a Muslim's life is marriage. The Prophet has told us that marriage is half of faith. Sometimes we misunderstand this. We think that if we get married, we don't have to do anything else. But if marriage is half of faith, then marriage is half of what we need to struggle with to engage ourselves in surrender before Allah. When the difficulty is over, we should still be striving. We still strive because our Lord is the goal, as Surah al-Inshirah says:

> Hence, when you are freed from your distress,
> Remain steadfast and turn to your Sustainer in love. (Q. 94:7–8)

As long as we are human beings, we are always in the struggle to attain some level of understanding and love of the Divine. It is an ongoing process because Allah is our goal, and we can never be finished with our surrender and engagement.

Engaged surrender goes on at all times, at all places, and for all circumstances. So we should think of our marriages and family lives as part of engaged surrender. We should not perceive of the situation in such a way that when the *nikah* (marriage agreement) is over, then that part of our lives is over. We should not think that once we sign the marriage contract, we can now put all of our attention and energy into our jobs, or business and political affairs. Instead, we should look at our family lives as half of our engaged surrender for the sake of completing our *din* (way of life or religion) on earth.

Your spouse—your wife or husband—is a new person every day. You should take the time to get to know that person—every day. That is part of engaged surrender. If she or he changes every day, you must engage anew in knowing him or her. It takes a certain kind of consciousness to treat him or her with respect. Sometimes, we think, we already know what she or he is going to say, so we do not listen. Consequently, we do not hear.

Part of the engaged surrender of marriage is that we must come to our spouse every day as if they are who they truly are—a new person every day. They have not attained their full Islam; they are also engaged in surrender, and we must respond to them as if they were. We must not assume they are today the same as they will be tomorrow, because Allah has also challenged and tested them, in the name of Islam, to engage in surrender.

Perhaps they have been more successful with some aspects of it today than they will be tomorrow. So part of the engaged surrender in marriage, part of fulfilling half of the *din* in Islam, is that we come to that relationship every day, with engaged surrender: with our minds intact and our hearts open. Our minds will engage in accepting that person anew, in respecting that person and honoring that change. Our hearts will open up to loving that person and will surrender and give that person the love and care that is due.

Allah says in the Qur'an:

And among His signs is that He has created from your own selves mates. And He has made between the two of you love and mercy. (Q. 30:21)

There's that *rahmah* again. *Rahmah* is supposed to be one of the characteristics of how we engage in surrender in our marital lives. We should not take the other person for granted. We should always extend loving care and mercy to him or her.

Remember the image of the mother—love is both holding and letting go. I must not tell another person how to coordinate his or her life. I, being just another human being, must allow that person to experience life. I must let that person go, and sometimes he or she may fall. This is also what I have to do with my children. I cannot live their lives for them. I must teach them, but I must let them go so that they can also experience engaged surrender.

We must never assume that marriage gives us the right to dictate the life of another person. It is half of *din*, half of what we have to engage in consciously, as Muslims, to surrender to the will of Allah. It requires more than a few quick commands at the beginning and end of each day. It requires listening and hearing, respecting and honoring, loving and caring. It requires us to be Muslim.

The idea that we must accept another person unconditionally does not mean we will not make mistakes. Surely, we make mistakes each day, and we ask Allah for forgiveness. And He has guaranteed that He has the capacity to forgive. Likewise, others in the path of their own engaged surrender might make errors. If we open our hearts as part of our engaged surrender, as part of our Islam, we will have the capacity to respect and acknowledge that perhaps they have erred, and tomorrow they may be able to correct that error. Then again, perhaps I have erred in my judgment, and tomorrow I can correct my error.

So the perspective we have on marriage should be one of engaged surrender. And we should come forward with the consciousness and surrender in our hearts. At the end of the day there is a possibility that this task will be a successful completion of what we know as our Islam.

I stand before you to remind you and to remind myself that the task of a Muslim is to continually engage in surrender. Sometimes we forget this task. Should we ever forget that we must consciously be engaged in surrender, surely Allah never forgets. He is always available for us, always accepts our *du'a* (prayer), and always accepts our effort to engage ourselves in surrender to Him.

amina's Journey to the Minbar:
"Raised with the God of Love"

A QUARTER OF A CENTURY has passed since August 1994 when I was first invited to South Africa—one of many "firsts." The country was marking the first one hundred days of the new democracy under President Nelson Mandela after the end of Apartheid. This was my first travel below the equator, with seasons reversed; my first time away from my children for two weeks. Most importantly, it was my first major public role with what I later call "embodied ethics," when words are not enough to achieve justice. I was asked to deliver the Friday khutbah to a mixed-gender congregation at the Claremont Main Road Mosque in Cape Town.

Embodied ethics requires full bodily enactment, which, as I reflect on that historical event, is established by two criteria: love and longevity. As for the love, many of the activists and scholars I met then have become lasting friends. No matter the challenge, this road was walked in love. As for longevity, in the twenty-five years since this groundbreaking event, it is clear this was the foremother to a new spiritual awakening beyond Muslim patriarchal hegemony. It was an affirmation of the Divine Feminine.

I am the fifth of eight children, born to a poor African American Methodist minister who raised us with the God of Love, al-Wadud. My father also taught me the integrity of faith. "I cannot go to the Judgment for you; you have to go for yourself," he once told me. He planted in me the seed of faith as ethical responsibility more than sixty years ago. When I was eleven years old, he took me to the March on Washington where the Reverend Dr. Martin Luther King Jr. made his historic "I Have a Dream" speech. Thus, there has never been a separation between faith and the struggle for justice in my memory. Embodied ethics is my heritage.

Arriving in South Africa was not easy. I left my three younger children with their father, whom I had divorced. I purchased his airline ticket and provided money for the duration of his stay with them. One week after my departure, he contacted me to complain that the air conditioner in my car had stopped working and the money was nearly spent. Although I'd heard it said that the man is the provider in Islam, this had not been my experience. Yet when the woman is the major provider, she is rarely acknowledged as guardian of the family, nor is she granted the authority of the provider. A question on my mind was: What do fixed gender roles mean against the survival of real families in present-day communities?

I was faced with the heaviest travel responsibilities in my life, and still I was called upon to care for my children from afar despite their dad being present. Participating at a conference on "Reformist Islam" in Pretoria, I met some progressive South African Muslims, including Rashied Omar, imam at the Claremont Main Road Mosque, who wanted to challenge fixed and unequal gender roles in public ritual worship. I agreed with this idea, but with no further details I did not know what was at stake. Not long after I arrived in Cape Town, those details were presented. With just a few hours before I was to embody an ethic of gender equality, Rashied told me I was invited to present a khutbah to a mixed congregation at the Friday *Jumu'ah*. It was both awkward and thrilling.[1]

At that time, I was not a public figure. I still feel uncomfortable with high visibility or controversy. That I was to ethically embody two of the most controversial events in the contemporary history of Islamic spirituality and gender justice still stuns me. Before this experience, I had offered lectures only in Muslim confessional contexts, mainly African American, and also for academic audiences. I used a set formula: write out the entire lecture, practice aloud a few times, and remember to smile. As a nerdy introvert, who reflected deeply on Islamic theology and ethics, I was not naturally inclined toward standing out in public or in sacred rituals; I preferred solitary worship. I could not have imagined that this major step outside my safety zone would signal the start of a global movement challenging restricted gender roles in Islamic worship.

For my first khutbah I chose a topic I knew well. A mother five times over, I focused on the female-only act of childbirth as metaphor for Islam as engaged surrender. While that khutbah celebrated pregnancy, labor, and de-

WADUD, "ENGAGED SURRENDER"   25

livery, it was not an illusive endorsement of motherhood with confining re-
ductionism. It elevated a female-centric act to the place of communal liturgy.
It was delivered in a male-dominant mosque, with mostly male congregants,
although the women prayed on the main floor for the first time. The khutbah
was women-centric, with a perspective that gave due attention to women,
but it was not about women.[2] My focus for the khutbah on female-only experiences was thus integrated for the whole community during the most public
level of Islamic spiritual practice. This topic alone marked a major transformation in the public performativity of Islamic spirituality. While women giving birth are indispensable to our communities, their voices had long been
silenced.

This khutbah disrupted the continuing legacy of exclusive male-
embodied experiences to reflect all of Islam and Muslims; it reminded us that
all human experiences reflect the potential of *al-insan al-kamil,* or the complete human. I remember once, during a family-centered celebration of Eid
al-Adha, I listened to a sermon about Abraham circumcising himself without
anesthetic. I could not recognize myself in that topic. Men's exclusive experiences have been celebrated from the minbar with little or no thought about
their impact on women. If both childbirth and male circumcision are part of
the human embodied experience, then both can be used to promote deeper
spiritual reflections. I intentionally used a woman's perspective and experience of childbirth as liturgy and metaphor by aligning it with the meaning of
the word *Islam.* With the topic of this khutbah we were taken to the precipice
of a new order where Muslim women's experiences matter.

All ideas about Islam must be interrogated for their inclusivity or ex-
clusivity. The idea of Islam as engaged surrender had only recently become
part of my understanding of the fulfillment of radical inclusivity. Once, when
I was overwhelmed with feelings of seasonal depression, a Sufi friend and
academic had written to me, "You must ask yourself: How is Allah nurturing me now?" I found the question ludicrous because I did not endorse the
idea of suffering as higher spirituality. Yet as time passed, I grew to greater
equanimity. The presence of Allah is unconditional; Her eternal Love and
Compassion unfold before us at all times, in all places, and under all conditions, including in the body. This was my introduction to Islam as engaged
surrender.

This 1994 khutbah was delivered amidst public furor from the more
conservative sectors of Cape Town's Muslim community, not for what was

said, but for the embodied female who delivered the words. This act disrupted fixed gender norms in Muslim ritual patriarchy: the same body that had safely delivered five children, without the father as provider, was invited to stand as imam. Gender roles are neither fixed nor divine. While this act of disruption, engaged surrender, and embodiment did indeed signal transformation, I consider the content of the khutbah to have been more radical than the context. At the time, I had never imagined Islamic spiritual practices outside their fixed gender forms. This event was both fluid and organic; I experienced it as both sublime and innocent. Although unprecedented in contemporary Muslim history, it could have happened only when those with exclusive authority permitted it. Why have only men held such authority?

The next major invitation for me to embody the ethics of engaged surrender was the well-publicized Friday *Jumu'ah* in New York, eleven years later in 2005. It was also viewed as controversial and precipitated protests from the more conservative members of our Muslim communities—this time globally. I was asked to perform all the major rites heretofore exclusively assigned to a male imam: deliver the khutbah and stand in front as the imam to lead the prayer. In the intervening decade I pursued deeper spiritual reflection on engaged surrender, aligned with additional critical research on gender and Islam.

Islamic ritual practices are always in a direct and unmitigated relationship with Allah, accepted or rejected on terms that transcend formulas erected by community. While they require full-bodied or embodied performance, one who is wheelchair-bound is neither less nor greater in their performance. Likewise, if I stand in a lush green field, am surrounded by stately trees in a dense forest, or perform in the special prayer space of my home, my worship of Allah is not elevated or demoted by circumstances of spatial coincidence. Thus, to stand in front of the congregation changes nothing about the human-divine axis of worship. No worshipper is closer to or farther away from Allah purely on the basis of spatial hegemonies. My acceptance to pray in front of others as *imamah* garners no lesser nor greater Divine Presence than my preference to pray alone. Both locations are equal. Sacred worship is non-hegemonic. Acts of devotion to Allah are not conditioned by restrictions placed by men unjustly wielding their authority.

In the years that have passed since these two public events of embodied ritual worship, a global trend of queer-inclusive mosque initiatives followed by the women's mosque movement have furthered the move to affirm women as *imamahs* and *khatibahs*. Their religious authority in worship is no longer beyond our imagination. Sacred worship is nonhierarchical because devotion to Allah is not conditioned by restrictions placed by men unjustly wielding their self-ascribed authority.

Amin

Feminist Ontologies
Rahmah and *'Adl*

An-Nur (Divine Light)
SHAYKHA OUMOU MALIK GUEYE
(Senegal)

In the name of the Divine Truth, by the flourishing light of our most beloved guide Muhammad, may peace and blessings be upon him, his family, companions, and community.

Iqra: (Read, speak, teach) in the name of your Lord who created. (Q. 96:1)

The divine command to read and speak His Truth was the first word revealed to Prophet Muhammad brought by the angel Jibril (Gabriel) for humankind. This enabled humanity with guidance to learn and preach the wisdom of scripture. This initial summons descended upon Prophet Muhammad's heart as a mercy to all: "I have sent you only as a mercy for the universes" (Q. 21:107).

The words sent to him are destined to all as a single humanity without discrimination. The revelation "the most Merciful taught the Qur'an, created the human, taught him eloquence" (Q. 55:1–3) takes us back to the filtering point, the main purpose for creation, which is to speak eloquently in loving guidance. The emphasis on "created human beings" does not differentiate on any basis, including gender. So standing in the pulpit to share and receive the Truth is a calling incumbent on all human beings, male and female. Muslim women's authority to teach, guide, and deliver sermons is our inherent gift, part of being original *insan* (humankind).

The broad calibration of women in the Qur'an provides us with prominent female figures in Islam with whom we share common beliefs and realities, including about gender. In the Qur'an, the fourth chapter, titled "The Women," exhorts humans to be conscious of God's Essence and Lordship as God created us from a single soul, one initial existence, one soul not differentiated as male or female.

The divine wisdom informs us of a unique soul from which creation sprang forth, and the human path being that of return, the cycle is complete only when one reaches again that fundamental oneness. The single state that emanated from the deistic beatitude is that state free from duality and separation, the condition of being embodied by this khutbah-giving servant and all other humans. When one has been set on the route of conveying the commands, exhortations, oaths, and promises of Allah *subhanahu wa ta'ala*, it is incumbent for the chosen, emblematic servant to polish the vessel of reception and dispensation—the self—so it can mirror the Divine Truth. On a more personal note, the wisdom of the Qur'an through the mystical trail of Sufism provides a method for attaining such a state of receptivity, especially for teaching. Such a state has an axial point around which rotates the idea of a genderless soul—that single, original, unified soul, or *nafs al-wahida*.

In the time of the Prophet Muhammad, prominent women like his beloved wife, Mother of the Believers, A'ishah (may Allah be pleased with her) were reputed teachers to scholars in Madinah. The Muslim community was instructed by the Prophet Muhammad to take lessons for one-half of their religion from Mother A'ishah. Her intrinsic intelligence and primordial disposition (*fitrah*) as *khatibah* were relied upon by Prophet Muhammad to help convey Allah's commands. She also gave the call to prayer (*adhan*) and led prayer (*salah*) in women-only congregations. Another female authority and wife of the Prophet Muhammad, Umm Salamah (may Allah be pleased with her), also led women in ritual prayer and lent him support in his religious mission. When Prophet Muhammad, in transcendent wisdom, signed the capitulating Treaty of Hudaybiyyah to preserve a commonwealth, even though his army was overwhelmingly stronger in moral and military forces than that of his opponents, the soldiers were dismayed. Faced with the unprecedented discontent within the ranks, Prophet Muhammad sought advice from Umm Salamah to restore the army's cooperation. Following her wise strategic counsel, a burden was lifted from the community, and hearts realigned.

The ways of Prophet Muhammad are the sunnah, providing an example for Muslims to follow. The stories of the earliest Muslim women are blueprints of female authority at the minbar and examples for acceptance in the contemporary period.

There are many illustrations of this in Prophet Muhammad's journey (*sirah*), starting with his first wife, Khadijah (may Allah be pleased with her), who was the first Muslim. When Allah's revelation descended on Prophet Muhammad in the cave of spiritual retreat, he was overwhelmed and went to the ennobled Khadijah, who consoled and reassured him of the Truth he had received in very trying times. Many reflect that Islam started in the arms of a woman, and I would add that the prophetic revelations also ceased in the arms of a woman, his beloved wife A'ishah, in whose lap he laid his noble head and took his last breath.

Yet another amazing early Muslim woman was Shifa bint Abdullah, given charge of Madinah's busy marketplace, the center of Arabian commerce. Asma bint Umays was consulted as a wise counselor in Umar's caliphate. Fatima bint Khays was nicknamed al-Najud, or the woman who comes to your rescue, by the noble companions of Prophet Muhammad. Last, but not least, the most cherished daughter of Prophet Muhammad—beloved of Ali, Mother of the Moons of Islam, Imams Hasan and Hussein—Fatima Zahra, the illuminated, was an admirable extension of prophetic guidance and teachings. (May Allah be pleased with them all.)

The list is long as Islam displays many authoritative female figures in its formative years. The Prophet Muhammad is said to have embodied the noble Qur'an and was a walking book of mercy. His way of life is the Muslim path to Truth. Time and space do not alter the legitimacy of Qur'anic acceptance of women's leadership in the original teachings. Muslim women's religious authority is not a new phenomenon but emerged from the very deepest roots of Islam. Different schools of thought (*madhahib*) have applied societal biases to the pristine, original teachings and exemplars, thus ostracizing women from religious oratory.

Yet today we are witnessing groundbreaking creativity freeing the victims from this lower reality of pronounced duality and boundaries related to gender. In 2000, Shi'i leaders in Iran lifted the ban for women to deliver sermons and lead prayer in female-only congregations. In China, women's mosques (*nusi*) have existed for more than a hundred years, with women leading other women in prayer and religious guidance. The Prophet Muhammad's paradigm thus has not shifted; it has just been veiled by a base patriarchy whose adherents seek in this social power structure the means to hide their own weaknesses or *nafs* (lower self), instead of striving to transcend them.

Call upon me as Allah or as al-Rahman (most Merciful). (Q. 17:110)

This divine command connects Allah's essence to *rahmah* (mercy), from the Arabic root *rahm* (womb), which God ingeniously projected into women, to be embodied solely by women. Divine mercy as the basis of all being is thus reflected in the depths of woman as receiver of Mercy, carrier of Mercy, giver of Mercy, women of Mercy. The decree of our Lord—*Iqra bismi Rabbik al-ladhi khalaq*—is to "read, teach in the name of your Lord who created" (Q. 96:1).

In the name of Allah, the most Beneficent, the most Merciful, may Allah bestow abundant blessings on the mercy and guide for humanity, Muhammad with his family and companions, peace be upon them all.

> All praise belongs to Allah.
> I praise Him, and seek His support and forgiveness.
> I beg Him alone for His guidance and compassion.
> I have utter faith in Allah alone.
> Do not reject Him.
> I bear witness that there is none worthy of worship but Allah,
> He is the One, He has no equal.
> I bear witness that Muhammad is His servant and messenger
> Whom he sent as a source of guidance,
> The way of Truth, the Way of Divine Light.
> —Extract from Prophet Muhammad's first *Jumu'ah* khutbah[3]

O humanity, may peace and blessings be upon you. We are gathered here today on this blessed day of *Jumu'ah* to give praises to Allah and support each other with love and guidance.

In the Qur'an, profound attention is drawn to the popular verse of Light:

> Allah is the Light of the Heavens and the Earth
> The parable of His Light is as a niche and within it a lamp
> The lamp made of glass
> The glass as a brilliant star
> Lit from a blessed tree
> An olive tree
> Neither of the East nor of the West
> Whose oil will glow forth though untouched by fire
> Light upon Light
> Allah guides to His Light whom He wills
> Allah sets forth parables for humankind
> Allah is all knowing (Q. 24:35)[4]

Dear community of Muhammad, our Lord and Cherisher refers in this verse to His essence as the magnificent Light of the universes. This all-encompassing radiance, that macrocosmic luminescence, is an abode for the chosen microcosmic beloved, none other than the children of Adam—us, beloved siblings. Whoever is guided to our Creator and Sustainer's Light will indeed be in eternal bliss. This verse does not differentiate between women and men, young and old, rich and poor for "Allah guides to His Light whom Allah wills." Beloved community, we may rejoice in the comfort of knowing that our Creator did not deprive any of us nor relegate any of us to a lower status; neither women nor men are a subclass for His utmost privilege or favor.

Ibn Arabi, a renowned twelfth-century scholar, shared in his mystical philosophy that women and men are absolutely equal in terms of humanity and spiritual potential.[5] Male and female are in synergy for the necessary cosmic unity at the level of creation. His teachings forge the grounds for reclaiming a holistic concept of humanity and gender in Islam. Thus, maleness and femaleness are sine qua non conditions in the human state, not a primordial reality that is the condition of oneness with the original divine soul from whence creation emanated.

Eve (Hawa), created from Adam, has two denominations—the first being male by virtue of origin, the second in appearing as female by reason of contingency (read as possibility, eventuality) to physical existence, an acquired Adamic distinction, that is, both for pairing with Adam and for completing their descendants.

Thus humanity, in the creation of both Adam and Eve, unites both male and female, which constitutes the root of gender equality and reciprocity. This deep understanding of the *shaykh* is exemplified by ibn Arabi's obedience to his female teacher and spiritual guide, Shaykha Fatima bint Muthana, who had attained perfection and was imbued by divine light. Her maleness and femaleness were annihilated in a gender-free unity of being, which allowed her to assume her true purpose of vicegerency and inculcate him with some of the most profound spiritual teachings in history.

We are reminded in the Qur'an:

Allah told the angels I am appointing my representative/vicegerent on earth [Adam and his progeny]. (Q. 2:30)

Beloved community, we are those heirs, and our challenge is not competing with each other for positions of religious oratory but rather for attainment of vicegerency through working on refining ourselves, our souls, because when embodied, our subtle selves dwell in the realm of separation and duality. If our souls are not freed, segregation will forever be apparent and unduly limit our understanding and endeavors.

Femaleness is not a fortification but a fortitude, and so too with maleness: both are a God-given sovereignty. There is a cosmic principle impregnated in every child of Adam and Eve, "the maleness of Adam" and "the femaleness of Eve." Human beings each have female and male within them. Existence depends on these two orders.

Yet this prime state of servanthood has become subjugated by gender polarization in limiting servitude. Theological restraints have become fueled by the personal interests of hearts, by the misunderstanding of the function of gender in creation.

Remember, my dear friends, Allah's Light is neither from the East nor from the West; religious teaching and authority come from that luminous beam and not from binaries of duality in all aspects, including gender. May we seek to be submerged within and reflect on that equal spark in all human beings.

May we practice acceptance and tolerance as all is encompassed within the divine mercy of the cyclical breath that always reenacts the creative process.

Utmost praise is due to Allah. *Allahu Akbar*, Allah is greater than our limitations. I seek refuge in Allah for any rendering veiled by my condition and thank Allah alone for any enlightenment to this audience.

Shaykha Oumou's Journey to the Minbar: *"In Truth I Was Never There"*

I WAS BORN IN SENEGAL into a beautiful Sufi Muslim family. The youngest of six children, I always felt as if I were bathed in the golden nectar brewed by my older siblings from the abundant, ripe fruits of our nurturing parents. I was immersed in love, caring, and gentleness, in which the teachings of our Islamic faith guided us as a family.

My father was a political figure—a man who was the vice president of congress and, at the same time, a spiritual guide in the Tijani Sufi *tariqah* (order) in Dakar. He made sure that we children grew up knowing the need for balance in mindfulness between worldly obligations and spiritual affairs. Similarly, my mother was a natural pioneer in social and spiritual affairs. She worked as a nurse at a hospital, organizing a charity foundation within the hospital that provided for the medical, psychological, and social needs of deserving families in our city. She later successfully established a *dargah* (meeting place) for Sufis at our home, laying the basis for us children being integrally involved in the activities of the Tijani *tariqah*. Later, my mother also served as the first female president of Tijani Sufi women in the capital city of Dakar and surrounding towns. This position was a major recognition of female spiritual leadership in our Muslim community, which tended to be profoundly male-centered in the rearing of spiritual leaders.

Under the canopy of my devoted and energetic parents, I grew up rather customarily. Religion and spirituality were seamlessly part of our daily routine, as were serving and taking care of others. I remember as a child helping in food drives for the needy and distributing water to the thirsty on hot days. It was all part of our family life. As expected of us children too, I met all my educational milestones. After graduating high school, I studied law in Dakar before traveling to the United States for further studies in business management. When I began my career in business, I also started spiritual training in the Halveti Jerrahi Sufi order. My beautiful teacher, Shaykha Fariha, was a vessel for dispensing God's mercy. Her profound guidance and teachings led me to experience many spiritual openings bathed in divine grace.

As my whole being resurrected through my spiritual life, so did my work. I moved to working with a charitable organization, the Mumin Foundation, whose work focused on responding to the needs of vulnerable groups in society. After years of training with my Jerrahi family, building on my Tijani upbringing, I received the authority and permission to guide seekers to the love of God as a *shaykha*.

In 2007, I returned to my native Senegal and opened the first female-led *dargah* for divine remembrance in the town of Mbao. Since then, our group has expanded to other locations in the city, *al-hamdu lillah!* Needless to say, my leadership as a Sufi was not a walk in the park within a patriarchal society. The memory of my mother's achievements in the past and her impact on seekers inspired me. I endeavored with the certainty of divine support, never hesitating to seek companions on the path.

In my journey, I experienced an abiding, innate sense of predisposition—of being destined to undertake the spiritual work I set out to do. I have always felt assured that I must remain steadfast in my purpose and that divine support will pave the path before me. In fact, I have always felt I was born for this purpose. This feeling or attitude is typical of those who believe they have found their calling in life. It is always with a deep sense of humility, sincerity, and clarity that I undertake all my spiritual work. It is with keen knowledge that I must serve God's creatures, particularly girls and women believers. It is equally clear to me that I must do this work to the best of my abilities.

Times were different in my mother's day; female leadership tended to err on the side of being subtle and cautious, women accepting it as their lot to be overshadowed by men. But my training with a female teacher in a non-traditional, North American community made it more natural for me to assert and mirror the leadership of my beautiful teacher Shaykha Fariha. I believe firmly in the crucial value of female spiritual role models for young women in all journeys they undertake. Female teachers in Muslim societies do not always enjoy broad acceptance, but we must rest assured of God's support and guidance—always. I have never really feared the challenges on my path, nor have I spent time grieving failures—these are inevitable.

In Truth I was never there . . .

Those who have walked into our gatherings to gauge or defy us have found themselves inevitably transported to a place where there is no duality—neither male nor female—just being in the divine essence of unity.

I have surrendered my will to God's and constantly work to be freed from praise or blame. I hope, always, for divine sustenance along with guidance. To me, this is the meaning of true Islam.

ꙮ

Khutbah al-Muwaddah lil Ghuraba— For the Love of the Queer Strangers
GHAZALA ANWAR
(Pakistan)

This khutbah is addressed to the *ghuraba,* queers and strangers, who do not find a mosque where they are welcomed and treated with dignity, and for whom there is no time or place in the dominant circles of our *ummah.* Through this khutbah, may Allah console their hearts, renew their faith, and manifest for them the *barakah* (blessing) of the four-arched portal of *rahmah*—Divine Love and Mercy, which is the foundation of our *din,* and its protection from egos immersed in self-worship.

The first arch of this portal is the *basmalah*—*bismillah al-Rahman al-Rahim* (in the name of Allah, the Most Loving, the Most Kind)—with which the journey of our faith begins and continues and through which every encounter with the Qur'an begins. It inseparably conjoins the Divine Name of Essence, Allah, with the divine attributes of *Rahman* and *Rahim,* formed from the order of the letters *ra-ha-mim*, primarily associated with *rahm* (womb) and *rahmah* (mother's love). Allah, the Rahman, creates and sustains all out of an overarching Love.

Allah, the Rahim, cares for each one of His creatures with continuous, particular, and repeated acts of Love and Nurturance. The *basmalah* is a supplication for *rahmah* predicated on our commitment to it. Invoking the *basmalah* over the Qur'an, we commit ourselves to reading with a *rahmanic* bias, to prioritize the understanding that is most *rahmanic* in its attribution to the Divine and its consequences for creation.

The second arch of the portal of *rahmah* is *"kataba 'ala nafsihi rahmah"* (Q. 6:12), Allah writing *rahmah* upon HimSelf in exquisite gender-balanced grammar:

> *kataba: He wrote*—masculine singular
> *'ala: upon*—gender neutral
> *nafsi: self*—feminine singular
> *hi: him*—masculine singular
> *rahmah:* feminine singular

This invites us to also write *rahmah* upon ourselves, to bind ourselves by the law of *rahmah* toward ourselves and all of creation. One instance of this conscious self-binding to *rahmah* is reflected in the articulation of a vegan Muslim theology and praxis, especially since this divine self-inscription is disclosed in Surah al-An'am (The Cattle).

The third arch of the portal of *rahmah* is accessed through the Qur'an by believers. If Allah wrote *rahmah* upon HimSelf, then the entire *kitabullah*—Book of Allah—must necessarily be *rahmah*, as declared in many verses:

> We send down in the Qur'an healing and *rahmah* for the faithful,
> and it does not increase the wrongdoers except in loss. (Q. 17:82)

The ability to access *rahmah* from the Qur'an is predicated on the reader's *iman*—faith. The depth and expanse of our *rahmah* are the measure of the state of our *iman*. If we believe in this Book, then we must read it with the eyes of *rahmah*.

The fourth arch of this portal is the prophetic *rahmah*, for the Qur'an says of Muhammad:

> And We have not sent you except as *rahmatun lil 'alamin*—(*rahmah* for all realms of existence). (Q. 21:107)

As emulators of the Prophet, who is *rahmatun lil 'alamin*, we must also strive to become *rahmatun lil 'alamin*. This prophetic title and mission provide the criteria by which to assess the relevance of *sirah* and hadith literatures as communicators of his model, prioritizing what is *rahmanic* for emulation and suspending judgment on what appears un-*rahmanic* by contemporary human standards. Using this criterion, we can access theologically significant resources for personal and *ummah* formation. Our commitment is to remain true to the prophetic mission of *rahmatun lil 'alamin* and not practice blind obedience to a vast body of literature with highly variable and even contradictory accounts of prophetic words and deeds.

It is reported that a companion said to the Prophet, "Ya Rasul Allah, I was about to slaughter a sheep but was overcome by *rahmah*." The Prophet replied, "Since you took *rahmah* on the sheep, Allah will take *rahmah* on you twicefold."[6] The Prophet speaks here from the throne of *rahmatun lil 'alamin*, against which all other hadith related to killing animals for food ought to be measured in order to determine their relevance for emulation.

I am proposing that our readings of the Qur'an and hadith must internally pass through this four-arched portal of *rahmah* before we allow ourselves the authority to consider them sources for Islamic sciences, including *tafsir*, *fiqh* (jurisprudence), and *tasawwuf* (Sufism). When we encounter verses and hadith that seemingly violate the Qur'anic command for justice (*'adl*), equity (*qist*), and goodness and kind consideration (*ihsan*), we have the Qur'anic portal of *rahmah* to help us negotiate this apparent challenge to our faith. A *rahmanic 'adl* is not blind: it has clear vision and is visionary; it has exceptional insight and foresight. It not only heals but also restores that which has been lost. In the process of reconciliation and compensation that ensues from our efforts to establish *'adl*, *qist*, and *ihsan*, on occasion, a measured retribution might be unavoidable. This applies to gender *rahmah*, gender justice, as well.

Gender *rahmah* ensues from the gender-fluid complementarity of Qur'anic grammar that encompasses divine and human names. The Indescribable, Incomprehensible, Unseen, Transcendent Reality, which is beyond gender, is referred to by the *ism dhat* (the name of the essence) "Allah," which is a name not shared by any other. The term *dhat* itself is feminine, and the *ism dhat*, the name of the essence "Allah," is feminine. The qualities or attributes—also known as the *sifat* of "Allah"—are called the *asma al-husna* (the Beautiful Names). All the *sifat*, meaning all the Beautiful Names in their individual forms, are masculine, but the collective term *asma al-husna* is feminine. To summarize: "Allah," although feminine, is referred to by the masculine inclusive pronoun *huwa;* and all of "Allah's" attributes, such as *Rahman* and *Rahim,* are described by masculine nouns.

> Allah [feminine gender specific] there is no god but He [*Huwa,* masculine gender inclusive], to Him [masculine gender specific] belong the Beautiful Names [feminine gender inclusive]. (Q. 20:8)

This layered gender-fluid complementarity between Divine Essence and Divine Names is mirrored in the two Qur'anic names for humans: the feminine *nafs* (self) and the masculine *insan* (human), occurring even in the same breath. Gender-fluid complementarity is the source of gender *rahmah*—the gender-just balance of compassion that holds the masculine and the feminine in fluid relation with each other, within each individual, within all of humanity, within all creation, and within our descriptions of the Divine, who is beyond gender and beyond Qur'anic descriptions.

> And whoever does good deeds *whether male or female,*
> and he [*huwa,* masculine gender inclusive] is a person of faith [masculine gender inclusive].
> They [masculine gender inclusive] shall enter the garden and shall not be wronged
> even as much as a speck on the date seed. (Q. 4:124)

Reference to all human individuals, regardless of their place on the gender spectrum, as both *nafs* and *insan,* articulates a contoured, ever unfolding gender fluidity and attendant complementarity, which negates all oppressive hierarchies based on gender.

> O ye who believe [masculine plural] fear Allah [feminine singular]
> and let each *nafs* [feminine singular] watch what she has sent forth for
> tomorrow and fear [masculine plural] Allah [feminine singular].
> Verily Allah [feminine singular] is Aware [masculine singular] of what you
> [masculine plural] do. (Q. 59:18)

The gender complementarity between the feminine individual self and the masculine collective of faith in the above verse is one example of the myriad ever-transforming gender fluidity in the Qur'an, which is essential for the survival and well-being of humanity. The intrahuman and interhuman play of the feminine and masculine unleashes the creative potential of individuals and collectives, of which human procreation is only one manifestation. Gender-fluid complementarity unravels all concretized, impermeable gender categories and makes present our gender proximity with each other in *rahmah*, recognizing the other in ourselves and ourselves in the other. So their Sustainer responded:

> I will not waste the work of any worker among you, male or female.
> *You proceed from each other.* (Q. 3:195)

Gender *rahmah* sees the sheer permeability of the *barzakh* (barrier) of gender difference.

The fourfold portal of *rahmah* effects the transition from *thinking Islam* to *being Muslim* and helps one move toward attaining a *qalbun salim*—a sound heart.

> The Day when neither wealth nor children will be of any benefit,
> Except for him who comes to Allah with a sound heart. (Q. 26:88–89)

Nothing matters except a sound heart in a state of Islam in the presence of the Divine—not our ethnicity, nationality, social status, gender expression, or sexual orientation. While we individually strive toward cultivating a *qalbun salim* during the week, on Fridays we come together to pour whatever we have earned throughout the week of a peaceful heart into a collective heart.

We ask Allah to bless our efforts so we return from the *Jumu'ah* having gained much in the treasure of a peaceful heart and a *nafs al-mutama'inna* (Q. 89:27–30)—a tranquil *nafs*—both of which while cultivated in divine presence are yet earned in the battlefield of life where we constantly pass all our acts, thoughts, feelings, and intentions through the fourfold portal of *rahmah*. As we continuously submit ourselves to *rahmah*, we enter upon the unseen realms of existence and become *ghuraba*, or strangers, in this *dunya*—this temporal, myopic life lived in oblivion of *rahmah* and the unseen realms of existence. It is such *ghuraba*—strangers, queers—who continue to draw divine blessings and healing into our *dunya*.

The *qalbun salim* (sound heart) and the *nafs al-mutama'inna* (tranquil self), born out of this meta-ethic of *rahmah*, develop an inner and outer aesthetics and etiquette of *ihsan* that is articulated in an *adab*—an etiquette emanating from the heart that effects healing in all the concentric circles of our existence. The aesthetics of a mosque, or lack thereof, is an indication of the degree of soundness of the hearts of its builders. A house built for the remembrance of Allah through the recitation of the Qur'an which is *shifa* and *rahmah* (Q. 17:82) must necessarily be an inclusive healing place, excluding none who enter peacefully and respectfully to worship in communion with others.

A mosque must also include the sky and the earth, even when part of it provides shelter from inclement weather. *Salah*, timed according to the movement of the sun, places our earthly body among the planetary bodies in communion with the earth and the sky, as does the *tawaf* around the Ka'bah; the hajj in the plain of 'Arafah, followed by the prayerful night under the open sky in Muzdalifah; and the two *salah al-Eid* gatherings in open grounds. The traditional mosque's courtyard with prayer rows and a place for *wudu* under the open sky are an attempt to remain in nature even in highly urbanized landscapes.

Dissociation of our rituals from nature alienates us from our bodies and ourselves, with disastrous consequences for the earth and her inhabitants. *Salah* performed under the sky on bare earth affirms our primordial, embodied coextension with nature. As we prostrate with the stars and the trees, we reaffirm our commitment to the cosmic, natural balance: the *mizan* of *rahmah* of which we are an integral part (Q. 55:5–9). The aesthetics of the Great Mosque of Djenné in Mali, hand built of adobe (mud bricks) and maintained by the local community, honors the earth, as does the earthen mosque built by the Prophet in Madinah. It invites us to reclaim the simplicity of the sunnah so as to make ample room for what matters most—affirming our earthen nature and righting our relation with the earth and all earthly creatures.

The *rahmanic* aesthetics of the inner being of the imam is as important as the aesthetics of congregational space and the physical *wudu* before *salah*. The *imamah/khatibah* must have dedicated her life to cultivating a *qalbun salim* and a *nafs al-mutma'inna* in order to lead the *salah*. She must have committed herself to upholding the witness of her inner truth in all matters, regardless of whether that brought worldly gain or loss. She must not have been afraid to ask her Creator and her tradition the honest questions that arose in her heart, having the conviction that her questions are worthier in the divine balance than half-hearted conformity to the inherited understandings of her faith. She must have come to the realization that a *qalbun salim* can be sustained only by a *jawfun rahim*—a merciful digestive receptacle—which voluntarily abstains from ingesting any food that had caused harm to Allah's creatures.

She must live the correspondence between the sanctity of the purified "caves" of her abdomen, chest, and mouth and of the caves of Kahf and Hira. Her heart must be open and clear, with no misgivings toward anyone, and she must have a voice capable of recalibrating to a higher frequency the vibrational fields of the hearts being led by her recitation to a different realm of being and consciousness. It is the responsibility of the *imamah*, by Allah's grace, to lead the congregation into an ascension of consciousness that allows her followers in *salah* a glimpse of the *mi'raj*, as when the Prophet ascended through the heavens during his Night Journey. As it is said: *Al-salah mi'raj al-muminin*—*salah* is the ascension of the faithful.

Ghazala's Journey to the Minbar: "*The Prophet Is Approaching, Give Your Salam!*"

WE TURN TOWARD ALLAH, and Allah turns us toward fellow seekers, human and nonhuman, to learn and to teach, to be led and to lead. Teacher and leaders are themselves in fact taught and led by the needs, aspirations, and sufferings of those who invite them to lead toward the Divine. Finding oneself on the minbar is one of the most humbling experiences one can have in one's lifetime; for me, this is the truth about being a *khatibah*. As I reflect on my journey to the minbar, I am reminded that it is the things of everyday life that enable this journey and calling.

I was born and raised in a Muslim family in Pakistan whose religiosity was submerged in a Westernized lifestyle. Our basic religious education in an enthusiastic neighbor's living room consisted of being taught to read the Qur'an in Arabic. It was not a language we understood; we memorized short *surahs* with translations for a small liturgical repertoire to conduct our prayers meaningfully. We were taught to pray but not told to pray.

A modern couple, my parents had planned only two children—a boy and a girl. Then I appeared in my mother's womb, unexpectedly. I was almost aborted, but my mother had a dream that intervened the night before she was due at the clinic. This dream not only saved my life but ensured I received tender love from many during my childhood. My mother loved to retell the dream that formed my sense of self from early on. She had dreamed she was walking down a street with my father and saw the Prophet Muhammad walking toward them with two companions flanking him. She nudged my father and said, "The Prophet is approaching; give your *salam!*" When the Prophet came closer, my mother noticed he was frowning and did not return her greetings. She awoke knowing the Prophet disapproved of her plan, so she bore me.

Prayer and fasting came abundantly to me as a young child. I was a seeker unto the Divine for as long as I can remember. But as I grew older, the dominant understandings of Islam began to choke the garden in my soul. Eventually, oppressive interpretations of Islam caused me to reject "Islam" so I could remain spiritually alive and true to myself. I became a refugee fleeing from the violation of Divine Compassion, the core of Islam and of all faiths; I fled from the abuse and misappropriation of god-talk used to oppress us. First, I turned to Buddhism; its abstention from god-talk provided healing. Then when I yearned to see God, I was led to the Hindu icon Mahalakshmi, who graced my life with the Divine Feminine—*rahmah*. When I yearned for communion with the earth to honor her, I was invited into indigenous circles. All faith traditions serve both as refuges and as purgatories, depending on whether or not an interpreter has arrived at *rahmah* at the heart of each tradition. My *sa'ir al-adyan*, or quiet journeys, through the hearts of various faith traditions were a sign of Divine Mercy and continued, even as I was being called back to Islam.

One day I entered the Bawa Muhaiyaddeen fellowship to perform the Eid prayers, since I missed the festivities and community of the tradition in which I had grown up. Being greeted by a deep inner peace, a sign of Bawa's presence even after he had transitioned behind the veil, I began to attend the morning *dhikr* there regularly and then afterwards humbly and gratefully accepted the bowl of vegan *kanji* (soup) for sustenance. For a long while, my body refused to take in anything except the offerings from the communal kitchen of the fellowship. I woke up one morning to discover I had begun menstruating, and thinking that my condition barred me from entering the mosque and participating in the *dhikr*, I went back to sleep. In my dream, Bawa, wearing his *ihram* clothes and sitting cross-legged, scolded me: "Why haven't you come?" I protested, "I don't have the key." He replied, sternly, "You have the key." So I awoke and ran to perform *dhikr*.

Around the same time, as keynote speaker at the al-Fatiha Foundation conference in New York (1999), I declared, "Islam and homosexuality can be reconciled, simply because they have been reconciled in individual people's lives."[7] The queer, all-gender communal prayer I led there bore witness to the reconciliation of all aspects of our being with our faith; acceptance with gratitude for who we are in our inner knowing and offering ourselves back to the Divine is Islam.

On January 8, 2003, I was returned to my ancestral tradition as suddenly and as undeniably as my firstborn child was returned to the Divine

Source in a car accident. When I led her funeral prayer, the entire congregation—including Bawa's children, the very conservative circle of her father's friends and relatives, and my queer community—prayed as one, moved by the spirit of compassion. Surrendering our ego's expectations and desires from life to the Will of the Divine with acceptance and gratitude is Islam. Whatever the situation, the response is *al-hamdu lillah*.

ᗺᚖᙅ

Ethics of Gender Justice
OMAIMA ABOU BAKR
(Egypt)

We begin in the name of Allah, the Compassionate and the Merciful, Lord of the heavens and the earth, Creator of everything, *al-hamdu lillah*. Prayers and peace be upon the beloved Prophet Muhammad, Seal of the prophets, his family, and progeny; and blessings upon his companions and all followers.

> God commands justice, goodness, and giving to kinsfolk,
> and He forbids indecency, wrongdoing, and transgression;
> and He admonishes you, that you may remember. (Q. 16:90)

Many commentators on the Qur'an have considered this verse the basic foundation and seed of ethical values and righteousness that are illustrated throughout the revelation. In a straightforward, condensed form this verse ought to be a believer's guiding light, presenting a comprehensive way of ethical life. Three essential virtues here are commanded by God, *subhanahu wa ta'ala*, and three vices forbidden by Him. Justice comes first and foremost, which is also, we must remember, one of Allah's Beautiful Names, al-'Adl, and is closely associated with the virtues of goodness (*ihsan*) and generosity (*ita dhi'l qurba*). The enumeration moves from the general to the specific and from the abstract to the concrete. Thus, to pursue and embody justice means, among many other things, to do what is good, what is morally beautiful, as the Qur'anic word *ihsan*, derived from *husn* (fair and beautiful), signifies.

One does not simply sing the praises of "justice" in theory and claim love of justice without actualizing it in conduct and life, or without acting justly. The Qur'an is not a tract of theoretical, abstract philosophy, only to be admired from afar like an ornament; it is a book of guidance and inspiration for a lived ethics of engagement within our communities. And what better example than the third commandment in this verse—being generous to one's kinfolk or relatives. Generosity is the ultimate embodiment of being fair, good, and helpful because individual responsibility for social support is simply the "right" thing to do, the Muslim beautiful thing to do.

And then there are the following three counter vices that God forbids. In a way, they are there to define further the virtues mentioned at the beginning of the verse—only by contrast. "Indecency" (al-fahisha) denotes a certain shameful or foul excessiveness that is opposite to the spirit of justice as moderation and righteousness of the "Straight Path." Again, moving from the general to the particular, munkar are the wrong deeds that cannot be denied as such and are recognized by anyone with sound mind or moral sense as inherently wrong. The classical commentator Razi specifies munkar as harming people and doing evil unto them,[8] while Zamakhshari qualifies it as that which "minds/intellects reject as untrue."[9] It is an action so opposed to good reason that it is reprehensible and unconscionable. Even more specifically is baghy, defined as pride, insolence, a sense of superiority and power over others that leads to infringement upon rights and hence injustice, that is, the opposite of the spirit of giving and generosity, as in the example of reaching out to one's kin. The verse ends with a confirmation that this is an important reminder and exhortation from God to believers.

Is there anything more comprehensive, beautiful, and clearly put than this verse? Its symmetrical, balanced syntactic structure embodies the notions of justice and uprightness, which are central Qur'anic imperatives. It recalls another Qur'anic image, that of the mizan, the scale, which appears in nine different verses with interrelated levels of meanings: (1) the actual scale used to measure in buying and selling, (2) the cosmic scale of the heavens, and (3) upholding fairness and an egalitarian ethic: in one verse associated with al-haqq (truth) (Q. 42:17) and in four other verses with qist (Q. 11:85, 21:47, 55:9, 57:25), qist being another term for acting justly, in fairness, and giving each and every one their due rights.

Qist is mentioned twenty-two times in the Qur'an, in many cases referring to the treatment of orphans, women, helpless children, and the downtrodden and regarding reconciliation among quarrelling Muslims. This is in addition to the fourteen times that 'adl is also mentioned as a commandment, three of which urge the just treatment of women. But these are not merely numbers and lists, sisters and brothers, not just words to compile; they are Allah's integrated imperatives for action and practice. The Qur'an is whole, living, and indivisible. God warns us against breaking the Qur'an into fragments, *'iddin* (Q. 15:91), or believing in parts of the Qur'an we like and rejecting others (Q. 2:85); thus, we ought to think of justice specifically for Muslim women within our communities and countries.

Women during the Prophet's time and the descent of revelation rightly understood the central message of this great *din* and expected its application to them, initially in the form of inclusion in the affairs of the *ummah* and in God's revelation itself. Three accounts reported in the tradition inform us of this. The first involves Umm Salamah, a wife of the Prophet, who once heard him calling from the minbar "O people!" and prepared to respond to the call, only to be cautioned by her maid who said, "He called upon the men, not the women." Umm Salamah sharply replied, "Verily, I *am* from the *people*."[10] The second account also involves Umm Salamah, who inquired of the Prophet whether the reward for the *hijrah* is bestowed only upon men since there is no *ayah* that specifically acknowledges women's participation in the early struggle of the *hijrah*. This was the occasion of the revelation where God states:

> I will not let the work of any male or female be in vain
> Each of you is like, and from, the other. (Q. 3:195)

The third occasion of revelation involves Asma' bint 'Umays, who, having returned from Habasha (Ethiopia), asked the Prophet's wives, "Did a revelation descend concerning us?" to which they said no, so she went to the Prophet and exclaimed, "O God's Prophet, women are in such failure and loss because they are not mentioned in righteousness as the men are mentioned."[11] And thus verse Q. 33:35 was revealed in which God assures women that their voices are heard and efforts acknowledged, including them forever *within* the Revealed Text. Every time we read these verses, we are provided with a clear sign for our communities to continue practicing this egalitarian ethic. And of course we also recall Q. 9:71, which explicitly states the equal, participatory ideal presenting believing men and believing women as protectors and supporters of one another in managing the religious affairs of the *ummah*.

All God's words, commandments, exhortations, guidance, principles, and signs are to be reflected upon so that they may be heeded and applied, not just recited and admired. This is the *tadabbur* (reflection) that God urges us all to engage in:

> Do they not reflect upon the Qur'an?
> Or do (their) hearts have locks upon them? (Q. 47:24)

We are exhorted not to fall upon His signs "deaf and blind" (Q. 25:73). One commentator, Tabari, explains the former verse as people who are supposed to be "with awakened hearts and discriminating minds,"[12] while Zamakhshari likened those described in the verse to the *munafiqin* (hypocrites) because they might show great concern and enthusiasm for hearing God's words without any awareness or insight.[13]

So we must ask ourselves: Why is it that Muslims rarely associate these three specific gender-equality verses with the *'adl*, *qist*, and *mizan* verses? Is not the equal humanity of women in Islam an inseparable part and application of these values? Is not injustice to women a form of *zulm* (injustice) too? Why do we not make the links and view the Qur'an as a whole? Why do Muslims end up saying that men and women have spiritual equality in the eyes of God and in worship but not in social and domestic lived reality? In our societies, Muslims are still convinced that authority, power, and leadership belong to men. Indeed, we can all quote the Prophet's saying that women are the "sister-halves" of men—meaning they are on par with them or of equal status—and at the same time quietly and politely exclude these sisters when it comes to activities of either authority or management or religious legitimacy.

Most of our mosques—including the Grand Ka'bah—are dominated by men; they belong to men, are managed and supervised by men, are almost "ruled" by men. Women are merely guests whose presence can be tolerated but is marginal, often regarded as a nuisance and intrusion. They can be granted—yes, begrudgingly *granted*—a small area where they can pray but can see nothing nor be part of anything. Most of our institutions of religious knowledge and official channels of Islamic learning and the study of tradition are dominated by male scholars. Women scholars are not regarded in this area as the "sister-halves" of male scholars or of equal level; they are not trusted with the grave task of producing and disseminating Islamic knowledge, or with the full legitimacy and authority that this activity provides.

Is that justice? Is that equitable, *qist?* Or is that *baghy*—an overpowering infringement on rights of inclusion and equal opportunities to be part of and contribute to the *ummah?* What about our practices in our homes and families? Do we really practice *tadabbur* and reflection upon all the inter-related Qur'anic notions and injunctions of *qist*, *'adl*, and upholding the balance or scale of equal rights in order to apply them to rulings of marriage and divorce? We notice that the verses related to women in the Qur'an have all descended to us in revelation to redress the slanted, uneven balance of gender relations; to undermine patriarchal authority, and the resultant abuse and deprivation of rights; to teach Muslims both the wrongness of inequality and discrimination and the equal dignity and human worth of women. But Muslims still manage to distort this core message and Allah's intent—to turn it around, in fact, by unjust and unfair practice of His commandments that are related to women or via outright false application that is counter to the basic Qur'anic egalitarian ethic.

Sadly, we sometimes manage to do exactly what the Qur'an describes in the example of *tatfif* (cheating, which is the opposite of the *mizan*), that is, to obtain one's own full rights while at the same time not recognizing the same rights for others. We are quite happy to shortchange others yet forget this injunction:

Woe unto those who give small measure.
They are those who, in receiving their rights from people, demand them in full
Yet when they measure what they owe others, give less than the rightful
    amount. (Q. 83:1–3)

As Qur'anic commentator Muhammad Asad observes, this does not only refer to commercial dealings but "touches upon every aspect of social relations (and applies) to every individual's rights and obligations."[14]

In general, Muslims refer to themselves as *ahl al-Qur'an* (people of the Qur'an). So let us also pride ourselves that we are *ahl al-qistas al-mustaqim* (people of fair scales; Q. 17:35, 26:182) and *ahl al-tadabbur* (people of reflection). Let us live the balanced life of coherence and moral consistency that God wants for us.

I seek forgiveness and repentance from You, my Lord, *la ilaha illa anta subhanak;* You are our Guide and Refuge; may You make us see clearly what is *haqq,* what is beautiful, what is right.

Omaima's Journey to the Minbar:
"Because You Were Sure"

ON THE WALL above my study desk in my girlhood room, I pasted a page on which I wrote in big Arabic letters with green ink: *ana 'inda zann 'abdi bi* ... ("I am as My servant thinks I am. I am with him when he makes mention of Me").[15] I had heard it from my mother, who always reminded me: "Allah will never fail you when you truly believe and think of Allah in that way."

This was a central belief that shaped my early religious sentiments. It was not a Qur'anic verse but a sacred, divine communication, a hadith *qudsi* relayed to the Prophet Muhammad (peace be upon him).

What touched me about this famous hadith *qudsi* is its implied meaning of intimacy and direct relationship between God and oneself—long before I grew up to learn about Sufism. Whenever a wish came true, my mother would say: "See? Because you were *sure* that Allah would not disappoint you, Allah granted this to you." This was heart-warming, in every sense of the word. The belief that Allah will not disappoint me equally created my desire not to disappoint Allah, echoed in Q. 55:60:

> *hal jaza al-ihsan illa al-ihsan?*
>
> Is the reward for good (anything) but good?

This brilliant, shining verse combines goodness, beauty, and fairness; the idea that beauty you give, you will receive, is nestled within Surah al-Rahman, the Compassionate. Unconsciously at that early age, I promised to always read Allah's words carefully, to understand, feel, recite, love, and live them as best I could.

In the years following, Sufi poetry and the voices of historical women *sufiyyat* (female mystics) and their passion for Allah stole my heart. Yet the unfair monopolizing of religious expression was baffling and disenchanting. Where in the Qur'an or in the life of Prophet Muhammad can some people possibly derive the view that women are less than men? Or that women are to be ruled and disciplined by men? Or that women's religious ideas are not to be taken as seriously as men's? Or that we cannot be teachers of God's words and guidance to all? Where in the Book does it state that God has given this as privilege and opportunity to only one branch of the created *ummah?*

My long years in schools and universities directed me to the path of studying the spiritual, sublime, and aesthetic powers of the Qur'an, finding inspiration and comfort there. This also led me to the pleasure of sharing that inspiration, the love of God's beautiful words, when I became a teacher. I taught literature, showing students the art of finding meaning and beauty in a human-made text, teaching Sufi poetry and stories of women *'ashiqat* (lovers of the Divine).

Later, I found myself sharing with young girls reflections about the beauty and justice of Allah—the compassion, mercy, and utter fairness of our Creator. *Zulm* is made by people, not God. One has only to read and reflect for oneself upon what God is really telling us. Those I shared my teachings with were unsettled souls; but I would see their eyes light up and feel their yearning to experience both the love *and* fairness of Allah, the faith and dignity of belief in the revelation, and in their equal worth and validation.

Throughout the years, I kept meeting such young devout hearts and souls, who were keen to maintain their faith but confused by the injustices and unexplained bias conveyed to them as part of religion. They confessed that if they asked questions, they were made to feel they were abandoning religion itself. They felt reassured and empowered to hear from me about Qur'anic gender justice and egalitarian ethics, about finding our own discourse as believing Muslim women against indigenous patriarchy, Western colonizing and orientalizing disdain, and secular opposition.

I feel my readings of the Qur'an and perspectives on Allah constitute knowledge to impart, or at least convey. My mother had planted in my consciousness the seeds of trusting in Allah—al-Rahman, al-Latif, al-Karim; thus it has become my natural duty to show younger women that our *din* originally descended upon humanity to shake the arrogance of power, inspire resistance against all forms of oppression, and redress the balance of rights and dignity for the "weakened" and disempowered. It is this truth about Islam and the Qur'an that inspires my writing, teaching, and preaching as a *khatibah*. May God accept my endeavor. *Al-hamdu lillah.*

<hr>

Resisting the Satanic Principle, Recovering *Maslahah*
RABEYA MÜLLER
(Germany)

The following episode in the Qur'an is familiar to many Muslims:

> Your Lord said to the angels: Truly I am One Who creates a mortal from clay. So when I have shaped him, and breathed into him My Spirit, then fall to him in prostration. So the angels prostrated, all of them together, except Iblis, who grew arrogant and was among the ungrateful ones. He said: Iblis! What prevented you from prostration to that which I created with My hands? Have you grown arrogant, or are you among the ones who exalt themselves? Iblis said: I am better than the human being. You have created me from fire while You have created him from clay. (Q. 7:11–12)

From this story we clearly know that Iblis is the one who established the idea or principle that human beings might be considered less on the basis of their creatureliness. But who actually is Iblis? And why exactly must we repudiate his idea?

Iblis ("the disappointed one") belongs to the jinn, beings created by God from smokeless fire, who can choose to be good or bad. Jinns who move away from God and the common good are regarded as devils (*shaytans*). Iblis is traditionally believed to have once held a high position in creation—guarding the gates of paradise. He fell out of God's favor through his rejection of God's human creation as exalted. His fall is degrading, to the extent that his name, Iblis, and the term *devil* are often used synonymously; thus, his principle is called the Satanic Principle.

It is a lesson in how relationships with God and His creation should *not* be handled. Obviously, most people naturally reject it, for who in their right mind would want to act according to the principle of the devil? Nevertheless, despite assertions to the contrary, people still find ways and means through which to consider themselves better than others, or relate to other human beings as lesser. By setting themselves apart from other humans—on the basis of skin color, religion, gender, or sexuality, for instance—they emulate Iblis in arrogantly refusing God's exalted status bestowed on every human being.

Criteria that place human beings on arbitrary hierarchies endorse the Satanic Principle, even informing legal texts that over time have become very difficult to repeal. This is evident in the laws that allowed slavery, apartheid, and discriminatory legislation of many religions and ideologies (including Jews under Nazism and, recently, the Rohingya people in Burma and Muslims in India). Thus, we see the Satanic Principle spread globally, overriding the divine imperatives for human equality.

The Satanic Principle violates the dignity of another and creates injustice by denying the equality of human beings as creatures of God. It is a clear example of what *not* to do since God explicitly condemns and sanctions Iblis for this violation. Thus it is important for all Muslims to evaluate our actions in relation to this code of value. Discrimination in any form is nothing other than the Satanic Principle in action; it is not acceptable and deeply contradicts Islamic principles.

God is just and the Satanic Principle is unjust, even arrogant, for personal interests should not outweigh divine will. Patriarchal leaders and their followers find this difficult because they have invested in a power structure developed over centuries that they won't relinquish. Among other things, this has led to Muslim women believing that they are violating "divine values" if they insist on an emancipatory approach to life.

Advocates of gender hierarchy should recognize that unequal treatment of women contradicts gender justice demanded by the Qur'an and also is contrary to the common good (*maslahah*), which requires that everyone be fairly treated in society. To resist gender inequality we need to explicitly recognize and unmask the fact that male supremacy reflects the Satanic Principle—it is the opposite of the inherent dignity and equality that Allah has granted each human being. However, egotistical personal interests are often accompanied by emotions that overshadow rational assessment.

That the Qur'an should be understood in its historical, time-specific context is perhaps difficult to reconcile with the view that it is considered to be God's word for all times and for all people. This is a false binary, however. Seen more holistically, the Qur'an assumes the place of being simultaneously contextual and eternally relevant. Such an approach allows us to do justice to the Qur'an and better gauge the ethics it contains.

The Satanic idea of people's elemental superiority or inferiority stems from the moment of creation and has become deeply rooted in us. It contradicts the Qur'anic revelation that God created all humanity from a single soul, a single substance—*nafsun wahidatun*—and from it its mate, *zawjaha* (Q. 4:1). Nowhere does this speak of Allah having created one sex superior to the other; the term *zawjaha* in Arabic grammar is more accurately translated as *her* wife, suggesting a corresponding partner. The verse leaves open or ambiguous which gender was created first, reinforcing the idea that gender has no hierarchical meaning. All important, however, is that Allah is the Creator and human beings are the creatures.

"Adam," moreover, means earthling, that is, the human being created "from the earth." The biblical view, often held in Muslim circles too, is that the woman appears as the seductress enticing the man to eat fruit, causing their exodus from paradise. Yet in the Qur'an it is Satan who is the seducer, and it is unclear whether man or woman succumbed first:

> Satan whispered evil to him. He said: Adam, shall I point you to the Tree of Everlastingness and a dominion that shall not decay? Then they both ate from that so their intimate parts were shown to them, and they took to stitching together for themselves tree leaves from the Garden. Adam rebelled against his Lord and erred. (Q. 20:120–21)

These gender conundrums would not be of great significance if social or legal norms had not developed to discriminate against women. The very idea that woman is created to be subordinate to man enabled implementation of the Satanic Principle in real life from the early days of Islam until today. The consequences are far-reaching, with regulations barring women from certain offices, including spiritual leadership, even though the Qur'an and the sunnah demonstrate the opposite.

In this context, we ask: What is the idea of God's justice? God explicitly claims:

> God bears witness that there is no deity but God
> And the angels and those with knowledge (testify)
> God provides for justice.
> There is no God but God
> The Almighty, the All-Knowing. (Q. 3:18)

How is it possible, then, that God should allow one category of creature, "man," to assert himself as better than woman, believing even that he is entitled to chastise women?

A Qur'anic verse used to justify man's superiority over woman is Q. 4:34, interpreted by conservative scholars as follows:

> Men are in charge of women
> by virtue of what God has favored some of them above others
> and because they support them from their wealth.
> Therefore, the righteous women are devoutly obedient,
> guarding in [their husbands'] absence what God has guarded.
> As for those from whose recalcitrance you fear,
> admonish them, leave them in their beds, and beat [*idribuhunna*] them.
> Then if they obey you, seek not a way against them.
> Truly God is Exalted, Great.[16]

However, here is another interpretation:

> The men stand up for women
> because of what God has rewarded each one before the others,
> and because they [economically independent ones] spend from their assets.
> Therefore, loyal women are devoted [to God],
> those who keep the secrets in marriage [what is not made public and is to be
>   protected from outsiders with regard to the relationship of the spouses],
>   according to God's instruction.

Each Qur'anic text is interpreted differently, and verses should not be understood without reference to broader social contexts and surrounding verses. Qur'an scholar Kerem Adıgüzel warns readers, "Tearing verses out of their context is the biggest mistake . . . and can be used to legitimize any wish or viewpoint, no matter how ungodly it may seem."[17] The Arabic term *idribuhunna* in Q. 4:34, translated in the first interpretation as "to beat," allows for several other interpretations, including "to depart from" or "to go away from," both of which provide more ethical and consistent interpretations, particularly when read in light of the verse that follows Q. 4:34, which states:

> And if you fear a break between the two
> Send an arbiter from his family and from her family.
> If they wish to reconcile, Allah will make peace between them.
> God is Omniscient, All-Knowing. (Q. 4:35)

It seems logical that "a break" alludes to a separation between a man and a woman; why would an arbitrator mediate when one party of the conflict has been beaten by the other? This refers to a question of attitude and shows how the lens of gender hierarchy informs one's understanding of the higher concepts of the Qur'an, such as the justice of God and the inviolability of the body; these are set completely aside to focus on the one-sided interpretation of *idribuhunna* as "to beat." This also disregards other Qur'anic principles such as the unambiguity (*muhkam*) and ambiguity (*mutashabih*) of verses, and their connection with the reasons for revelation (*asbab al-nuzul*), which are important for producing holistic readings of the Qur'an. Why are these traditional interpretative methods discarded or used rarely in the so-called women's verses?

Qur'anic interpretation has been dominated by patriarchal assumptions for almost fourteen hundred years, but this is no excuse to continue this trend. It is important to be critical, especially for those things the Qur'an leaves open-ended or ambiguous, which offer opportunities for varied interpretations. We need to break these long-standing patriarchal "rules" of interpretation that create injustice, precisely because the Qur'an demands justice.

The principle of justice also applies to gender justice. Apologetic statements that "the Qur'an has already given women all rights" without social application can no longer be tolerated. Our readings of the Qur'an should return the holy text to being the dynamic Word of God and a living guide for Islamic ethics, focusing on its overall respect for the innate dignity of each life. A gender-just understanding of the Qur'an for the common good (*maslahah*) is at the center of scripture, and we must take responsibility to discern the *maslahah* in the Qur'an, for every generation. Allah has commanded believers "to stand up for justice" (Q. 5:8). We must unmask the Satanic Principle of patriarchy as injustice disapproved by God.

Rabeya's Journey to the Minbar:
"This Fight for Justice Is Worthwhile"

EVEN BEFORE I STARTED UNIVERSITY, I was actively involved with feminist issues in various organizations and the women's movement. In my late teens, the spiritual and religious side of my life remained neglected. But after school, I began to think deeply about what I believe, and slowly, my Islamic faith came to the fore. I dedicated myself to studying Islamic theology and religious education, wanting to teach children and young people about Islam.

The field of didactics provided me with teaching skills to inspire my students to deeper understandings rather than learning by rote. I was motivated by my experience in a mosque when a little girl asked me, "What does all we have learned about Islam have to do with our lives?" She articulated the problem incisively: How do we transfer the spirit of Islamic teaching to our daily lives? This challenge endures.

As director of the Institute for Interreligious Pedagogy and Didactics, I put my energy into creating teaching materials to ignite in children the pleasures of learning about Islam, including encouraging careful and critical reflection on everything they are taught. Justice has always been key for me in the teachings of Islam, which I strive to include in my materials, guided by the injunction:

> You who believe! Stand up for Allah as witnesses for justice.
> And let not the hatred of a group lead you to act otherwise than justly.
> Be just, that is closest to being God-conscious.
> And remain conscious of God.
> God is aware of all that you do. (Q. 5:8)

Islamic feminist theology also beckoned; I saw so much injustice against women, so much abuse of the Qur'an to advance men's rule and having nothing to do with the message of Allah. Allah is just. How can that same God be so unjust to women, who are as much a part of divine creation as men? Tragically, many women also believe they are less than men. Many have no real access to the Qur'an because only men in their societies are allowed to read, interpret, and teach Allah's revelations. Such patriarchal Muslim communities believe that Allah wills bias and favoritism—that this is divine justice.

These issues still move me today. I have not stopped working for justice, even as my anger has given way to serenity as I realized the importance of acting to encourage women to empower themselves. To me, education is the key to women's freedom and self-determination. I focus on education for and about women, especially at the Center for Islamic Women's Studies in Cologne.

It is gratifying to see girls and women wanting to study the Qur'an, their direct engagement opening up new perspectives for them, even as they are aware that it is often a struggle to have their views engaged with meaningfully. My work is to support them in their struggle and to fight for those who do not (yet) have the strength to do so. If we believe that Allah is just, then this fight for justice is worthwhile. It is important that my students understand that some of the insights we acquire are not always in accordance with the traditions. But many ideas the Prophet Muhammad taught were also against the traditions of his time!

Allah has gifted us a natural sense of justice; it is in our *fitrah*, our innate human nature. To me, it is important to know that in the history of Islam, Muslim women have always resisted injustice; for example, an ordinary woman contradicted the Caliph Umar when he wanted to abolish the *mahr* (marriage gift) to a bride. How many women today would dare stand up in the mosque to contradict the leader? How many Muslim women are actually able to enter a masjid? If we are no longer able to exercise the freedoms that women had during early Islamic times, then we must recognize we are falling back into the times of *jahiliyyah* (ignorance).

Since 2014, I have been serving the progressive Muslim community in Cologne as an *imamah*, putting many of my convictions into practice. The congregation views itself as a role model for others. I, too, would like to see young women leading such congregations. The men in my *ummah* are very brave; they are often called weaklings by other Muslims because they pray behind a woman. And why should they not pray behind a woman, having being born from a woman? Incidentally, the hatred and resistance some men display regarding being led by women is incomprehensible—nobody is *forced* to practice prayer this way. Every person must be free to choose.

We dare not forget that the Islamic tradition for centuries has been shaped by male thinking, which is not synonymous with the divine will and certainly not with Allah's injunction for us to uphold justice. I encourage all Muslims to use their minds to discern and resist injustice.

Allah is the essence of justice; to be on the side of the Divine is to *not* be on the side of patriarchy! This, I believe, so I will never give up.

ꙅ᙭ᙅ

This Speaking Earth
RABIA TERRI HARRIS
(United States)

Bismillah al-Rahman al-Rahim.

Idha zulzilati al-ardu zilzalaha
Wa akhrajati al-ardu athqalaha
Wa qala al-insanu ma laha
Yawma idhin tuhaddithu akhbaraha
Bi-anna rabbaka awha laha
Yawma idhin yasduru al-nasu ashtatan li-yuraw a'malahum
Fa-man ya'mal mithqala dharratin khayran yarah
Wa man ya'mal mithqala dharratin sharran yarah.
Sadaqa Allah al-'Azim. (Q. 99:1–8)

The Qur'anic scholar Yusuf Ali translates these verses, known as the Surah al-Zalzalah, as:

When the earth is shaken to her (utmost) convulsion,
And the earth throws up her burdens (from within),
And man cries (distressed): "What is the matter with her?"
On that Day will she declare her tidings:
For that thy Lord will have given her inspiration.
On that Day will men proceed in companies sorted out, to be shown the deeds that they (had done).
Then shall anyone who has done an atom's weight of good, see it!
And anyone who has done an atom's weight of evil, shall see it.[18]

Al-hamdu lillah alladhi la yansa man dhakarahu
Wa la yakhibu man da'ahu
Wa la yaqta'u man rajahu.

All Praise belongs to Allah
who does not forget one who remembers Allah
and does not disappoint one who calls to Allah
and does not cut off the hopes of one who hopes in Allah.

Many of us are familiar with the text of Surah al-Zalzalah and use it in our *salah*. When we think about the meaning of this *surah*, our minds often jump immediately to the events of the Last Day when all the graves will open and all the dead will rise, and every act will be connected to its final consequence. And surely we are right to be conscious of that terrible hour, and surely that is one of the meanings this *surah* carries within it. But Allah *subhanahu wa ta'ala* reminds us:

If all the trees on earth were pens and the ocean (were ink),
with seven oceans behind it to add to its (supply),
yet the words of Allah would not be exhausted. (Q. 31:27)[19]

And so we can be confident that a single meaning does not exhaust the mighty words before us. I therefore invite you to explore with me another level of this *surah*, one that also demands engagement with our consciousness and our conscience. For do we not today see the earth shaken and throwing up her burdens? Are people everywhere not exclaiming, "What is the matter with her?" Is she not in fire, in flood, in famine, in drought, in enormous storms, in appalling loss of countless communities of creatures, for as we are reminded:

There is not an animal (that lives) on the earth nor a being that flies
on its wings but (forms part of) communities like you. (Q. 6:38)[20]

Is she, the earth, not speaking to us directly now? Has her Lord not inspired her to confront us with what we do to her?

Yusuf Ali translates the earth's declaration of her tidings as "inspiration," but the verb is *awha*, from *wahy*, the very same word used for the revelation given to the prophets. The *surah* suggests that the earth will speak to us as the prophets speak—with prophetic authority, offering the divine witness that she alone can provide. If that is what is happening now and people alive today are not listening, we are no different from those other peoples who ignored the warnings of their prophets. How, then, do you suppose we will be judged? Allah says:

If Allah were to punish human beings for their injustice,
He would not leave on the earth a single living creature. (Q. 16:61)

We may well fear that the punishment for our injustice is approaching, because living creatures—plants, insects, birds, and animals—are now being removed from us for our sins at the rate of 150 to 200 species *every twenty-four hours,* according to the United Nations Environment Programme. And what are all these communities that are vanishing out of reach? They are communities of praise.

> The seven heavens and the earth, and all beings therein, declare His glory:
> There is not a thing but celebrates His praise;
> And yet ye understand not how they declare His glory! (Q. 17:44)[21]

Brothers and sisters, do we truly grasp what this means? It means that with every species that becomes extinct we lose a unique and priceless opportunity to deepen our understanding of Allah. With every species that goes extinct the world becomes not just biologically but spiritually more impoverished and bleak. If our actions are directly responsible for the extinction of species, then they and we are directly responsible for the extinction of worshipping communities. When the Last Day arrives, what do you suppose will be the price?

Al-hamdu lillah wa salatu wa salamu 'ala rasulillah. Praise to Allah and salutations upon the Messenger of Allah.

You will recall that Allah created the human being to be His *khalifah* on earth—to be the active representative of the All-Merciful. That is the work for which you and I were designed. To turn away from or to abuse the earth is to turn away from and abuse Allah's commission of the human being. And we see this very clearly in our time.

Now some of us believe that turning away from the earth, her communities, and her burdens is the spiritual thing to do, citing Qur'anic and prophetic warnings about the dangers of becoming too entangled in the things of this world. But such a view arises from confusing *al-ard*—the earth—with *al-dunya*—human society. *Al-dunya,* which we are obliged to inhabit, is indeed dangerous to us if we become too attached to it beyond the service of justice, mercy, and the love of Allah. But *al-ard,* the Qur'an tells us, over and over again, belongs solely to Allah and remains, altogether, *always* in Allah's care. There is no spiritual danger to us in also caring for what Allah cares for, thereby also entering into divine care. From the day of Adam's creation, we were *intended* to be on this planet and to take care of it. That is the express wish of our Creator. Where is the danger in this?

The last part of Surah al-Zalzalah speaks to *taqwa* (God-consciousness). Taken seriously, it provokes in us acute awareness that we will ultimately know the consequences of our *khayr* and *sharr*, our good and bad actions, and that Allah knows them too. It is often difficult for us to know the state of our *taqwa* as we live, in the present. Thus the best measure of human *taqwa* that we can see is the state of the earth. While it is not an encouraging view, how may we apply this sobering knowledge?

Brothers and sisters, the state of the earth mirrors the state of all our relationships. If we believe our destiny is to dominate, then we remain just so many little pharaohs, so many little *shaytans*, or devils, declaring, "I am better." May Allah protect us all from that!

> Art thou not aware that it is God who has made subservient to you
> all that is on earth . . . ? (Q. 22:65)[22]

The secret of these divine words is that it is not necessary for us to try to dominate or conquer anything; creation, as it is, already serves us. Our benefit does not lie in trying to overpower anything that exists but in listening to it:

> There is not a thing but celebrates His praise. (Q. 17:44)

The present time in which the earth aches is not necessarily the end of the world, but it could be. This should inspire *taqwa* and action, for the whole earth is our witness.

Perhaps Surah al-Zalzalah prophesies to us today not the end of the world, but the end of *a* world. In these days, many fear for the earth; yet we are reassured:

> His Throne encompasses the heavens and the earth, and their pres-
> ervation tires Him not. (Q. 2:255)

What is in immediate question is ourselves—whether our societies will be permitted to survive or will fall, victims of their own injustices, like so many societies and worlds that preceded them.

We do not really know whether these are the last days of all days or the lesser days of recompense for heedlessness; nobody knows this but Allah. We must, however, know and act on all possibilities that fulfill the commission placed on us by the Divine to take care of the earth. We are not free to abandon our responsibility to act—this is what being a *khalifah* means.

The Beloved of Allah, peace and blessings be upon him, advised that if someone comes running with news that the Last Day has arrived while you are in the middle of planting a tree, do not stop; go on planting the tree. We need to plant many trees: planted with *taqwa*, each tree becomes a prayer— and we need that many prayers.

May the earth bear witness for us and not against us; may we act and become worthy of having been created as *khalifahs* of Allah al-Rahman, al-Rahim.

Rabbana atina fi al-dunya hasanatan wa fi al-akhirah hasanatan waqina 'adhab al-nar (Our Lord! Grant us good in this world and good in the next world, and save us from the torment of the Fire).

Wa salla Allahu 'ala sayyidina Muhammadin wa 'ala ali Muhammadin wa ashabihi wa sallim (Allah's blessings on Muhammad and the companions of Muhammad).

Rabia's Journey to the Minbar:
"Interesting Answers Are the Children of Interesting Questions"

SOMEONE ONCE ASKED the renowned spiritual teacher Junayd, "How did you get to be a teacher?" He replied: "I sat with the Sufis for twenty years, never differing with them in anything. Then one day, somebody asked me a question."

I am thankful for Junayd's testimony because it was like that for me. I always knew I had something in me to share, but also that it was not yet ripe to share; I also had serious concerns that this something would never be ripe. Then one day, it was ready—people began asking me questions to which responses flowed from me that appeared to be useful to them. I take no personal credit for that; the phenomenon of teaching something useful to someone continues to amaze me.

I have given many talks, in classrooms and less formal spaces, but for a long time not a single khutbah. Talking from the minbar was never something I particularly wanted to do. Friday prayer, for me, has always been about praying in solidarity with others, about affirming community. I hardly paid attention to the khutbah, unless the *khatib* said something unusually annoying, which fortunately was not a common occurrence where I worshipped. Occasionally, he said something that moved me, upon which I reflected. But the best things I heard from him, the things that really struck a chord with me, I heard elsewhere than when he was at the minbar.

One day, years ago, at an interfaith summer camp where I acted as den mother for a week, I was approached by some South African young men who were students in the program. They asked me to serve as *khatibah* before the whole group. I felt humbled by their request, and very touched. How brave they were and what trust they were reposing in me! They were making a statement about Islam, *their* Islam. They wished to own their religion: they cared passionately about what Islam meant and ought to mean, and they needed my help to make this statement, to get there. I felt honored to oblige.

As I recall, the khutbah I gave compared Prophet Yusuf emerging from the dungeons of Pharaoh to become governor of Egypt with Nelson Mandela emerging from Robben Island to become president of the Republic of South Africa. I had never before thought about such a comparison, and I still find it an interesting one. Perhaps some members of that congregation still remember it; their presence produced it—interesting answers are the children of interesting questions.

Afterwards, relating this experience to a friend, a formidable Muslim woman scholar of a more conservative bent, I was met with her alarm. "However did you dare to do that?" she asked. "We have no hadith to validate women giving the khutbah!" "Maybe not," I responded, "but it was not all that daring. You know very well it is widely accepted that when there is no explicit prohibition, *mu'amalat* (lawful human transactions) may evolve to suit prevailing customs. It is only *'ibadat* (divinely accepted acts of worship) that need to be preserved from change." "Maybe so," she replied, "but how do you know that giving the khutbah belongs to the one category rather than to the other?"

This was and is an interesting question. And the answer is that actually, I do not know what category the act of giving a khutbah belongs to at all; I am not sure it *can* be known, at least in this life. But I am placing a bet on the intentions of God.

Now that I am much older and less worried about being too daring, I still find that an appropriate response to my friend's objection simply does not flow. If a person of faith is sincere, then her question is deep, and the territory into which my friend's questioning led stretches beyond the enclosed garden of my own spiritual education.

I am the adherent of a *revealed* religion; this means I accept that my path to God was not opened by a human wish, human reasoning, or even human aspiration—it was opened by God. The principle my teachers taught me is "follow the road that is known." The road opened by the question my friend posed enters into the unknown. Prudence (along with the sunnah) suggests that in matters of religion one should avoid anything that is doubtful. So why am I making an exception in this case?

Many elements of our practice, of our *din*, are regularly attributed to God with far fewer conscientious scruples, while the actual uncertainty surrounding them is not one whit less. Attributing things to God simply because those before us have done so is condemned by the Qur'an. The historical absence of *khatibahs* is no kind of argument for them not to exist in our lifetime. What if the opening of the public voice of women pertains to the force of revelation that in Surah al-Zalzalah God declares He will extend to the earth? What if the time for such revelation and extending is now?

Imagine that women's public voices have in fact become a divinely accepted act of worship, requiring careful preservation. That is not impossible, for revelation is revelation, and the affair belongs to God. We cannot know for certain, one way or the other. So how are we going to place our bets? And why would we decide as we would?

Friday is for consulting with the community. The Prophet teaches that whoever consults gains assurance about decisions.[23] And in times of uncertainty when there is no clear text or example, the Prophet has advised us, "Consult your heart."[24] Yet if we are honest, not much heart seems present in most of our Friday prayers; their relevance often seems so small—they are difficult to consult.

Do you wonder why that might be? If so, what are you going to do with the interesting question posed?

I have been a Muslim for more than forty years, in love with the subtleties of Allah. I pray my *salah*, pay my *zakah*, fast every Ramadan, and have made the hajj. I reexamine my profession of faith many times each day and hope very much that I will be permitted to die in remembrance. What more, really, is there to say about a life?

Subjectivity and Consciousness
Ihsan

The Gift of Four Human Births

NUR ROFIAH

(Indonesia)

Beloved congregants, *rahimakum Allah*. In this khutbah I will show that humans are born four times during their lives in the journey to becoming fully human and realizing the deepest message of Islam. First, a person experiences biological birth, when a fetus develops and a new human body arrives out of a mother's womb. However, the possessor of that life easily forgets the importance and merit of a woman as the mother of life. Therefore, Allah (*subhanahu wa ta'ala*) reminds us of this truth:

> And We have enjoined upon the human, good treatment to his parents,
> His mother carried him with hardship and gave birth to him with hardship,
> his gestation and weaning took thirty months. (Q. 46:15)[25]

> And We have enjoined upon man [care] for his parents.
> His mother carried him, in weakness upon weakness,
> and his weaning is in two years.
> Be grateful to Me and to your parents,
> to Me is the [final] destination. (Q. 31:14)[26]

In these two verses, Allah commands every human being to be filial and show loving regard to both parents. However, the command to care for parents is especially focused on the mother because of her pregnancy, childbearing, and breast-feeding. The verses express gratitude to the mother, and a child is considered grateful to Allah by thanking the mother of life. So as humans, we may grow up to become whatever we want to be—a businessperson, a state official, a politician, an engineer, a scientist, a farmer, a teacher, a worker. Yet we must never forget our essential debt to the woman who endured the challenges and pain of pregnancy, birthing, and breast-feeding us. By remembering the hardship endured by our mothers, the bearers of our very existence, and by expressing appreciation to her, we give thanks to Allah.

The second birth the human experiences is spiritual birth. The human is a creature like any other that has a body. After death, the body is devoured by the earth, yet the spirit remains alive and must take full responsibility for and be accountable to the life the human led. Thus, the most important identity of the human is as a spiritual being. Every human being has a distinct and inherent subjectivity as a servant only of Allah. So, we may not worship anyone and anything other than Allah, nor treat anyone and anything like a servant. To be a servant of Allah means refusing to give absolute obedience to anybody or anything else—not to oneself or other people, nor to wealth, power, sexual libido, nor any other worldly attractions.

The Prophet Muhammad reminds us that there can be no obedience to those who are created if it requires disobedience to the Creator, al-Khaliq.[27] When we fully recognize that we are created to be a servant only of Allah— that we are never to be servants to any other person or relationship, whether marital, family, work-related, or other social relations—then we are actually experiencing a spiritual birth.

The third birth the human being experiences is social birth. In addition to our inherent spiritual status, we also have an inherent mandate as *khalifah fi al-ard*, the recipients of the Divine Trust (*amanah*) on earth, to realize and embody the greatest benefit for all creation:

> Indeed, We offered the Trust
> To the heavens and the earth and the mountains,
> They declined to bear it and feared it;
> The human being undertook it.
> Indeed, he was unjust and ignorant. (Q. 33:72)[28]

Every human being, both male and female, has an obligation to treat themselves and other people with respect and dignity (with *maslahah* or a "beneficial" way), as best they can. This obligation is related to *tawhid:* recognizing Allah as the singular, absolute deity requires an attitude that also values all God's creatures. True faith in Allah requires decency, good deeds, and the greatest benefit directed toward all God's creatures. When we realize that each of us is at the same time obliged and entitled to the greatest benefit on earth, then we are actually experiencing social birth—we truly come into our social being.

The fourth birth the human being experiences is intellectual birth. Unlike other creatures, humans are given minds and hearts to consider what is and is not permissible, what is good and not good, and what is appropriate and inappropriate in our capacity as servants of Allah, gifted with the mandate to realize the greatest *maslahah* or benefit on earth. Thus, as Muslims we are always required to think many times before undertaking an action. First, we must ask, Is this action allowed by Allah? Only if the answer from within our moral conscience verifies that it is lawful and permissible may we proceed with spiritual integrity.

However, we all have unique life conditions; we may be responsible for children and parents, healthy and sick, or we may be in a normal situation or experiencing a crisis. Like the diversity of such conditions, not everything allowed by religion is always good. Humans are required to use their minds and hearts to discern whether an action permitted by a religion is good or not, in accordance with the specific conditions of their lives. In answer to the question that the intellect poses, the heart and the mind must indicate beyond doubt that the action is good (*tayyiban*). When we experience the mind and heart in this way, then we are experiencing true intellectual birth.

Finally, because social conditions continually change, what is good in one place is not necessarily good or appropriate in another; or an action might be permissible and appropriate in one place and at a certain time, yet in other places or at different times the same action might be inappropriate. Humans are required to use their minds and hearts to discern appropriate actions (*ma'rufan*) that enjoin the good. This capacity for wise discernment and suitable response is part of our inherent status and mandate with all other human beings as both servant of Allah and as *khalifah fi al-ard*. When the awareness arises to continuously use our minds and hearts as best we can so that we always take action in *halalan* (lawful), *toyyiban* (good), and *wa ma'rufan* (appropriate) ways, then we have been born as an intellectual or right-minded being.

Beloved congregants, *rahimakum Allah* (may Allah be merciful). Our first birth as a human is a necessity, and it is Allah who determines when we are born and from which woman's womb. However, our next three births—spiritual, social, and intellectual—are entirely in our own hands, within the realm of our endeavors and choices (*ikhtiyarat*) as humans. There are people who, until they arrive at death's door, function solely as physical beings, their lives occupied only in pursuit of physical happiness for themselves. They forget God, forget the happiness of others; they even use their human capacities and intellects to do damage on earth and take selfish actions:

> We have certainly created man in the best of stature,
> Then We return him to the lowest of the low,
> Except for those who believe and do righteous deeds,
> They will have a reward unending. (Q. 95:4–6)[29]

Conversely, some humans experience the four births from an early age. Their faith in Allah as the one and only God guides them to do good toward everyone and anything at any time, anywhere. Their presence becomes a gift to their surroundings, as a rare and precious sustenance to a person in need, or as a child is a gift to their parents, and a parent, a gift to the child; as a husband is a gift to his wife, and a wife, a gift to her husband; as a trader is a gift to a buyer, and a buyer, a gift to the trader; or as a leader is a gift to the people, and the people, a gift to their leader.

This relationship of gifting embodied in one's very being, life, and every deed is the state of the *al-insan al-kamil* (the complete human being), aspired to in Islam. Humans who exist as gifts to themselves, to their families, to others in their society, and to people everywhere are in fact giving birth to themselves to the fullest extent. This is the heart of Islam in accordance with the mission of the Prophet Muhammad as the messenger of Allah, and it is our life's mission as his loyal followers, for the Qur'an states:

> And We have not sent you, [O Muhammad],
> except as a mercy to the worlds. (Q. 21:107)

Friday congregants, *hafidhukum Allah* (may Allah protect us), let us pray together—may we strive to become human beings who are gifts to fellow Muslims, and to all the creatures of Allah.

Amin, Amin, Amin, Ya Rabb al-'Alamin.

Nur's Journey to the Minbar:
"Engage Deeply with Allah in All Situations"

I WAS THE YOUNGEST in my family, with five brothers and a sister. As two daughters among several sons, my sister and I were the children the family "accepted." Unfortunately, my mother passed away when I was nine years old. I do not have any memory of her in good health—she was always sick. My father passed away three years after her. Thus I had neither father nor mother at the final stage of elementary school. I followed my sister, continuing my studies in the same Islamic boarding school in another province; at least an uncle lived close by at the time. My sister is six years older than me, and after we were together for a year at the boarding school, she left for university. I think my spirituality began to develop when I found myself alone, without my sister, at the boarding school.

I began to make decisions for myself, including about me. Sometimes I felt as if I was all alone in the big universe, that no one worried and cared about my life—I imagined all parents do this for their children. This loneliness meant that I could not depend much on anyone, except Allah. Thus I started to engage deeply with Allah in all situations I found myself in, and I continue this.

Currently I am a lecturer in Qur'anic *tafsir* at Perguruan Tinggi Ilmu al-Qur'an (PTIQ—the Institute of Qur'anic Sciences) in Jakarta, Indonesia. The campus is well-known as a male campus because for decades it has mostly accepted males in its undergraduate and graduate programs, has mainly male lecturers, and accepts only a small number of female undergraduate students. The students, usually engaged in religious fields, go on to work in the Ministry of Religion or as religious leaders in their communities.

During the month of Ramadan, male students and staff are sent to mosques throughout Indonesia and abroad to lead *tarawih* prayer and other special activities—being the *muadhin, khatib,* or imam. In short, the male students, like their lecturers, hold the authority to become imams and *khatibs.*

As a lecturer in the field of *tafsir* at PTIQ, I have the professional standing to be an *imamah* and *khatibah*. I am eligible in terms of individual qualification as a doctor in the field of *tafsir,* an alumna from Ankara University (Turkey), and institutionally as a lecturer at PTIQ. All my fellow male lecturers are offered the opportunity to be *khatibs,* as are my male students. I, however, am not offered this opportunity. Instead, I am positioned as a *tafsir* lecturer of *khatibs* in training at PTIQ. I therefore can conclude that the only capital I do not have to become a *khatib* is a penis. I am not biologically male, which, unfortunately for me, counts as an absolute social condition for my exclusion. Ironically, as a woman with all the educational qualifications, I teach male *khatibs* but am not allowed to perform the khutbah in my community.

The majority of Indonesian society is Muslim—87.6 percent (2018) of about 267 million people. Many public religious platforms are available for women, for example, as preachers on national television, administrators of the Indonesian 'Ulama Council, lecturers at universities with mixed students or men-only students, heads of Islamic institutes (private and public), and owners of *pesantren* (Islamic boarding schools). Women are also owners and leaders of *majlis al-ta'lims* (organizations providing routine Islamic studies). Women perform informal religious duties, such as thanksgiving for pregnancy, birth, circumcision, graduation, marriage, and commemoration of the day of death, even religious holidays or giving religious advice. But they cannot perform the Friday khutbah or other sermons in front of men.

I lecture *tafsir* in all-male classes, undertake teaching in *pesantren* for thousands of male students, and train male employees at the Ministry of Religion on Islamic discourse. As a *tafsir* lecturer, I integrate gender in my teaching subjects, including Islamic studies, literature studies of the Qur'an, *tafsir 'ilmi*, classical and contemporary *tafsir*, social *tafsir*, and the history of *tafsir*. I include gender in the paradigm and method of *tafsir*, as an analytical perspective and as a specific discussion topic.

Since 2019, I have led an initiative that provides a discussion forum on Islamic gender justice, called Ngaji KGI (Keadilan Gender Islam), as a response to the lack of study forums on Islamic gender justice; the public can access it for free. Those who attend are mostly women. Nevertheless, I take every opportunity in any forum attended by men to talk about Islamic themes integrated with gender. I have noticed many men who feel a sense of unease regarding gender-biased understandings of Islam and the subordination of Muslim women. During a class discussion on polygyny, which elicits excitement in a men-only class, the atmosphere quieted when I asked, "What would you do if your mother became very ill and your father remarried?" One student burst out, "I would kill my father." In that moment, I demonstrated the adverse effects of polygyny on men too. Recounting this incident at an Ngaji KGI event, a male participant confessed that he had really wanted to kill his father who had remarried when his mother fell ill.

I am thankful for the opportunity to contribute a khutbah to this book. It has sparked within me an idea to compile my own collection of Friday khutbahs. For easier acceptance, I might perhaps have to publish such a collection under a male-sounding pseudonym—Nur Rofi, AH. Such a book might be one strategy for the message of Islamic gender justice to reach the Friday prayer *jama'ah* (congregation), who insists that to be its *khatib* you must also be a man!

ɔ፠ͼ

Spirituality of the Ordinary
SA'DIYYA SHAIKH
(South Africa)

Bismillah al-Rahman al-Rahim.

> When My devotee asks you concerning Me, I am indeed close
> I answer the prayer of every suppliant when they call on Me

Let them also willfully hear My call, and believe in Me
That they may be guided (Q. 2:186)

Two aspects of this beautiful Qur'anic verse stand out for me: first, the constant, intimate presence of Allah *subhanahu wa ta'ala* with the sincere seeker; and second, a mutual relationship between the Creator and human beings. Together, these present us with a mode of being in the world, a posture of seeking, of willingness to hear and to be guided, of intentional receptivity as we navigate the journey of our everyday lives. Despite nuances and sometimes complicated "gray" areas of life, on the path of spiritual transformation, human beings are each given a choice in every ordinary and seemingly mundane experience. Daily we make decisions about choosing a stance of seeking and surrender to divine guidance or succumbing to egotistical agitations.

Believers who yearn for inner transformation are assured by this verse that the Reality of the Divine is ever-present and ever-desiring to be known, and that we are meant to seek it always and to live in a state of receptivity to it. The clarity of conscious intention (*niyyah*) is critical in living faithfully. *How* to be in a state of receptivity is hence a key question for the sincere believer.

To begin with, we recognize that within every human there exists a higher consciousness; how much of it we each cultivate varies, but the central point remains that every human life, without exception, contains the spirit of God. A deep intimacy with the Divine is inherent to human *fitrah*, or created nature, as reflected in the hadith *qudsi* where Allah says, "The heavens and earth do not contain Me, but the heart of my faithful servant contains Me."[30]

Within the Islamic tradition, every person is created to know and manifest the Divine—this is our shared and collective existential purpose. Simultaneously, each human is a "unique filter of Divine light."[31] As such, all souls have their own distinctive pathway to God, in harmony with their individual nature and constitution. Hence, knowledge of *oneself* in the nonegotistical sense is key in a person's life journey.

Within human beings resides an exquisite balance between the universal and the particular. On the one hand, we must recognize the shared human possibilities that every person equally possesses and appreciate that the original divine light is scattered on all lives. On the other hand, we need a keen attentiveness to individual differences—where responsiveness to a person's particular nature and constitution renders this light either visible or less visible, depending on the investment in knowledge of the self toward the Real.

Importantly, the original divine light, cascading through myriad filters and personalities, is *never* lost. It is always among and within each of us, constantly accessible, seeking manifestation in our everyday lives. This divine light is the true source of self-knowledge and the basis of our most meaningful relationships.

When one is valuing the uniqueness of human beings, a helpful spiritual lesson is to surrender one's expectations of others. This might seem to be a commonsense insight, but it is amazing how many people suffer persistently because of their constant expectations of others. I am not suggesting that people indiscriminately accept bad, discriminatory, or abusive behavior from others, which is manifestly unacceptable. Rather, I am referring to instances when we are frustrated or unhappy because people close to us fail to fulfill our expectations of them. Thus we remain trapped in such thoughts of "if only" or "what if," believing that once others change, *then* things will be better.

Basic emotional intelligence teaches us that ultimately, we are powerless to change others; each person can do that only for themselves. Our expectations and frustrations are thus quite futile; for our own psychological health, relinquishing expectations of others is liberating. Significantly, too, this attitude has a valuable spiritual dimension, for amassing expectations of a person blinds us to their God-given distinctiveness, and to what they *do* in fact offer us.

Consumed by measuring others against our own internal calculus and resenting them for failing to meet our standards, we lose sight of their unique beauty and gifts. We might fail to appreciate those in our innermost circles of friendship and family because of the obfuscating deficit of our own need. Imbuing our spiritual lives with discernment requires that we set aside egotistical expectations, sometimes even real personal needs, to more fully apprehend the distinctive value of others.

My own experience has taught me that divine grace can manifest in unexpected ways. As a young graduate student of Islamic studies, which was part of an existential journey for me, I realized my spiritual hunger could not be sated by purely intellectual work. I began to zealously seek out a Sufi teacher, conjuring up a mental image of a powerful (*jalali*) spiritual teacher in whose *jalali* presence truth would be unveiled to me. During this same period, I undertook a doctoral scholarship in the United States with some ambivalence and uneasiness. I was excited to be studying Islam and religion with leading scholars in the world. But as a radical young activist, I was also uncomfortable about the capitalist, neocolonial empire of the United States, which I vociferously critiqued; thus I entertained a degree of negative stereotypes about American people.

It is both funny and edifying that in this place I had perceived as politically fraught, unethical, and without social virtue, I found my sought-after sublime, spiritual teacher. Shaykh Muhammad Raheem Bawa Muhaiyaddeen was not only a small-built Sri Lankan man who sang Tamil songs in a high-pitched voice, did not speak a word of English, and looked very much like the ordinary South Indian men I had grown up among in Durban, but he was also, rather inconveniently, no longer physically alive![32]

Given my fanciful preconceptions of my spiritual teacher, I failed to immediately recognize him or his teachings. Rather, it was through the living qualities and alluring fragrance in the character of his students that I was drawn to the source of their teachings; they embodied an intangible, compelling beauty that I aspired to. What mysteriously unfolded in the ensuing decades was an extraordinary spiritual journey that endures; relationships of deep love, wisdom, and transformation were gifted to me from Bawa, through his songs, writings, and closest disciples.

In this most surprising of places, through this teacher and his students, my deepest questions and hunger began to be sated. I had never expected my spiritual nurturing to unfold in this way, through a gentle, oh-so-ordinary-looking man who was rather ascetic—a vegetarian and celibate—choices I was personally not inclined toward! He was the opposite of my imaginary mental constructs of a *shaykh*. Yet he did and continues to awaken my heart, including through the living wisdom and beauty embodied by his students, a number of whom are also American. Humbled, I began to understand that when wisdom arrives, it sometimes emerges from unexpected places, breaking down walls of exclusion and stereotypes. I began to recognize that divine light and guidance are the birthright of every human being. Laying down my personal expectations enabled my heart to open to the abundance of divine beauty and grace around me, manifest in sometimes unanticipated ways.

Everyday life is the workshop of the spirit, the real locus of meaningful spiritual transformation. Shaykh Fadhlalla Haeri, another luminous Sufi teacher, cautions seekers against being captivated by otherworldly mystical experience as the marker of spiritual development, sharply observing, "If you have had some extraordinary visions or mystical dreams, good for you, but really, who cares?" In my experience, enthrallment by a specific state, or *hal*, could easily become "spiritual candy." Narrowing inner growth to a heightened spiritual state, delicious as that might be, blinds us to the core of spiritual work in our everyday behavior, in our *adab* and our ongoing and sustained relationships.

Ultimately, the specific labor one does is of little consequence; a street sweeper, a lawyer, a parent, a housewife, a teacher—in the field of the spirit and the light of the Divine, each role enables us equal opportunities for cultivating the heart, through practicing good qualities and purifying intention. No space is spiritually superior for the possibility of refining character. It is our egos that classify some roles and spaces as more valuable than others, for social recognition and prestige, neither of which is the metric of Divine Reality.

The qualities of primary importance relate to the manner with which one undertakes a task, the sincerity one gives to specific responsibilities, and the way one engages with other people. It is ultimately the kindness, love, compassion, and sense of justice in our interactions, the generosity we show in understanding the weaknesses of others as well as our own, and the embodiment of firmness and courage when needed that matter. These qualities and intentions require careful cultivation in the full range of our lives, from work in the sociopolitical arena to our daily domestic spaces. Cooking a meal with loving devotion is a form of *ibadah,* or worship; as ordinary as such an act might seem, by consciously inviting the One who is the source of love and nourishment to be present with and through you, the mundane chore is transformed into spiritual practice. It is we ourselves who must, by example, attempt to model the very qualities we desire in others. When our interactions are saturated by loving-kindness, these can set hearts alight.

Allah in Her infinite abundance resides in the detail; spirituality is embodied in our lives and relationships with others and not simply in the ritual prayers we perform on the mat or in a mosque. We are engaged in opportunities for spiritual refinement in everyday actions: in the manner of raising our children or interacting with those less powerful in our communities, in dealing with pain when wronged, in our artistic expressions that aspire to transcend form, in clothing our beauty with modesty, in being vigilant against spiritual pride, and in doing sincere service for others.

Let us always remember: spiritual refinement and beauty of character reside in the details. God is in the ordinary details. Love is in the everyday details. And the spiritual journey is always in the present.

Sa'diyya's Journey to the Minbar:
"Wisdom Sometimes Arrives from Unexpected Places"

I WAS BORN IN 1969 in South Africa and grew up in Durban with parents whose practice of religion had a significant impact on me. As a child, I was nurtured by a deep undercurrent of Islamic spirituality. My father regaled me with lively tales of the early female spiritual savant Shaykha Rabia Adawiyya, that intoxicated lover of God. I was fascinated by her wandering the streets of Basra, water in one hand and fire in the other, demanding that spiritual seekers douse the fear of hell and incinerate the lust for paradise from their hearts so devotion to God might emerge from sheer unadulterated love. I listened avidly to stories of the Baghdadi Sufi Abdul-Qadr Jilani, whose mother was a formative spiritual teacher. Her son embodied her teachings about constant awareness of God, and his courage, integrity, and virtue melted the hearts of even the most hardened criminals. These early Muslims were spiritual superheroes in my young imagination, and I yearned to be like them.

Another cherished memory is my mum leading *tarawih* at home for the neighborhood women while the men prayed at the nearby mosque. Her beautiful recitation captured the transformative power of listening to the Qur'an, and being part of that dedicated female congregation nourished my experience of female communal ritual. I also internalized the idea that men owned the public spaces of congregational worship, the masjid. My madrasah teachers reinforced ideas that men were in charge religiously and that God was to be feared. Fortunately, their teachings failed to affect me deeply, so fundamentally opposed as they were to the experiences of my childhood home.

The image of God gifted to me by my parents was filled with reverence, wonder, mystery, awe, love, and beauty, which later also helped me to view my parents generously when facing some difficulties with them. Indeed, Bawa Muhaiyaddeen, among my spiritual teachers, observes that our first image of God is formed by our early relationship with our parents. This gem has made me appreciate the importance of careful reflection on formative relationships on the path of spiritual unfolding and maturation in life.

As a young adult born in a community that originated in the Indian diaspora in South Africa, and based in the coastal town of Durban during apartheid, my relationship with religion was fraught. This was primarily due to prevailing sociocultural norms that made women secondary citizens in the family and society. Sexism intersected with racism and ethnocentrism, creating a suffocating community environment in which people were simultaneously victims and perpetrators of abusive racist, sexist hierarchies. I rejected an "Indian" identity, embracing instead Black consciousness. In these struggles, Islam was the matrix through which I wrestled with issues of human purpose, spirituality, politics, dignity, and social justice. The Qur'anic mandate to stand up for justice as witnesses for Allah (Q. 4:135) was my constant guide and companion. Islam constituted the existential skin of my being, even as I grappled to discern "Islamic" positions from competing Muslim perspectives and practices.

The antiracist politics of progressive Muslim organizations in South Africa strengthened my vision of Islam as both spiritually introspective and politically active. I increasingly came to see the quest for racial, economic, and gender justice as a religious obligation. Yet pursuing graduate studies in religion in Cape Town, I began to better understand the insidious ways that patriarchy infiltrates many traditions. I also learned how women from diverse religions resist and instead engage faith constructively as the foundation for justice and human dignity. Among Muslim scholars, I was invigorated by Professor amina wadud's pathbreaking work on the Qur'an.

Her 1994 talk at my local masjid, Claremont Main Road Mosque, deeply inspired the development of my Islamic feminism. Moreover, the mosque's invitation to amina opened a pathway for more public roles for women in our congregation. Subsequently, I have given *Jumu'ah* talks there, including this very khutbah. Elsewhere in the world and among local gatherings of likeminded people, I have led mixed *salah* congregations. My acceptance of leadership roles is driven by my experience as a young Muslim who desperately needed women leadership role models. My intent for initiating this volume with Fatima was to deepen the archive for Muslim women's leadership. Role models are critical for internalizing gender justice as a living reality and concomitant part of spiritual growth—as is the presence of ethically refined Muslim men, like those who nourished me, embodying their masculinity separate from toxic patriarchy. I am grateful to all these friends and teachers who have deepened my faith and perception: the stories of Muslim women such as Rabia Adawiyya; the female-led congregations in my childhood; the work of contemporary Islamic feminist scholars; my spouse, who embodies goodness effortlessly; and my children, whose existence inspires me to do the work with a heart receptive to the changing signs on the horizon.

ꙅꙥꙓ

The Overview Effect
SHEENA BAHARUDIN
(Malaysia)

Bismillah al-Rahman al-Rahim.

When asked, I found myself in a place of great uncertainty: Should I
volunteer to give a khutbah, or remain silent? There are so many things that
I have yet to learn that the very idea of standing in front of you feels tremen-
dously heavy. But the opportunity presented itself and I did not say no. Still,
I was immediately overwhelmed by a tsunami of fear, doubt, and joy at this
space that had suddenly opened up, so that my throat began to close up as I
attempted to swallow back the tears into that lump we are all too familiar
with. Mine was the size of the moon.

I knew I could not do it alone. I needed help. It was then that the story
of Prophet Musa (peace be upon him) came to me. I quickly turned to the
Qur'an to find Surah Taha. Reading its first verse, I knew that it was not a
coincidence:

We have not sent down to you the Qur'an that you be distressed.
(Q. 20:2)

I was indeed in a state of distress. Unlike the past decade spent writing
and performing poetry before different audiences, I had never until now been
given the same space to speak in my Muslim community. There was a clear
separation between my lived story and the sermons delivered from the pulpit
of my mosque.

Stories are important: First, because human beings are composed of
stories—from the minute of birth up until the last moment of life, we are
sharing, reading, and listening to each other's stories. Second, storytelling
has long been used by women to break the vicious cycles of human error and
transgression. We share the stories that have been passed down from one
generation to the next, driven by the purpose of remembering our cause for
justice, and uniting in the face of the injustices we experience.

I began writing and performing poetry as a Muslim woman for these
very reasons. Within the constraints of our society and its many manmade
rules, poetry (which is but another form of storytelling) has given me a platform to connect with and reach out to others. But I admit that it has not been

easy to do, nor will it ever be. Being here before you is proof yet again that the act of speaking involves not only courage but clarity of intention. Being among you, I also know I am not alone.

We have all found ourselves in situations where we must choose to speak or remain silent. When the Prophet Musa was given the heavy task of confronting Pharaoh to return to the path of righteousness, he prayed for strength, as reflected in these beautiful verses:

> My Lord, expand for me my breast
> And ease for me my task
> And untie the knot from my tongue
> That they may understand my speech. (Q. 20:25–28)

These are the same verses I began to repeat, over and over again, in my room. These same verses I repeated just before it was my turn to stand before you and present this khutbah. I may not know how exactly to begin or end a Friday sermon, but I do have a story I would like to share with you. It is a poem I have written, which goes by the title "The Overview Effect." It goes like this:

> There is a term used by scientists
> to describe the sudden shift of consciousness
> experienced by astronauts upon seeing the earth
> from space for the very first time.
>
> From this viewpoint,
> there are no more countries and borders,
> just the division of land and water.
>
> No more are the things that we think matter
> like money, sex, politics, religion or power
> because from this viewpoint,
> everything is clear
> and quiet
>
> except
>
> for the sound of breathing
> as it dawned upon the astronauts
> that this tiny blue planet is the only place
> in the entire universe they could call home.
>
> Scientists call this phenomenon:
> The Overview Effect

and though I may never get to see myself
in a space suit or go walking on the moon,
meeting You has shifted my entire worldview
from the singular to the plural.

From me to we, from I to us
getting to know You has made me more
than just a body of flesh and bones.

I am seeing things I never used to notice before.

Like how I was recently struck
by the story that occurred in the Cave of Hira
The story that Muslims refer to as Nuzul al-Qur'an,
the night when the Prophet Muhammad
received his first revelation.

What began as an evening meant for deep meditation
came to a sudden end when the archangel Gabriel appeared
out of thin air only to wrap their massive wings
around the poor, unsuspecting,
forty-year-old man.

It left him gasping for breath and shivering deep
in his bones as Gabriel proceeded to seal his body
into a vessel of prophethood.

"Read!" Gabriel thundered.
"Read in the name of God who created you from a clot"
and yet Muhammad could not for he was illiterate.

Three times, the angel tightened their grip.
Three times, the angel firmly repeated until finally,
sacred verses began spilling out from Muhammad's cracked lips
like a desert spring and the rest of the story,
as we are told, became *history*.

So, I thought I knew it all, inside and out,
but since waking up every morning
with the first thought of You,
I could not help but wonder aloud:

Now what if the Prophet was never illiterate?

It is no mystery that the human race
is best known for its propensity to forget

so perhaps he had only forgotten how to read
the words long inscribed within until the heat
from Gabriel's embrace made the invisible,
legible again.

If that was the case,
then perhaps we are all just breathing,
walking secret messages waiting to be deciphered
or we are poems, eager to be understood
by first being recited out loud.

Maybe all those times when we found ourselves
crying or laughing without reason, when we felt burdened
by the weight of irrational fears, or when certain places
felt like home even when we have never been there before

We were simply seeing glimpses of the writings
left on the walls of our souls.

Maybe we all used to read God
before we were taught to speak human
and all we ever needed to experience
the Overview Effect was to be held tight.

Now I bet,
that was what happened
the first time we embraced.

You were the fire casting light
in the caves of my existence.

Suddenly,
I am the archaeologist
resting my palms on the outline
of a 40,000-year-old handprint;
I am the mother
counting my firstborn's fingers and toes
[one, two, three, four],
my heart on board a moonshot,
I am the astronaut
mouthing the countdown,
wondering if I will ever get to feel gravity again
[four, three, two, one]

I am the Prophet
receiving my first revelation.

I am seeing things I never used to notice before:

Like how our bodies are libraries
filled with the memoirs of the dearly departed,
those whose lineage can be traced back to the Beloved,
those whose features still ripple on the surface
of our reflection and all we have to do
for us to see them is to be
absolutely
quiet.

Like that night when I first slept
in the warm stillness of Your embrace:

My Love,
I could read again.

I pray that in moments of distress and difficulties, we may always find
the courage and grace from God to have our hearts expanded, our tasks
eased, and our tongues unknotted so our shared stories can continue being
heard and understood.

    In sha Allah. All the good comes from Allah, and all the flaws are my own.

Sheena's Journey to the Minbar:
"Curves of the Qur'an's Exquisite Poetic Verses"

IF SOMEBODY HAD TOLD ME that I would deliver a Friday khutbah in
front of a congregation, I would have dismissed them immediately. The idea
had never crossed my mind, and why should it? In the thirty-six years of my
life before, I had never heard a single khutbah delivered by a woman. In our
society, women seldom attend the weekly Friday prayer; hence our exposure
to religious sermons is limited to Eid al-Fitr and Eid al-Adha. And all the
khutbahs I heard were presented by men, whose faces I could barely see because female members of the congregation were always segregated by a wall
or a curtain. Physically disconnected, I could never tell what the *khatib* was
doing, if he had a kind face or not—he was simply a voice I had been taught
to accept as a religious authority.

Ironically, these disembodied voices had a strong impact on my embodied experience as a Malay-Muslim woman in this country. I remember one sermon that made my muscles quiver with anger as the *khatib* reminded us neither about Islam nor God but instead spoke on the LGBTQI+ community as a threat to the Islamic way of life. For context, the past five years have seen increasingly aggressive targeting of sexual minorities as part of a vicious political discourse in Malaysia. I wondered whether the *khatib* might consider that a number of those listening to him were in fact queer Muslims. These were people who had made the effort to attend prayers as members of the community, only to be told that they do not and could never belong. The thought that his words could turn believers away from Islam hurt me to the core. How could this figure of authority forget the great responsibility that comes with delivering a khutbah?

Not soon after this troubling khutbah, I agreed to deliver a Friday sermon at the Musawah "Islam and Gender Equality and Justice" South East Asia Regional Course. It was a one-week program. Most of the participants had extensive experience in social activism, but I attended in my capacity as a female spoken-word poet to learn to contribute to my country's public discourse on Islam. From an early age, I have been fascinated by language—its letters and sounds, how careful arranging of these can create meanings and affect people in a multitude of ways. Poetry is recognized as the height of this art; once acquainted with it, I had made a conscious decision to surround myself with words and the worlds contained within them. It is not an exaggeration to say that poetry strengthens my love of and belief in Islam. Decades of tracing the curves of the Qur'an's exquisite poetic verses have convinced me of its inclusive, miraculous, and divine nature.

I also believe that a poet has a social responsibility to point out the imbalances and injustices in society. My poems tend to offer criticisms of gender inequality, racial discrimination, and injustice, in particular, patriarchal interpretations of Islam that attempt to subjugate rather than embrace women. Perhaps this is a reason I took my poems off the page and onto the stage. Spoken-word poetry is a form of storytelling. I did not want to be another disembodied voice in readers' heads. I wanted them to see and hear me in the flesh, to respond to me and give me feedback, interact with me as a poet sharing her stories through the medium of poetry.

It is fascinating that the Malaysian performance poetry scene is dominated by female poets. I believe this is because it is a platform for marginalized voices where various identities are seen, ranging from the religious to the political. It was through participation in the spoken-word scene that I grew to understand the importance of representation in public spaces, including the religious space. The absence of women *khatibs*, or *khatibahs*, reflects the larger issue of physically silencing women in Muslim communities. Yet this situation is manmade and thus can be rectified.

Admittedly, I struggled at first to prepare and deliver the sermon, simply because I had been consumed with feelings of inadequacy. *Al-hamdu lillah*, I remembered that I had been doing this kind of sharing via language for a full ten years already. My poems have always been extensions of my worldview, informed by my experiences as a Muslim woman. As with a sermon, the process involved in writing a poem also includes research and sensitivity to the effects of the words on an audience. This was why I decided to include a poem in my khutbah; the words of the poem I chose are carefully arranged with the clear intent of delivering the message of al-Rahman and al-Rahim.

I would love to describe the experience and the feedback I received after the first khutbah I presented, but it was one of those ineffable occasions when language fails. I look forward to more opportunities to present khutbahs inside or outside a mosque, as the Qur'an teaches:

> To Allah belongs the east and the west.
> So wherever you [might] turn
> There is the Face of Allah
> Indeed, Allah is all-Encompassing and -Knowing. (Q. 2.115)

Any space can be a religious space, with the right intention. *Salaam.*

Darkness to Dawn and the Spiritual Journey In Between

AMIRA QURAISHI
(United States)

You arrive at the masjid at midday to express gratitude to the Creator; we begin the *Jumu'ah du'a, inna al-hamdu lillah*. You come knowing it is not language, skin color, age, talent, or status but hope and conscience that draw you in community with others to affirm your faith. We acknowledge the unknown, *nasta'inuhu*, we ask Allah for help. We say *nastaghfiruhu*,[33] asking for forgiveness and believing that it is possible when we see others as ourselves.

Our sincere request for forgiveness requires willingness to enter the unknown to learn to self-correct with compassion.

We say *wa na'udhu billahi min shururi anfusina*, acknowledging our constant battle between choice and vice, seeking protection against negative traits turning into corrosive habits. *Wa na'udhu billahi min sayi'ati a'malina;* we acknowledge that our actions have consequences, even if we regret them. We take responsibility even if we do not see the impact of our misdeeds. We invoke the overarching protection of divine *rahmah*, compassion and mercy. Our responsibility is to seek the best choices and guidance from the One who is stronger than everything—*man yahdi-llahu fa la mudillalah wa man yudlil fa la hadiya lahu.* The All-Compassionate, the Most High, Allah *subhana wa ta'ala* guides us—with this, we cannot go astray.

Allah has promised us guidance always, and in many ways: one is the Qur'an, revealed to the Prophet Muhammad, Allah's messenger—*ash-hadu an la ilaha illa Allah ash-hadu anna Muhammadan 'abduhu wa rasuluhu.* This treasured book of guidance tells us,

> Oh you who believe, be mindful of God and speak a sound word.
> (Q. 33:70)

Today, beloved sisters, I want to reflect on some elements of our spiritual journey and relationship with Allah. The third part of the night is a special time to connect with Allah, as the Divine draws close and asks: "Who of my servants are calling to me? I will respond to them."[34] This mystical description is beautiful but somehow feels out of reach, like a difficult test that requires we pull ourselves out of deep slumber to receive an audience with our Creator. Indeed, much of Islam feels transactional in this way: one must overcome a test to receive a reward. One completes the five pillars and more, in a sort of checklist—we are left judging ourselves as "good" or "bad" Muslims.

Yet we ought not to miss the heart of our religion—the profound, personal exploration about who we are and our rootedness in the natural world, engagement with the world, and ultimate journey back to Allah. This is a journey about understanding the self as much as the Divine, as reflected in the hadith *qudsi* "When you know yourself, you know Allah."[35] Is it any wonder that our Islamic intellectual heritage is steeped in discussions about the differences between knowledge (*'ilm*), understanding (*fahm*), experiential gnosis (*ma'rifah*), and wisdom (*hikmah*)?

The natural world helps us imagine and experience the human condition in a state of unknowing. The hadith *qudsi* situates the believer in the last part of the night to be closer to Allah, the All-Knowing. Consider this through commonly used metaphors: We say we are "in the dark" when uninformed, or "reaching in the dark" when trying but failing to understand or make progress. We say "it is always darkest before the dawn" when yearning for hope in despair. Being in the dark, before dawn, mirrors our state before we have knowledge, information, understanding, clarity, and direction. Dawn indicates our state of consciousness, when our hearts and minds are a clear slate, not yet influenced by the day's activities. In this time, we cling to faith, trusting even though we cannot yet see. Thus, immersed in physical darkness, we are primed mentally and emotionally to trust Allah and receive guidance.

In the dark, a mystery is waiting to be illuminated. It is the experience of not-knowing that primes us to receive guidance. Moments of unknowing happen all the time, and these are precious invitations to deepen our faith and spirituality. Sometimes they occur in a new place or circumstance, in a new city or school. Not knowing our way around and being unfamiliar with the customs or language, we are constantly reminded that we are not at home; perhaps our clothes are inadequate against the cold, or we struggle to remember a name or directions.

Sometimes these moments of unknowing take us by surprise and are unsettling. Constantly taking in new information or questioning what we know is exhausting. When relationships are uncertain, finances strained, or health precarious, living in the unknown can be sad, lonely, and painful. It takes energy to deal with the loss of the familiar. The inability to anticipate what is coming next intensifies feelings of insecurity, anxiety, fear, and sadness. Uncomfortable with the unknown, we develop deflective behaviors and attitudes, demanding others provide us with guarantees. We rush to judgment, trying to fill the unknown with something we know, even if it is negative.

The Arabs who ridiculed the Prophet Muhammad's message demanded proof of the elusive Judgment Day, desiring to control their destiny. Allah's response is that the Day of Recompense can be revealed instantly in a flash of light but that it is better that humans receive it gradually:

> Humanity was created of haste. I will show you My signs, so do not impatiently urge Me. (Q. 21:37)

Spiritual development depends on heeding internal reminders that we do not know everything. Facing ourselves in the vulnerability of the unknown provides the space to grow in *taqwa* and *tawakkul* (awareness of and reliance on Allah). If too confident in knowing what is to come, we belong to the circumstance, but if comfortable in the unknowing and trusting in God, we belong to Allah. Finding oneself suddenly in a moment of unknowing is perhaps scary, but it is a gift—a precious opening to deepen faith and insight, a doorway toward receiving divine compassion and guidance, with treasures to be found.

Pausing in the unknown enables us to look outside ourselves and recognize ourselves in context. In a hadith, the Prophet Muhammad responds to the angel Jibril (Gabriel), questioning him about the meanings of *islam*, *iman*, and *ihsan*. The five pillars are the cornerstones of Islam, actionable and routine. However, only following these pillars may reduce one's spirituality to a mere checklist. *Iman* is faith in Allah, the angels, the books, the prophets, and the Last Day. In other words, these are the nutrients to a deeper understanding (*fahm*) of the story of humanity and eternal truths. *Ihsan*, which I translate as "beautiful presence," is living as if we are seeing Allah, or at least living as though Allah sees us.

By welcoming the moments of unknowing, we fold into our spirituality the richness of continual mindfulness and trust in Allah. This enables us to see ourselves as subjective beings, functioning within a context formed by particular historical, social, emotional, physical, and mystical elements. With such experiential knowledge (*ma'rifah*), we can live a life of beautiful presence (*ihsan*) in this world and the next.

A life based solely on knowledge of the five pillars is a sufficient starting point, but it is the exploration of one's unique nature and distinctive journey to *ihsan* that brings beauty into the world. Allah states:

Hal jaza ul-ihsanu, illa al-ihsan?

Can the reward for beautiful presence be anything but beautiful presence itself? (Q. 55:60)

The journey begins with *la ilaha illa Allah* (there is no power but Allah); there is nothing without Allah. There is no knowledge without Allah; therefore, the not-knowing is an open invitation to Allah's presence, the Divine Compassion.

In Surah al-Mulk, Allah tells our Prophet Muhammad that it boils down to this:

What does it matter if Allah chooses to destroy me and my followers? . . . Say: "He is the All-Compassionate, in Him we believe and on Him we depend." (Q. 67:28–29)

So welcome the unknown, negate everything but Allah; humble your-self to receive learning from the only Being with power to truly know, your Lord. Humility is not easy to attain, yet Allah says that mountains would have crumbled had the Qur'an been revealed to them (Q. 59:21). Instead, it was revealed to humans, a testament to the potential within us. The task of facing oneself in the unknown and trusting in Allah is not easy, but it is mar-velous! Rumi recalls the paradox of human existence, that each of us is the ocean in a drop, rather than just a drop in the ocean.[36]

Our spiritual practice (*din*) guides us and give us skills in moments of anxiety; our Prophet's supplication provides understanding of the emotions we cling to when facing the unknown:

Allahumma inni a'udhu bika min al-hammi wa al-hazan wa al-'ajzi wa al-kasl wa
  al-bukhli wa dala'il al-dayn wa ghalabat al-rijal.

O Allah, I take refuge in You from anxiety and sorrow, weakness and laziness,
  miserliness and cowardice, the burden of debts and from being overpowered
  by men.[37]

The unknown need not be scary. It can be welcomed, even loved, for it invites us to meet Allah there. Allah provides us with many tangible ways to contemplate unknowing, including the mystical *muqata'at*, disconnected let-ters *alif, lam, mim* in Surah al-Baqarah, which remind us of the limits of our knowledge.

Allah assures guidance in the Qur'an for those who believe in the un-seen, who pray and give charity from the bounty they receive. Remaining with the unknowing and surrendering ideas to which we are attached enables us to rest in Allah's presence and brings relief from constraint. Only then can we truly give thanks and give charity for the sake of God. Willingness to let go of resentments and negative thoughts about self and others is a tangible spir-itual practice that opens us to these higher possibilities. Facing yourself, truth emerges just as nature gently reveals the sun with the dawn breaking. What was previously in darkness become faint silhouettes against an indigo sky. Uneasiness persists from the still hidden shapes, but the growing light grad-ually provides depth and transforms perception. From the horizon, silhou-ettes begin to emerge as familiar figures, bringing a flood of reassurance— what was not seen in the dark has been there all along! You realize where you are, where you have been all along in relation to it all.

Being attentive to our hearts allows deeper comprehension of the Qur'an, including our experiences of nature. Allah describes the dawn as softly breathing (Q. 81:18) to focus on being present in the moment, bringing awareness to the breath and being in the natural world. As the breaking dawn's sun begins to illuminate the surroundings, so too does practicing intimate *du'a* at night illuminate a deep knowing within: that which is confusing becomes clear, and we experience Allah as "Light upon light" (Q. 24:35).

There is a rich journey of the self that can be undertaken between the darkness of night and the light of day. The struggle to embark on it can be overcome by viewing the unknown as a spiritual treasure, key to *taqwa* and happiness rooted in belonging to God. The Qur'an becomes a friend on the journey, reassuring us that in "the remembrance of God hearts are contented" (Q. 13:28). Embrace this, as you journey in perplexing and unfriendly spaces. Know that Allah is always present, even if you are momentarily blinded by anxiety. Do not lose sight of the tree in the darkness of night, for it is there, waiting to be revealed again at dawn. These are the beautiful illuminations, poised to emerge in us all.

Amira's Journey to the Minbar:
"Being Patient with the Unknown"

MANY SCHOOLS AND UNIVERSITIES consider spiritual spaces an essential part of a nurturing environment and healthy community. The majority of college students today are unaffiliated with a religious tradition yet consider themselves "spiritual." They are emerging adults, exploring their values and discovering what is meaningful to them. Muslim students too yearn for spaces that reflect who they are. As a culturally diverse, religious minority, these students need a place where they can safely explore life's questions and try to understand the multiple variations of Islamic practice, belief, and identity within their communities. The weekly *Jumu'ah* prayers I facilitate offer them a diverse and inclusive Muslim space.

Being a *khatibah* to young Muslim women over the years has given me the opportunity to understand the responsibility of the minbar. I wanted our *Jumu'ah* prayers to be uplifting and grounding, a space where students experience the support of other Muslims. I grew up knowing that prayer is the cornerstone to a Muslim's daily life and that Friday prayer is the cornerstone to establishing our community. My father instilled in me the second pillar of Islam, prayer (*salah*), making sure we stopped to pray whether in a neighborhood park or on a road trip. Touching my forehead to the ground in the middle of anywhere, nowhere, taught me that

Allah is with you, wherever you are. (Q. 57:4)

When I arrived at Wellesley College in 2013 to take up the position of the Muslim chaplain, I could not deny the feeling of religious obligation to establish the weekly congregational *Jumu'ah* prayers. It is what makes a community cohesive, allowing for discussion and shared experiences through the perspective of faith and spirituality.

I was aware that if men were present, it would likely fall on them to establish congregational prayers, as is so often the custom, but at this all-women's school, there were no Muslim men. Although I had written khutbahs for male imams in the past, I had never presented one to a congregation myself. It was likely that only one or two students would join me to pray on that first Friday, and I wondered about what approach to adopt in this space. Were students afraid to share their Muslim identities and join a congregational prayer? Was this too religious for them? Were they uneducated about prayer? Were they dismissive of the importance of women praying together? Did they not know it was happening? Were they all on their period? Was it me?

The first *Jumu'ah* arrived and passed predictably, and every week these questions pushed me to ask, "What am I not seeing?" I felt self-doubt and awkwardness as I called the students to pray and assumed they knew to sit and listen to a khutbah. The silent audience was difficult to get used to. I had no sense of whether this was beneficial except for the persistent reminder in my head to follow the sunnah of the Prophet Muhammad (peace be upon him). When we follow the Prophet, our Sustainer will help us. What also stuck in my head was a variation on a line from the movie *Field of Dreams:* "If you build it, they will come."

Each year I explored possible solutions to the awkwardness: I worked hard to create a routine for the students to feel comfortable with, improved my speaking skills, found more central spaces to pray, integrated a special *dhikr* (melodic supplication), cooked lunch, invited non-Muslims to learn about *Jumu'ah* prayers, invited students to lead, developed a teaching template and tutorial. Although I believe the success of a program is not always marked by its numbers, it has been gratifying to see the attendance of our *Jumu'ah* prayers grow from two to twenty students, becoming a true space for community to gather, for students to share their faith and to learn from each other to establish a cornerstone of Islam.

The most gratifying aspect of *Jumu'ah* prayers has been witnessing female students lead our community. The moment they take their words seriously in worship (*'ibadah*), they transform the experience for those listening. One *khatibah* shared how she connected to the Qur'an by learning the meaning of her name; another spoke of her gratitude for this community. This has truly become a community shaped by women for women, where women can hear their peers express what Islam means to them and how they struggle with their own spirituality. The space enables Muslim women students to feel valued in a way that seldom happens in male-dominated spaces. Congregants know they are equal partners in sustaining the spiritual well-being of our community, the shared responsibility of all. I see the students come to *salat al-Jumu'ah* with energy and commitment to the community, with confidence in their Muslim identity, and with deep faith.

Serving as *khatibah*, I have learned to practice my Islam with the authority of both a seeker and a guide. Both entail different commitments. The former has, at times, felt externally awkward but spiritually significant. The latter has revealed the opportunity to create a space for young women to explore their faith and provide spiritual leadership to their peers. The khutbah I offer here draws from my experience of walking through unfamiliar terrain in both commitments. The process has directed me inward—to be patient with the unknown and to turn toward Allah through God's Divine Names.

ꙮ

Ramadan:
The Divine Treatment

SHAYKHA AMINA TESLIMA AL-JERRAHI
(EDLÍN ORTIZ GRAHAM)
(Mexico)

So where are you going?
—Q. 81:26

Bismillah al-Rahman al-Rahim.

The first night of Ramadan was special for many reasons—one being the mystical body of dervishes unexpectedly attending the masjid to join us in greeting the arrival of this month. All generations of our community were present, from Abu Bakr, an eighty-five-year-old dervish, and his adorable grandsons, Anwar and Perceo, and their parents, Muzafereddin and Munevere, to the beauty, little Fatima, born only a few months before and still looking at Paradise. There was the sweetness of the *tarawih* prayers, the soul strength of the dervishes, the ecstatic sound of the Divine Names our voices chanted in unison. The falling rain cleansed the city as *maghrib* prayer arrived, a palpable flow of blessings poured from the Most High, a preparation for the arrival of the holy time of Ramadan.

This time that Allah has endowed with a nature like no other time is a Generosity and Mercy, a time that is Generous in Mercy. This time is when the strength and the power of Mercy flow over abundantly. And what is Mercy if not an extreme manifestation of the fullness of Divine Love? This reason, one among so many, is why Ramadan is a sacred time, a special time given to us from the Creator of space and time. In a hadith *qudsi*, Allah the Most High proclaims:

> The children of Adam misunderstand Me when they complain against Time, for I am Time . . . I alone cause the day of knowledge to follow the night of ignorance.[38]

The sacredness of this month was as intense from the beginning of our faith as it is at this moment. We are informed that Ramadan was a time when the archangel Gabriel met nightly with the Prophet, peace be upon him, to revise the Qur'an. Another hadith states that during Ramadan the Prophet became "more generous than the swift wind"[39] and urged an intensified state of generosity, saying, "Whoever provides the food for a fasting person to break his fast with, then for him is the same reward as is (the fasting person's), without anything being diminished from the reward of the fasting person."[40] And for those who did not have the means to do that, the Prophet encouraged them to share even a half a date or just some water.[41]

Not only is Ramadan an encouragement of profound open-heartedness among humans, but our tradition informs us that this sacred time also brings an intensification of Divine Generosity. All demons are kept chained, the gates of hell closed, and the doors of Paradise wide open. In this best of times, our teacher Muzaffer Effendi (may Divine Mercy embrace him) reminds us of the Prophet's khutbah on Ramadan:

> The month of Allah has come with its mercies, blessings, and forgiveness . . . the days of this month are the best among days, and the

nights are best among all nights, and the hours . . . best among all hours. You have been invited by Allah to fast and pray . . . Allah has honored you in it . . . every breath you take is a reward of Allah, your sleep is worship, your good deeds are accepted, and your invocations are answered.[42]

All too often, we lose sight of what is significant and meaningful about Ramadan if we are focused on the initial discomfort of the fast. Yet may our fasting be transformed into food for all those who fast in hunger and thirst all the long year because they have nothing to eat. For the mystery of Ramadan transcends the aspect of abstinence from food, water, and sex between sunrise and sunset. The fast is much greater than biological restriction—it is a way of bringing healing and illumination to the now naked self.

Our teacher Shaykha Fariha al-Jerrahi enlightens us:

> The fast in Ramadan brings us to the place
> where we realize we do not know
> we must come to this place to let go
> to become primal and empty
> primal, again *hyle*[43]
> to return to the Cloud where all is potential
> the original Chaos
> to be created again
> by Allah
> and the Beautiful Divine Vibrations
> "Allah creates as He desires"
> Allah desires to create
> in our breast
> as the Qur'an was revealed in the breast of the Prophet,
> may he be embraced in sublime love
> Allah created the Qur'an in the breast
> we are also the breast that opens and receives
> but it must become silent, submitted, empty
> to become the dough in the hand of the baker
> the earth under the plough
> Allah desires us empty of knowing to fill us.[44]

Ramadan is the divine invitation for us to deny some comforts to receive yet others. We easily become like an infant whose pacifier has been removed, sensitive and vulnerable, as the surface of the skin of the soul is cleansed.

Open and unguarded at that moment, we can see the pain hitherto not seen or resolved internally. Freed from the weight of our "issues" through *taqwa*, God-consciousness, we become aware of the Divine Presence at all times. At the same time spiritual dimensions, faculties, and skills—things that we do not know about ourselves or about the nature of Reality—are shown to us, as the highly subtle "divine treatment" unfolds. Waves of blessings just to give and give and give ceaselessly arrive from Arham al-Rahimin, the Most Merciful of those who show Mercy.

So we offer in this holy time all that we can offer to Love. Allah Most High informs us that the value of every action lies in the heart's intention; let us never think what we offer too little if it is offered with the loving and noble intention of the heart. If one is unable to perform the biological fast, another kind of powerful fasting—such as silence—can be followed. And the days that we do not fast can be replenished later. Let us remember that fasting is an utterly private thing between us and our Beloved Rabb. The Sufi tradition abounds with literature on fasting, with deep insights shared by the *awliya*, the friends of Allah.

It is said, for example, that 'Isa (Jesus), peace and blessings upon him, taught that there are demons that only fasting can expel from our soul structure. Sufi teachings about the seven levels of consciousness alert us that the most basic level, the dominating self, or *nafs al-ammarah*, is the nest of all kinds of low-level energies and subtle and not-so-subtle manifestations. An increasing number of nutritionists are now recommending fasting since studies show that intermittent fasting regenerates the body's systems and organs. The mind, it seems, has run out of arguments against fasting. Yet, too, as Shaykh Nur insists, it is only by Divine Permission that we may undertake a fast; in our case, we fast only for Allah, who tells us clearly, "The fast is Mine, and its reward lies with Me, " since no one but Allah alone sees it.[45] The Prophet clarified: "Allah said: 'Every deed of Adam's people is for them except fasting; it is for Me and I will give the reward for it.'"[46]

Unlike other religious activities, the faster, or *sa'im*, is marked by a special form of sincerity; her offering to the Source of Being remains concealed from the eyes of others. The nature of this concealed act confers the *sa'im* with protection from hypocrisy, such as, perhaps, social pressure to fast—there is simply nothing to show or to be seen. We who live in Mexico City, for example, do not have people around us who are fasting or who have even heard about Ramadan. What a powerful freedom to be who we truly are with Allah and with ourselves before Allah! The sole "pressure" here is a gift; it is our Love in the desire to connect with the Source of Love.

The Hidden and Manifest, the All-Loving Guide and the All-Powerful Teacher has issued an invitation. The lovers respond, satisfied with the call, to attend from their very own contexts, with her own spiritual practices, with his own degree of dedication, with her own degree of remembrance, with his own degree of absence and presence, with her own commitments, with his own efforts, with her own passions and wisdom, with his own external and internal struggles. Everyone, without exception, maps out their place in Ramadan. *Ma sha' Allah!*

We are informed that on the Day of Resurrection, the month of Ramadan will take on corporeal form and bear witness for us, her friends, about the journeys we undertook for our souls during this month—for the new understandings and expansions of consciousness, for the greater freedom and tranquility, for the greater internal space to receive without resistance that which we are presented at every moment, for the valuable skills and states for connecting to the higher spheres of Being, Pure Truth, and Essence. I secretly enjoy imagining that day when we will see a corporeal manifestation of something as mysterious as Ramadan. My heart remains in awe of the miraculous grandeur and the powerful subtlety of this blessed month.

Shaykh Nur teaches:

> Only through the open gates of the Paradise of *Ramadan* can the total flood of Divine Presence enter, awaken, and transform the heart. The fully flowered state of sanctity is hidden within a few human beings, but the noble month of *Ramadan* is open and available to persons at all levels of spiritual development. *Ramadan* reveals the intrinsic sainthood of every heart.[47]

And Shaykh Muzaffer reminds us to cherish this time:

> Appreciate it! It passes very quickly. Life itself passes very quickly too, as does the time for prayer. Do not say: "*Ramadan* will come again," because a *Ramadan* that has gone will never come again. The next *Ramadan* will be a different *Ramadan*. Maybe *Ramadan* will keep coming around until the Resurrection, but this *Ramadan* may be your last.[48]

Equally relevant is a memorable story that Shaykh Muzaffer relates about Ayaz, the beloved courtier of the eleventh-century Sultan Mahmud of Ghazna. The sultan once peeled a cucumber, which he shared with Ayaz. As he ate his own half, the sultan found that the cucumber tasted acrid and unpleasant, and yet Ayaz appeared to relish it. Nonplussed, the sultan asked Ayaz why he showed no sign of distaste, nor did he spit out the bitter vegetable. Ayaz responded:

> My dear Sultan, I have enjoyed so many bounties from your hands. After all that, how could the cucumber taste bitter? Would it not be ungrateful of me to spit out the good thing you have given me now, when your hand has given me tasty morsels by the hundred? Even if you did give me something bitter, it would taste sweet to me.[49]

Here is a poem by Mawlana Rumi:

> A new moon teaches gradualness
> and deliberation and how one gives birth
> to oneself slowly. Patience with small details
> makes perfect a large work, like the universe.[50]

This is the prayer that comes to my heart as we begin the holy month:

> May we give birth to ourselves in the most subtle way.
> May we grow to know in our own heart for God
> the spiritual state of Love that Ayaz had for his sultan.
> In this time, may each of us find this strength of Love
> by eliminating the superfluous.
> May our clarity reinforce our joy
> And our joy reinforce our clarity.

Ramadan Mubarak, dear companions on the Path of Love! Blessed *Ramadan Karim!*

Shaykha Amina's Journey to the Minbar:
"A Wide Door Was Opened to Seekers in the West"

IN 1982, almost forty years ago, I moved from Puerto Rico to New York to take up a journalist post and, more especially, to seek out a spiritual guide.

With this thought in mind, I arrived at Masjid al-Farah and found myself in the midst of an exquisite dervish traditional Islamic *tariqah*. This was the Halveti Jerrahi Sufi order of Shaykh Muzaffer Ozak Effendi from Istanbul. Islam was a universe absolutely unknown to me at the age of twenty-two. But at this masjid, a spacious Soho factory building, beautifully renovated, everything seemed familiar despite the fact that everybody was speaking and praying in a language I could not understand. I left the masjid at 2 a.m. with a deep sense of spiritual homecoming. It was in this community that I met Lex Hixon, or Nur, my spiritual director for thirteen blessed years.

My search for understanding the nature of reality, though, had begun many years before this event when I was growing up in Puerto Rico. Even as a six-year-old, I felt connections between this world and the next. Late one night, I heard a shuddering noise from our garden; birds were flapping their wings in agitation. The next morning, I learned that Don Francisco, our caretaker, had died during the night. A few days later, passing by his little house in the garden, I heard him calling me in the sweet way he did, "Little Star! Little Flower!" When I told my grandmother, she hastened with me to the spot, calling loudly: "Francisco, you do not belong to this world anymore. Please go toward the next!"

I took my first communion in the Catholic Church at the age of nine very seriously. As a teenager, I read voraciously—the Bible, Krishnamurti, Khalil Gibran, Allan Kardec's works on Spiritism, and Swami Yogananda's works on yoga. I avidly consumed books on spirituality in the bookstores of Ponce.

When the powerful mystic Muzaffer Effendi arrived in New York, thousands of spiritual seekers flocked to Masjid al-Farah to listen. His presence gave the impression of a towering, sacred mountain; he gave generously of himself to us seekers of Truth, some of whom undertook the spiritual initiation (*bay'ah*) with him. I myself plunged into the ocean of riches he offered, drinking for years spiritual honey, milk, water, and wine that flowed from him. Once, after spending a few hours with him and his dervishes, I was elevated into an extraordinary spiritual state. Walking back home in the cold autumn night, I could not feel the bitter cold wind in my face; my body moved as if carried and suspended beyond gravity—I experienced utter lightness and Living Presence. Thus began many gifts of realization and awakenings transmitted to me by my teachers. Muzaffer Effendi soon declared me his khalifa and guided me to open a very wide door as a seeker of Truth as a member of the Halveti Jerrahi Order (founded in 1706 by Pir Nureddin al-Jerrahi, may his secret be sanctified, a remarkable Turkish saint of the late Ottoman Empire). Muzaffer Effendi exuded a deep love for the Prophet Muhammad, narrating Sufi tales full of ancient wisdom with contemporary relevance. I have been honored to serve and train in his community of dervishes in New York.

Lex Hixon, who was appointed *shaykh* at the new mosque in Soho, was an ocean of light, named Nur, or "Divine Light." With him, I developed an ever-deepening appreciation of all the sacred traditions and the core teaching of Oneness within them.

In 1984, I began studies on the Advaita Vedanta tradition, under the direction of the late Swami Aseshananda, a senior Indian monk of the Ramakrishna Order of Calcutta based in Portland. Later, I also explored Zen Buddhism with Roshi Tetsugen Bernard Glassman of the Japanese Soto lineage, and with Roshi Ejo Takata, a Zen teacher from Japan residing in Mexico City.

At the beginning of 1995, Nur was diagnosed with colon cancer. Three of his students traveled to Istanbul to pray for his healing at the tomb of the founder of our *tariqah*, Pir Nureddin al-Jerrahi. There, Sefer Effendi, the successor of Muzaffer Effendi and spiritual head of the *tariqah* in Istanbul, who was also my direct teacher for fourteen years, handed me the *khilafah*, or permission to transmit the light of this spiritual lineage as an official representative of the Jerrahi Order. On my return, Shaykh Nur was elated that his woman student was confirmed as a *shaykha* in Istanbul. Now the community that he lovingly founded in Mexico City had an officially recognized spiritual guide within the old Istanbul *tariqah*.

The new dervishes had dreams transmitting blessings for the newly born mystical body in the midst of Mexico City. The first thing that Shaykh Nur did before he opened a Sufi *tariqah* on the land of Maryam, in the form of the Virgin of Guadalupe, was to visit her, carrying with him a relic, a hair of the Prophet Muhammad. He named the new masjid Mariam an-Nur, or Maryam of Light. For the past thirty-three years I have been leading this community and representing the Sufi Islamic tradition in the Americas as well as internationally in various interfaith organizations, including Religions for Peace, United Religions Initiative, and Zen Peacemakers.

In 1992, we founded, together with an orthodox Ashkenazi rabbi and the Catholic archbishop of Mexico City, the first Interfaith Council of religious leaders of Mexico. After arduous interfaith work, the council produced the "Code of Ethics for the Religious Associations," a document without precedent in Latin America, which outlines the guiding principles of respect and harmony among spiritual communities.

After Shaykh Nur's passing, a remarkable woman student and dedicated dervish, Fariha Fatima al-Jerrahi, received permission from both Muzaffer Effendi and Shaykh Nur to awaken hearts and lead our community. Shaykha Fariha was the person who had originally invited Muzaffer Effendi to the

United States. In a profound way, we all owe our collective and individual spiritual journeys to her glorious initiative. I continue to gladly and gratefully serve her in any way I can, as we walk together with many other Circle Servants and Dervishes on the Path of Divine Love.

Sociality and Difference
Maslahah

Knowing in and through Difference
FATIMA SEEDAT
(South Africa)

This khutbah focuses on the nature and place of difference in our spiritual, political, and personal lives. It begins in the first realm of separation—between the Divine and Creation—and concludes in our daily abilities to include different ways of being and thinking in our communities and families. I show that the ways in which we know and the ways in which we differ are intimately aligned—indeed, our ways of being and knowing are determined through one another.

The creation of humanity marks the beginning of difference. In the hadith *qudsi* where Allah explains our origin to the Prophet, Allah says:

> "I was a hidden Treasure, and desired to be known; thus I brought
> forth creation, that I may be known." (*Hadith Qudsi*)[51]

Allah is the origin and the conclusion of everything, "*inna lillahi wa inna ilayhi rajiun*" (Q. 2:156). We emanate and come into being because Allah wants to be known. Thus the first point of ontological difference is at the moment of creation when human and Divine are separated; thus differentiated, the first soul arrived into being as clay, enlivened by the breath of Allah. The purpose of this separation and new creation is to know Allah. The Qur'an (Q. 2:31) explains further that once we came into being in our originary singular humanity or our Adamic form, Allah taught us the Divine Names; thus began our processes of knowing. Through the names of all things we were given knowledge, and collectively we came to know.

Next came the differentiation of humanity from a single soul into pairs of souls and further into communities, differentiated by our ways of being, our different bodies, our colors, and our customs. Again the Qur'an tells us that the purpose of this difference is to know:

> Verily we have made you male and female and peoples and tribes so
> that you may know one another. (Q. 49:13)

And so, there is a chain of differentiations; first there is separating from the Divine and coming into our human being, next separating from our originary soul and coming into our bodies, until finally we multiply and differentiate into communities. Each differentiation is marked by knowing, perceiving, thinking, or becoming aware of the diversity revealed. And so our ways of being (our ontology) are intimately connected to our ways of knowing (our epistemology). We gain human existence as we separate from the Divine to know the Divine. From the Divine form to the Adamic origin, and from bodily pairs into communities, these three linked moments of creation are our ontology, forged in difference, the knowledge of difference, and the knowledge that comes through difference. Created through kaleidoscopic diversity, we come to know via difference.

We might well have been created all as a single entity, yet here we are in our billions, each with unique ways of knowing the Divine and knowing each other. And our differences seem to bring out the worst forms of division among us. Much of our collective quest is for supremacy of our own way of being, whether as sect, religion, or ideology. We have lost sight of the connection between knowledge and ontological separation through which we ought instead to have forged a robust ethics of living within difference.

Among world religions, Islam and Judaism are often considered nomocentric religions, meaning their principle focus is the law. A key element in Islamic legal sciences is the facility of disputation and argumentation. *'Ilm al-jadal,* the science of dialectics or argumentation, is a formative dynamic of premodern Islamic legal systems evolved into Islamic legal thought. Guided by a series of formal steps, *jadal,* or *mujadalah* (disputation), and *munazarah* (debate) present systematic forms of argumentation developed through a question-and-answer format to prove or counter a thesis. The final assessment is in the form of both the debate, which requires adhering to its rules, and its outcome, which is aimed at providing a proof. The ethics is cooperative, and the aim is to pursue truth, not to win or feed the ego. Proper disputation is truth-seeking; improper disputation is legal sophistry.[52]

An early form of *jadal* is reflected in Surah al-Mujadila (Q. 58), in which a woman disputes with Allah, who, responding through the Prophet, makes this disputation a form of Qur'anic guidance. Khawlah bint Tha'laba is "the woman who argues," the *mujadila,* when her ill-tempered husband took a purportedly irreversible pre-Islamic oath, *zihar,* renouncing her sexually, thus placing their marriage in limbo. Even though neither Khawlah nor her husband, Auws, wanted to separate, there was no socially sanctioned expiation for this oath. Khawlah sought out Rasulullah for help, complaining of her dilemma. Despite her strenuous argument at the injustice of this practice, he was disinclined to rule in her favor, given the weight of social custom. Dissatisfied, Khawlah begins her disputation and eventually demands that Rasulullah return to Allah for a solution, all the while making a *du'a* with her women companions: "O Allah, reveal through the tongue of your Prophet something that will have comfort in it for us."[53] Allah hears and responds through Surah al-Mujadila:

> Certainly, has Allah heard the speech of the one who argues with you, [O Muhammad], concerning her husband, and complains to Allah.
> And Allah hears your conversation; indeed, Allah is Hearing and Seeing.
> (Q. 58:1)

The revelation offers Khawlah options for Auws to expiate his oath, none of which is practically possible: Auws cannot afford to feed the poor, free an enslaved person, or fast for months. After rigorous negotiations with Rasulullah, whom Khawlah co-opts into assisting Auws to expiate his oath, she successfully negotiates a way to resume her marriage. 'Ai'sha bint Abu Bakr reports that those of the Prophet's family who were with them wept "in compassion and empathy" for Khawlah.[54]

The *mujadila* teaches us the possibilities and power of argument, engagement, and counterargument, even with Allah and Rasulullah. Khawlah, the woman who disputes, presents us with a compelling and critical model of fidelity that pushes for new ways of thinking that resist customary hardship. While the prophetic community did not disparage Khawlah's disputations nor accuse her of disbelief, today Muslim feminists who dispute destructive forms of traditions are denigrated as unbelievers.

Fortunately, Khawlah had direct access to the Prophet and revelation. For those of us who do not, there is nonetheless a rich and vast history of various legal schools and a myriad of differences within each school. In the combination of *'ilm al-akhlaq* (knowledge of virtue) and *'ilm al-fiqh* (knowledge of norms) is an ethical code for refining individuals in their relationship with the Divine and in society.[55] Combining the legal and spiritual sciences brings together the internal and external moral codes of the self.

The history of the *madhahib* (schools of Islamic law) began with a large variety of scholars until they coalesced through scholarly consensus into a much smaller group. This illustrates that Islamic law and its *madhahib* are a historical human-made phenomenon, fluid and dynamic, contingent and varied; and despite suggestions otherwise, they have historically changed and adapted with time and circumstance.

Takhayyur and *talfiq* are two among various legal mechanisms that allow legal scholars to employ legal difference for the improvement of society. *Takhayyur*, the practice of choosing a ruling from another school, is used when the legal opinion of one's own school is inadequate to new circumstances and social need. This means that it is especially valuable to know various available legal options and opinions. *Talfīq*, the practice of combining rulings from different schools, is also designed to provide legal ease for believers. Further, a fatwa within a single school of law may be followed by a second one with a different opinion, both within the same school, and the believer may choose between the two.

These valuable tools of legal difference reinforce an ethics of difference and disagreement. Indeed, more than one position can be right, and two things can be true and valid at the same time. Our challenge is to remain connected through these multiple truths and diversity—as with the difference regarding our human ontology with which I began this khutbah.

Rasulullah was also clear when he said that difference in the *ummah* is a mercy; while legal consensus is considered definitive proof, divergence of opinion is also considered "a vast mercy."[56] Our challenge today is in dealing with different opinions and our toxic reactions that associate disagreement with disbelief despite the Qur'anic caution against constructing others as unbelievers and casting others into sects or schisms:

> . . . and be not like those who ascribe (God) partners, those who split up their faith and create (differing) parties, each rejoicing among their own (claims). (Q. 30:31–32)

The Prophet envisaged that his community would eventually be divided into seventy-three communities; the one moving toward Paradise, he explained, would be of those who follow his example—submission to the Divine, to the Sublime Creator. Clearly, this is not submission to a *madhab* (school of law) or an *alim* (scholar), but to the difference that constitutes our humanity from divinity and the human collective from our individuality. Knowing each other through our differences enhances our relationships with each other and refines our relationship with the most Sublime, until we come to know Allah as the Essence of all that differs.

Fatima's Journey to the Minbar:
"Twenty Years and Forty Women's Khutbahs Later"

GROWING UP IN A COMMUNITY of many faiths I was schooled from an early age in male religious privilege. I knew there was no easy way to be a woman and religious. So I was fortunate for guidance that flowed from three streams. First, there were women who stood out for their faith, like my drama teacher, who loved her life at the ashram; our school's Mother Superior, with her peaceful countenance; and my grandmother, the first of my paternal grandfather's two co-wives. Erudite and well-read, she taught us afternoon madrasah. History was my favorite, especially learning about women's courage on the battlefield. I loved Khadija the most—smart and certainly not shy, like I was then. With my grandmother-teacher, Ayesha Meer, our "Mosque-Nani," I got excited about faith.

Then there was *tarawih* in Ramadan with my mum at the Isipingo Hills mosque, which was special even though we couldn't pray in its central, beautiful sections, with soft arches and the names of Allah ornamenting its borders (I know because I snuck in once). I wanted to be near the minbar, rather than in the dreary basement. But we'd enjoy the ninety-nine names anyway, humming to the tape recorder on our drive home. With my mum I learned divine quietude and gratitude.

Finally, I was "Daddy's girl," but he wasn't much for mosques—not unless they included the regular *qawwals* (singers) that visited Durban's shrines, or *mazars*. With my dad I forgot about the barred minbar, and instead watched as his heart disappeared into the ecstatics and aesthetics of the Divine.

I got an undergraduate degree in religion, and my plans for graduate studies in Islam quickly fell apart when studying "womanhood" in the Qur'an seemed too maverick for my supervisor. Moreover, it was 1993, and we needed to organize for South Africa's first democratic elections. At the University of Durban, Westville, having received the most votes, I was elected to lead the Islamic Society but subsequently couldn't take on the position because it was reserved for men. Though irritated by the ridiculousness of it all, I soldiered on in a "deputy" position, scarf tied tightly under my chin. Through the combination of Muslim gender politics and anti-apartheid student resistance, I eventually found my political location; pan-Africanism, Steve Biko's teachings on oppression and Blackness, and a revolutionary Islamic politics embraced me.

By 1994 I was based in Cape Town and was an excited congregant witnessing amina wadud's historic arrival at the minbar. What a heady moment that was! And the next year I had the joy of a communal Eid prayer, this time in Zarqa, a small town in Jordan, and of learning Arabic with twenty-five young women—the "Jordan girls." Taken by the beauty of congregational prayer, we planned to one day hold our own Eid prayers, attended by entire families.

Returning to Durban, mundane busyness enveloped me for years. I would swaddle my little niece, and together we'd attend Eid *salah* in the women's sections of a Sufi mosque. The room bore the messy remnants of the previous afternoon's madrasah class, but it was a chance to meet the Jordan girls, who were almost the only ones there.

Through the campaign for recognition of Muslim marriages in South Africa, I focused on the intersections of race, gender, and religion. These struggles showed me that my spiritual and professional lives would align cohesively only once both squared with my instincts for equality.

In 1999 I received my first invitation to a minbar at Claremont Main Road Mosque on Women's Day. Excited but nervous, I wrote a note to myself: "What should I say and how? What do I wear—must it be more modest than usual? How/where should I stand? Should I make eye contact with women only? Can I look toward the male section? How?" Clearly, it was not so much the content of my first khutbah but my presence, form, and behavior at the minbar that filled me with anxiety. Invited again over the years, I have trained my eyes and strengthened my voice to encompass the entire *jama'ah*—and I have also acquired brightly colored khutbah clothes!

Back in my hometown of Durban, our regular Eid *salah* space at the Sufi mosque was moved. Instead of trudging up what seemed like a hundred stairs, we now filed past garbage bins into a squashed room behind the male *wudu* facility. Interrupted by the sounds of gargling and spitting water, we strained to hear the khutbah—ever anxious that the sound system would fail and cut us off from the minbar entirely.

Those unpleasant experiences compelled us into action; with their families, some Jordan girls organized an outdoor Eidgah near the beach. It included families and two khutbahs, one each by a man and a woman. Despite the death threats and name-calling (the "bikini Eidgah"!), it was a beautiful and gratifying moment. In the years following I hoped to collect and compile a book of all the women's khutbahs—a hope that continued for almost two decades and more than forty Eids in what has become the "TIP Family Eid Gah." Although the congregation has been nurtured by the ideas and knowledge of as many *khatibahs*, women still, sadly, do not offer the Arabic khutbah or the *salah*.

In 2019 Taking Islam to the People (TIP) invited Professor wadud to address the Family Eidgah, a first for Durban. Alas, we came under attack from within; the community took offense at her commentary on the story of Hajar and refused to let her speak. And so, in my most reluctant presentation at a minbar, I spoke about how easily women's work comes undone, is hidden, censured, and erased. The irony of it all was maddening!

But my dream of compiling a book of women's khutbahs has come to fruition. After years of resisting the exile of marginalized religious subjectivities from the beautiful spaces of Muslim public life, through this virtual minbar it is possible that we may access and adorn them again, as we do these pages, with God's most beautiful names.

ﷺ

God's Command for Justice in the Qur'an
GWENDOLYN ZOHARAH SIMMONS
(United States)

Women's scholarship on the Qur'an and Islamic law has grown into an identifiable field, making inroads into the formerly all-male domains of Qur'anic interpretation, the writing of fatwas, and the performance of the Friday sermon, whether one lives in Muslim-majority states or the West. Muslim feminist scholarship has endeavored to show that the patriarchal exegesis of the Qur'an is not the only possible interpretation of many passages in the text that have been used by male exegetes for centuries to create laws and uphold cultural practices that deny Muslim women equal rights.

How enlightening are the many Qur'anic references to God's creation of the human pair, without qualifying one as superior over the other. This beautiful verse reveals the intended relationship of equality between the earthly pair:

And among His signs is that He created mates for you from among yourselves,
that you might find rest in them,
and He established affection and mercy between you.
Truly there are signs for a people who reflect. (Q. 30:21)[57]

Yet the Qur'an also speaks of inequality between the sexes. For example, Q. 4:34 reads:

Men are the upholders and maintainers of women
by virtue of what God has favored some of them above others
and because they support them from their means.
Therefore the righteous women are devoutly obedient,
guarding in [their husbands'] absence what God has guarded.
As for those from whom you fear discord and animosity,
admonish them, leave them in their beds, then strike them.
Then if they obey you, seek not a way against them.
Truly God is Exalted, Great.[58]

Thus there are clearly tensions between the different ideas of gender relations presented in the Qur'an. The latter verse (Q. 4:34) is disturbing for feminist Muslims and their allies. Even many of the classical exegetes were troubled by the punishment section of the verse, as it contradicted the Prophet Muhammad's own practice. How convenient that those using the verse as "proof" of male superiority ignore the Prophet's practice in this regard—a Prophet who never resorted to physical chastisement of his wives, even in periods of intense marital discord.

Some contemporary Muslim scholars have also contested these andro-centric verses. Fazlur Rahman, a prominent Muslim reformer, promoted independent reasoning, or *itjihad,* arguing the rationale for Q. 4:34 as historically based upon socioeconomic factors, which change dramatically over time.[59] Even more powerfully rejecting male dominance, Nasr Hamid Abu Zayd, a scholar of Qur'anic hermeneutics, noted that "on the cosmological level, human equality is stated in the opening verse of the chapter 'Women' (*al-Nisa*)":

O Humankind! Reverence your Lord
Who created you from a single soul
From which He created its mate
And from them two, countless men and women
Reverence Allah through Whom you demand your mutual rights
And (reverence) the wombs (that bore you), for Allah ever watches over you.
    (Q. 4:1)[60]

Ziba Mir-Hosseini explains the term "soul" (*nafs*) in Q. 4:1 as feminine and "husband" as deriving from the masculine *zawjaha,* also translating as "twin," meanings that are often overlooked.[61] These scholars collectively argue for elevating God's teachings of unity, reciprocity, and justice as central divine prescriptions reflecting the general ethos of the Qur'an.

Understanding the historical context in which gender discriminatory *tafsir* emerged is vital. Gender-equitable verses echo our contemporary knowledge of the physical, mental, and spiritual equality between men and women. We know and experience men as our peers, sometimes even outstripping them in physical and mental accomplishments. Women can do things that men cannot—carry in our womb and give birth to a new human, and produce food from our bodies to sustain it. As a mother, I remain amazed that we are not exalted for these "miracles" but instead are abused in almost every society.

Our knowledge, which has expanded since the seventh century when the Qur'an was revealed and classical *tafsir* began, requires us to abrogate androcentric verses. This will, of course, be rejected by many; Muslim scholars promoting gender-equal *tafsir* suffer. In 1995, an Egyptian shari'ah court declaring Nasr Abu Zayd an apostate issued a judicial divorce from his wife. He was subsequently forced into exile because of death threats. Mahmoud Mohammed Taha, a Sufi and religious thinker, was executed in Sudan for his innovative approach to Islamic legal ethics, which prioritized the more egalitarian Meccan verses rather than the pragmatic and socially conditioned Medinese ones. The former, he argued, should be used to develop legal rulings as they represented the ideal ethical trajectory of Islam based on freedom and equality.[62]

The pursuit of freedom and equality in the Qur'an and Islam is powerful. Even earlier, some classical exegetes attempted mitigating the gender-conflicting verses through specific hadith, an accepted exegetical principle by the ninth century. *Naskh*, or abrogation, in Islamic legal exegesis deals with contradictory material within the Qur'an and between the Qur'an and sunnah by arguing supersedence of earlier material, or prioritizing prophetic interpretation and practice. In the Qur'an, God commands justice from all believers in their dealings with others, whether friend or foe:

> O you who believe! Be steadfast for God
> Bearing witness to *justice*,
> Let not hatred for a people lead you to be unjust.
> Be *just*; that is nearer to reverence.
> And reverence God. God is aware of whatsoever you do. (Q. 5:8)[63]

Justice in our context is aligned with *equality* as a balance between rights and duties.[64] Yet this is often overlooked in Islamic laws dealing with personal status where women are made "legally" subject to their husbands, who have "power and authority" over them. As scholars Ziba Mir-Hosseini, Mulki Al-Sharmani, and Jana Rumminger observe, male authority is based on medieval *tafsir* concepts of *qiwamah* and *wilayah*.[65] Sa'diyya Shaikh criticizes these concepts as patriarchal and "not the only or most benevolent ways that Muslim jurists could have interpreted the sacred texts."[66]

Medieval jurists, Kecia Ali explains further, saw nothing wrong in legally positioning a wife's sexuality as "owned" by her husband, interpreting the dower as a form of payment for his sole access to her sexuality and divorce by him a form of release of his ownership of her.[67] Mir-Hosseini reminds us that marriage, according to classical *fiqh,* is a contract that makes the female vagina the husband's property![68] Through such concepts male dominance in classical legal thought has established itself as "natural."

This is a significant challenge for contemporary Muslims. Shaikh asks: How do we transcend, in both spirituality and *fiqh,* these historical discourses that have assumed universal, transhistorical, and religious authority? According to her, hermeneutics, or the study of interpretation, makes us aware of the historically shaped nature of all reading, that is, that the gender-biased contexts and preconceptions of jurists and Qur'an scholars influenced the meanings they gave to authoritative texts. This allows us to be critical of medieval-based *fiqh* regarding marriage and divorce, which are harmful to women.[69] Discerning universal Qur'anic values of an inclusive human dignity and justice while applying these to changing social norms is a vital spiritual exercise for Muslims.

The Qur'an's call for justice exposes interpretations of unequal gender relations in *fiqh* as the opposite of the divine will. Consider the following *ayah:*

> Truly God commands *justice*, virtue, and giving to kinsfolk,
> God forbids indecency, wrong, and rebelliousness
> And admonishes you, that perhaps you remember. (Q. 16:90)[70]

A recent exegetical compilation shows that the Qur'an considers justice a supreme virtue, representing moral rectitude and fairness. Justice is a basic objective of Islam, next in priority to belief in God's existence and God as the Only Being to whom worship is due. The exegetes suggest that the injunction to "give to kinsfolk" is meant to maintain good family relations, which is impossible when there is injustice and worsened by the claim that God sanctions a husband's tyranny. The *ayah* is clear: God forbids *indecency, wrong,* and *rebelliousness.* Fakhr al-Din Razi, a classical period Persian Sunni theologian and philosopher, interprets "wrong" as sins rooted in love of power and violence.[71] Tyrants, whether in nations or the family, rule via injustice, fear, and violence.

God abhors *zulm*—injustice—and certainly does not intend unjust spousal relationships. Instead, the Qur'an emphasizes peace, affection, and mercy in the divine plan for family harmony:

> And among His signs is that
> He created mates for you from among yourselves,
> That you might find rest in them,
> And established affection and mercy between you. (Q. 30:21)[72]

Razi, still referring to Q. 16:90, explains sin as indulgence of human pride, ambition, and injustice. As commentators have noted, the Qur'an identifies Satan as being unjust, being the first creature to rebel against God and His commands; the sin of injustice thus derives from Satanic illusions.[73]

Justice is an obligation in Islam and injustice is forbidden. Consider the following:

> We sent Our Messengers with clear signs
> And sent down with them the Book and the Measure
> In order to establish justice among the people. (Q. 57:25)[74]

The Qur'an also exhorts:

> O believers!
> Stand firm for justice as witnesses for Allah,
> Even if it is against yourselves, your parents, or close relatives,
> Be they rich or poor. (Q. 4:135)[75]

According to classical Qur'anic exegetes, these verses link bearing witness to God's Oneness and Lordship with standing for justice, which should be free from such influences as unchecked loyalty to family, questions of social status, hatred, and enmity[76]—and I add also free from irrelevant bygone cultural traditions.

The Qur'anic command for justice extends unapologetically to justice for women and should lead to direct amendment of personal status laws sanctioning male authority over women. The idea that God has given men authority over women, emanating from the classical jurists' concept of *qiwamah*, is called by Lynn Welchman the "qiwamah postulate"—a set of rulings, or *ahkam*, based on Q. 4:34 that allow male-centered definitions of social power to take root in Islamic law.[77] Thank goodness most Muslims repudiated the institution of slavery, albeit relatively late in the abolition movements. Given the seventh-century context, the Qur'an never abolished slavery but instead tried to ease its harshest practices. It was Muslims who discerned the logic that the abolition of slavery was a logical and ultimate ethical end in the reading of the Qur'an. It is our hope that the community of Muslims moves in a similar direction by addressing the androcentrism of the Qur'an.

Critical of the poor treatment of Tunisian women in the 1930s, the scholar and journalist Tahir al-Haddad, in his contribution to gender-equitable exegeses, made distinctions between Qur'anic verses that reflected essential, eternal norms and prescriptions and those that were contingent or bound by time and context.[78] He highlighted the important concept of gradualism in the Qur'an, which governs its view of Islamic legislation. For example, since slavery was endemic in seventh-century Arabian slave-owning society, it was economically unfeasible for slavery to be immediately abolished. Yet the Qur'an and the Prophet encouraged the freeing of slaves, emphasizing the enduring divine principle of freedom. Similarly, al-Haddad argues, although patriarchy was tolerated, the Qur'an and the Prophet emphasized the key principles of equality and justice in Islam.

Muslim feminist scholarship in the contemporary period has developed along a similar trajectory and contributed to deepening foundational Qur'anic teachings whose highest aims are justice and equality among all humans and God's creatures. I, too, believe this fervently, and offer my khutbah in this spirit.

Zoharah's Journey to the Minbar: *"Who Am I? Who Is God?"*

I AM AN AFRICAN AMERICAN MUSLIM WOMAN who converted to Islam as a young adult under the guidance of my Sufi *shaykh*, Muhammad Raheem Bawa Muhaiyaddeen, from whom I learned about the beautiful qualities of Islam. At the time that my spiritual search brought me to my beautiful teacher, I had already traversed numerous paths, looking for answers to my questions about life, death, and God. This search had begun for me at the age of twelve.

I was raised Christian, in a devout home, and had grown up studying the Bible with numerous teachers. However, I was searching for deep answers to life's questions: Who am I? Who is God? Why am I on this physical plane? What is the relationship between God and me?

The Islam taught to me by Bawa provided answers that resonated with my heart and mind. It was an Islam of infinite love, compassion, and justice for all. Most important for me, it was a religion that accorded women equal status and rights with men. This was salient for me as a person working as a social justice activist in the African American civil rights and women's rights movements in the United States, fighting for my rights as a Black person and woman.

I headed a delegation to the 1995 Fourth World Conference on Women in Beijing and spent time with Muslim women delegations from around the world. At that time, I was a graduate student in Islamic studies at Temple University, still deciding on a topic for my thesis. It was a rude awakening; during two intense weeks, Muslim women from around the globe shared their stories about mistreatment by the men in their families and societies, purportedly based on Islamic teachings. I heard how imams and other religious teachers taught an Islam that treated women as second-class people to be ruled over by their fathers, uncles, brothers, and even grown sons.

I knew that this was untrue, or certainly a misinterpretation at best. I decided to focus my postgraduate studies on women in Islam. I learned in Beijing, and subsequently, undertaking two years of living and researching Islam and women in Egypt, Jordan, Palestine, and Syria, that shari'ah law is the main instrument families and the state use to discriminate against women through Qur'anic misinterpretation that has become embedded in the law. These misinterpretations, buttressed by hadith, many of which were not authentic but were still included in numerous hadith collections, are the materials from which *ulama* have built their teachings that marginalize women. These sources often contradict the words of the Qur'an, yet they are given precedence.

Studying Muslim women scholars inspired in me an urgent need to see Muslim women who are feminists and progressives becoming religious authorities in their communities. Our misogyny-free interpretations of religious texts are needed in all Muslim societies. Instilling our perspectives, formally, into Muslim communities was and is still difficult. There is tremendous resistance to women *imamahs*. On those rare occasions when a woman is asked to give a khutbah, her doing so is often met with virulent objections and sometimes even violence, whether in Muslim-majority countries or in the West. A prime case in point is Professor amina wadud's 2005 *Jumu'ah* prayer and khutbah, coorganized by the Progressive Muslim Union and the Muslim Women's Freedom Tour, to a mixed-gender congregation in New York City. No mosque would open its doors to the assembly, which eventually gathered in the Episcopal Cathedral in Manhattan. She endured protests and death threats. A decade earlier, in 1994, after she gave a pre-khutbah talk at the Claremont Main Road Mosque in South Africa, she had experienced similar attacks, including attempts to have her fired from her university position.

I have never been invited to give a sermon at a mosque, but I have been verbally attacked at my talks at universities and conferences where I have questioned interpretations of the Qur'an. I challenge the authenticity of hadith used to justify discrimination against women and explain that *fiqh,* often mistaken for shari'ah, is a human product of male interpretation of the Qur'an and hadith developed into legal codes. The vitriol from men (and occasionally women) is upsetting, to put it mildly. Even more shocking, perhaps, have been aggressive reactions from male Muslim students in my university classes on Islam. A number have been so verbally abusive that I have had to ask the chair of my department, a male Jewish rabbi, to threaten them with expulsion from the university if they did not stop. Their outbursts ceased, but their disapproval of a woman *teaching* Islam still hung palpably like an angry cloud above them in my classroom.

Let me be clear: I prioritize my personal sensibilities on the matter of justice and human rights for women as a frontline activist in the struggle for both African American and women's human rights. I bring to my readings of the Qur'an a fully formed sense of what justice and injustice are, and what human rights are. I, like the classical and modern male exegetes, have been shaped by my historical, social, and cultural milieus. As an African American convert to Islam, born in the United States in the middle of the twentieth century and active in my country's civil rights, Black power, and women's rights movements of the 1960s, 1970s, and 1980s, I have helped to precipitate the changes that have made life infinitely better for African Americans and women in my country. This is the personal history and experience I bring to my every endeavor; this is the lens through which I read the Qur'an, and through which the Qur'an has been meaningful in my journey.

The need for a book of khutbahs by women is urgent, as the doors to most mosques remain closed to women as religious authorities and *imamahs.*

This is an important way to have our voices heard. I offer in this book my first khutbah, written and yet to be presented.

ﺷﻮﻩ

Rethinking Shari'ah—A Guidance and a Mercy
SHERIN KHANKAN
(Denmark)

Beloved sisters, I salute you with the greeting and blessing that has been handed down to us by generations of devout seekers who, in all times and places, have worshipped and celebrated the One True God: *assalamu alaykum wa rahmatullahi wa barakatuhu*. Today I address notions of shari'ah, Islamophobia, and European secularism and then offer a rethinking of Islamic practices relating to interfaith marriage and divorce.

Shari'ah in the West is often associated with antidemocratic behavior and is allegedly incompatible with human rights. Politicians, the media, and some academics equate shari'ah with criminal, premodern practices, insinuating that Islam is tyrannical and opposed to secular democracy. They dismiss the fact that shari'ah is a central part of Islamic practice, providing guidance for inner spiritual practice and expression of an external religious framework for Muslims to serve God. Shari'ah is in fact a form of ethics focusing on *maslahah*—that which best serves community and public interest. Shari'ah stems from the Qur'an and is key to Muslim understandings of the mercy of Allah. Containing the five pillars of Islam, it teaches Muslims how to live daily life. Shari'ah is defined variously among Muslims and non-Muslims—as Islamic law, a guide to mercy, an ethical code of conduct, or a method of reaching God. The holy Qur'an reveals:

> Certainly, we have brought to them a book [the Qur'an],
> Which we have explained in great detail with knowledge,
> A guidance and a mercy to those who believe. (Q. 7:52)

In addition to being a source of divine guidance, for many Muslims shari'ah is intrinsic to practicing a just Islam. Because Islam emerged before the contemporary nation-state and legal system existed, framing Islam as a set of laws fails to understand it as a fundamental source of spiritual and ethical guidance. Shari'ah corresponds to instructions and moral codes given by Allah in the Qur'an and must be differentiated from *fiqh* (jurisprudence), which refers to the temporal or human interpretation of the shari'ah. *Fiqh* is a tool for human understanding of shari'ah in practice. Essentially, Allah's instructions and Islamic jurisprudence must dynamically combine to produce meaningful answers to believers' questions and the challenges of their lived contexts. Belief in the Qur'an as the sacred word of Allah does not exclude common sense, criticism, and new knowledge.

The Qur'an and hadith are dynamic sources, open to reflection and interpretation by the *ulama*, and in fact, all believers; this means the Qur'an must not be read simply or as a definitive code of law. Both sources provide the universal rules of conduct for ethics and spirituality, as well as philosophical and political aspects of a Muslim society.

Of the approximately 6,000 Qur'anic verses, legal scholar Hashim Kamali observes that only 350 have direct legal content.[79] Islamic law principles are not fixed but function as general guidelines for people to intelligently apply in order to serve the community's best interests. Thus, humans must grasp their destiny and choose, in accordance with the eternal principles, the form of government best suited to their realities. As with the Decalogue, or Ten Commandments, shari'ah sets general principles, which some Muslims read literally and others metaphorically, as we do, at the Mariam Mosque to which I belong.

In part, the shari'ah's negative reputation stems from problematic uses by pseudo-Islamist states and groups that twist shari'ah toward narrow political ends. Some European politicians and so-called experts of Islam point to this egregious use to motivate abandoning, wholesale, the Islamic legal code of conduct as a prerequisite to Muslims living in Europe. By making belonging contingent on renunciation of the core of Islam—the Qur'an as the revealed word of Allah—they effectively marginalize Muslims in their midst and support warped understandings of shari'ah and Islam.

Yet there is nothing contradictory about being a "secular Muslim believer," provided secularism does not intrinsically signify nonreligiosity. Religious legal arguments are acceptable, provided they refrain from becoming state law or claiming political primacy. While presented as a barrier against all forms of dogmatism, and emerging historically as a form of resistance against the church holding political power in the West, secularism does not require banishment of religion from the public sphere, but rather, assurance that all religions are treated equally.

Many Muslims rightfully criticize problematic forms of shari'ah practiced in some Muslim-majority countries, unwittingly also reassuring the pseudo-experts and Islamophobes. Indeed, Muslim leaders and activists must oppose the literal and tyrannical institutionalized shari'ah forms that threaten Muslims and non-Muslims alike, as these are not proper expressions of Islam. The solution is not to force Muslims to renounce shari'ah, which is equivalent to demanding Jews and Christians abandon the Ten Commandments. Rather, it is best to focus on shari'ah's historical and spiritual meanings, highlighting the theological and etymological viewpoints that relate to mercy and equality.

The Qur'an is a text reflecting the context and norms of its revelations that has both limited historical application and universal relevance for the spiritual guidance of believers across time. When these two registers get mixed up, some verses can certainly be interpreted as discriminatory against women. However, such verses must be reread metaphorically to resolve the harm caused by literal, problematic interpretations.

To illustrate, Surah al-Nisa's specific reference to *Al-rijalu qawwamuna ala an-nisa* is used by both Islamophobes and Muslim patriarchs to present Islam as oppressive to women:

> Men are the protectors and maintainers of women
> Because God has given the one more (strength) than the other
> and because they support them from their means. (Q. 4:34)[80]

Qawammuna is often translated to mean "the man is above the woman." This translator, Yusuf Ali, argues that the term can also mean one who stands firm and protects; at the Mariam Mosque, we understand *qawammuna* to mean the man must support his wife in her dreams, visions, and actions. He must not dominate her, but like a pillar, he must stand next to her as an equal partner and supporter. We argue that this supportive role reveals the underlying equality between them, rather than the man being the maintainer of the woman.

In terms of the relevance of shari'ah in a European context, we also find that shari'ah is compatible with and already coexists with European legislation, for example, when Danish Muslims give alms, pray, or marry. Islamic marriage exists parallel to civil marriage; the latter carries the strength of law and has priority from an official point of view. From the spiritual, religious, and psychological viewpoints, though, the religious marriage has priority for practicing Muslims. This is because shari'ah, or the Islamic system of law and guidance, stems from the Qur'an and designates "the path" toward or "the way" to respect divine law. It offers a code of conduct regarding Muslims' individual and collective duties, establishing rules, prohibitions, and sanctions. Yet in practice, the *fiqh* of manmade laws often contradicts the Qur'anic ideas of equality and justice in marriage.

As a European female *imamah* fighting against growing Islamophobia on one hand and Muslim patriarchal practices on the other, I see one of the biggest challenges facing Muslim youth in Europe as the prohibition of inter-religious marriage between a Muslim woman and a non-Muslim man. This causes great sorrow for young Muslims who fall in love with a Christian, Jew, or other non-Muslim. We *imamahs* at the Mariam Mosque have tried to find Islamic solutions to this, drawing on this Qur'anic inspiration:

> O humankind! We have created you from a single pair
> Male and female, and made you into tribes and families
> So that you may know one another.
> Surely the noblest and most honorable of you in God's sight
> Is one best in piety, righteousness, and reverence for God.
> Surely God is All-Knowing, All-Aware. (Q. 49:13)

Drawing on the essence of this verse, we embrace the divine teaching that *all* humans are God's creation. Two of my four children are girls, aged nine and sixteen; the chances that my daughters might grow up and fall in love with a non-Muslim are huge since we live in Europe. Many, including their father, think that having raised our children well, this will never happen. Similarly, a rabbi in Denmark informed me during an interfaith debate that religious Jews do not fall in love with non-Jews, because they know it is impossible to marry outside Judaism. The dogmas of apparent incompatibility between belief systems and the superiority of one's own religion are a universal problem.

In response, we at Mariam Mosque celebrate interfaith marriages because we recognize the reality of Muslim women in Europe marrying non-Muslim men. We have responded by respecting Qur'anic legality, which does not oppose such unions. I have officiated at more than fifty Islamic marriages between faithful Muslim women and faithful Christian men. Our mosque has a long waiting list of couples from all over Europe, as most male imams refuse to perform rites for Muslim women marrying outside Islam.

Further, even though Islamic law allows for Muslim women's right to divorce, these are not generally included in most marriage contracts, thus trapping many women in unhappy or abusive marriages. The Mariam Mosque's marriage contracts, therefore, include women's right to divorce. Women trust us, consult with us, and dare to open up to us if their husbands abuse them. We accept women's right to Islamic divorce, based on the Qur'an:

> O you who have chosen to be graced with belief!
> It is not lawful for you to force women into marriage
> Or hold them in marriage against their will.
> Pressuring women to remain in wedlock
> By threatening to take away the marital gift is forbidden.
> A wife could forfeit the right to the marital gift
> Only if she has indulged in clear lewdness.
> You shall treat your wives honorably, even if you dislike them,
> It may happen that God has placed good in what you dislike. (Q. 4:19)[81]

Our *nikah* (marriage) contracts also exclude polygyny, and the preamble renders the contract invalid in cases of physical violence or emotional abuse. Fusing Danish legislation and Islamic guidance, we ensure that a woman undergoing civil divorce also instantly receives Islamic divorce. The divine knowledge bestowed upon humanity by the Prophet Muhammad imbues our work with the ethical imperatives for justice required by the Qur'an. Most traditional schools of *fiqh* allow divorce only through the husband's pronouncement granting divorce. This applies generally, only changing when extenuating circumstances apply or when other grounds for divorce are found valid, such as the husband's cruelty (*darar*), impotence (if undisclosed at the time of marriage), or inability to provide his basic marital obligations, such as shelter and maintenance. The marriage contract promoted at the Mariam Mosque focuses on women's rights instead, making divorce equally available to both parties.

Muslim feminist rereadings of the Qur'an and shari'ah can potentially change conditions for Muslim women. Rereadings have always formed part of Muslim practice, and they still reverberate globally in our mosques and communities. There *will* be resistance when women challenge male dominance; families are disrupted and marriages dissolve—this is the price of change. I should know, as this is the price I have paid for insisting on my rights as a Muslim woman. But I also know that justice and full dignity of each and every believer is an intrinsic goal of Islam and one in which we must persist.

Sherin's Journey to the Minbar:
"Long Live the Female Imams!"

I GREW UP HEARING MY FATHER, a political refugee from Damascus and a Muslim feminist ally, say, "The perfect man is a woman." He was quoting Ibn Arabi, an Islamic philosopher and Sufi known for challenging patriarchal structures and *tafsir*. My poetic childhood has inspired my own gender activism in Islam.

The family provides the first memories and experiences of community, often the foundation for the communities we create in the future. Our first community is dramatic because we do not choose it but are born into it. Indeed, a game of chance, family can take many forms. I was lucky in the lottery of family because my parents succeeded in uniting East and West, Christianity and Islam, village and city. My mother is a Finnish Christian immigrant; it was my father who introduced our family to a spiritual interpretation of Islam and the shari'ah that holds possibilities of hope and justice. My father's spiritual approach is not unique or rare, but it is widespread throughout the Muslim world of which I am a part.

In the authoritative biographical lexicon *Kitab al-tabaqat al-kabir,* Ibn Saad, a Persian historian, tells us that at least three women led the prayer in Madinah at the time of the Prophet and after his death. A woman serving as *imamah* is not a new phenomenon or reformation of Islam. In the broader religious context in Denmark, the country of my birth, and my current home, the first female priests were ordained in 1948 in the Protestant Church of Denmark. Today the gender ratio of priests is about equal, with more women in theology faculties at Danish universities. Among Danish Jewish and Muslim minorities, male and female scholars have long been calling for full-time female rabbis and *imamahs.* The Mariam Mosque, to which I belong, is an all-inclusive mosque, but its *Jumu'ah* prayer is exclusively for women. At all other times, men are welcome to join its women-led prayers and Islamic Academy.

Women *imamahs* are not limited to Denmark; female *imamahs* are active in China, Somalia, France, Belgium, South Africa, Canada, Germany, the United Kingdom, and the United States. In the contemporary period, Professor amina wadud gave the first khutbah by a woman in South Africa and led the first *Jumu'ah* prayer by a woman in the United States and various European countries. Morocco educates female religious leaders, or *murshidahs,* to teach and give Islamic spiritual care.

The al-Azhar University in Cairo and three (out of four) Islamic legal schools acknowledge women-led prayers for female congregations. Classical Islamic scholars of *fiqh*, philosophy, and the Qur'an al-Tabari and Ibn Rushd also affirmed women-led prayers as acceptable. Umm Salamah and A'ishah (may Allah be pleased with them) led the prayer for women in Prophet Muhammad's mosque in Madinah, the first house mosque in Islamic history, and the Prophet requested that Umm Waraqa lead the prayer for her household. Women in the Prophet's time were valued teachers, warriors, and *imamahs*.

On Friday, August 26, 2016, a group of female and male activists and I opened the first women's mosque with female *imamahs* in Scandinavia, the Mariam Mosque. The title "imam" until this day in Denmark has belonged exclusively to men. With the making of the Mariam Mosque, "imam" would transform into *imamah*—a woman who leads prayer, who leads the mosque, a spiritual or religious leader who offers Islamic spiritual care. Little did we know that soon news of our mosque would spread from Copenhagen to China, and farther. The Mariam Mosque challenges the conservatism and paternalism reigning supreme in the heart of our society where men have all the power. Younger Muslims desiring to fully live out their faith do not see themselves in patriarchal *tafsir* and Islamic practices. We offer alternatives to transform Islam in Europe and beyond to show the world that Islam is a justice-loving and peace-inspiring religion. We will change things from within, and we will take as long and go as far as needed to put an end to the current age of ignorance.

Nothing has predisposed me to becoming a woman *imamah*. I never imagined such a destiny for myself. Yes, my father was born in Syria and grew up in a house in the historic part of the city, twenty yards from the Great Umayyad Mosque of Damascus where my grandfather, Naim, was a *muadhin*. Married to my grandmother, Wajiha, and father of six children, he worked hard to support his family. Still, every sunrise he would climb the thousand steps of the minaret to call the faithful to prayer. I often imagine his voice rising in the crisp early morning, soaring over the Damascene rooftops: "Prayer is better than sleep."

The morning the Mariam Mosque is to open, I get ready to lead the Friday prayer. I put on my white Syrian *galabiyyah*, a long-sleeved garment that falls down to my ankles—a gift from my father that I have transformed into my *imamah* clothing. I drape my white headscarf. Halima Mariam, my youngest, and her friend are watching me. The friend whispers loudly to Halima, "Do you know what an imam is?" Halima looks at her with proud tigress eyes and responds, "It is a woman who does very important things!" Yes! It is possible to change a millennium of fixed narratives in the mind of a five-year-old!

My sons, Salaheddin and Djibril, play chess every week. I teach them that the Danish word for "checkmate" has Arabic and Persian derivations—"*Shah mat,*" "*Shaykh ma't,*" "*Skatmat*" means "the *shah/shaykh/*king is dead." My oldest daughter, A'ishah, laughs and teases: "Watch out, brothers. The *shaykh* is dead. Long live the female imams!" She is right. Patriarchal understandings of Islam are being challenged by men and women everywhere. Among this new generation, there is growing awareness of gender equality as an intrinsic pillar of the faith. Halima Krausen, from Germany, wrote, "Things will stay the same until someone comes along and just creates that change." I and other Muslim women are doing that.

ꙮ

No Justice, No Peace:
Social Justice as an Islamic Imperative
TAMSILA TAUQIR
(United Kingdom)

At the core of the message of Islam is social justice, and working toward it in our everyday lives is a source of spiritual peace.[82] I will elaborate on the intrinsic relationship between justice (*'adl*) and peace (*salam*) through the guidance of the Qur'an and our lived experiences as minority communities in the Muslim diaspora.

One day, Prophet David (peace be upon him) was praying, having ordered his guards not to allow anyone to interrupt him. Nonetheless, two men entered, disturbing him. "Who are you?" he asked. One replied: "Do not be frightened. We have a dispute and need your judgment." Prophet David asked, "What is it?" The first man related, "This brother has ninety-nine sheep and I one, which he gave to me but took back." Prophet David replied immediately: "He did you wrong by taking back the sheep, and many partners oppress one another, except those who are believers." The two men suddenly vanished.

This Qur'anic account proceeds:

> And David realized We have tried him
> And sought forgiveness of his Lord
> Falling and prostrating to God in repentance
> So we forgave him that, and for him is a near access to Us
> And a good place of final return to Paradise
> O David! We have placed you as a successor on earth
> So judge you between humans in truth and justice
> And follow not your desire
> For it will mislead you from the Path of Allah
> Those who wander astray from the Path of Allah
> Shall have a severe torment
> Because they forgot the Day of Reckoning. (Q. 38:24–26)

It strikes me in recalling the experiences of our prophets how *imperfect* they were in action and behavior, but also how keen to reflect and repent, despite their failings. In this example, Prophet David is presented as innately human and not above making some fundamental mistakes—he did not listen to the perspectives of the different parties in the dispute. His hasty response, judgment, and presumptions in assessing the relationship resulted in an error. Realizing this, he sought and was blessed with forgiveness from God. Prophet David subsequently became known for his just and peaceful rule.

The Qur'anic story of a prophet learning the skills of truth and justice has lessons for us. First, and most important, that Allah is ever-generous in Her Mercy; second, that we must not be afraid to admit our weaknesses and fallibility and to seek forgiveness. Allah is clear: we as vicegerents on Earth must avoid judging others pejoratively, and our judgments must align with truth and justice. Importantly, we should not follow our vain desires that mislead us from the path of Allah.

This story powerfully reminds us that our social relations must reflect our spiritual selves, that our everyday behavior and interactions are entwined with our relationship with the Divine. There is no separation in Islam between public and religious life; our lived realities are guided by the spiritual goal of moving closer to Allah to be the best versions of ourselves.

Repentance and self-reflection in social relationships are vital, and it is important to hear all sides in a conflict. Prophet David's mistake was assuming he could understand and pass judgment using incomplete information; he was tested so as to teach him and us to listen and hear all aspects of a conflict. And so, Prophet David learned to be just. Please join me in a supplication for guidance so that we too may learn to be just and to work for a world that is just:

> On no soul doth Allah place a burden greater than it can bear.
> It gets every good that it earns and it suffers every ill that it earns.
> (Pray): "Our Lord! condemn us not if we forget or fall into error;
> our Lord! Lay not on us a burden
> like that which Thou didst lay on those before us;
> Our Lord! lay not on us a burden greater than we have strength to bear.
> Blot out our sins and grant us forgiveness. Have mercy on us.
> Thou art our Protector; help us against those who stand against faith."
> (Q. 2:286)[83]

"No justice, no peace!" We hear this slogan at rallies to counter the Islamophobia we experience. But what do justice and peace actually mean in our daily lives? What is the Islamic relevance of peace and justice? How can Islam become a daily spiritual and practical resource against injustices in Islamophobic environments?

In the Islamic worldview, justice means situating things in their rightful place; morally, it links with the human personality and the drive to achieve fairness, aligning equality through carefully balancing rights, duties, responsibilities, and social roles.[84] Equality is related to justice when differences among people are not stratified in a hierarchy that excludes some members of society. Thus, adults' social responsibilities are different from children's, and the young and able-bodied have duties toward elders and those with disabilities. The link is logical as justice is an indispensable prerequisite for lasting peace. A hadith *qudsi* reports that God stated:

> O My servants, I have forbidden oppression [*al-ẓulm*] for Myself and have made it forbidden amongst you, so do not oppress one another.[85]

In the Islamic tradition, social justice demands our moral rectitude and fairness.

Today, Muslim communities all over the world experience multiple forms of injustice, prejudice, exclusion, and violence. Muslims living in the West have a unique experience of this. Sisters and brothers in Islam, you each know how deeply and directly anti-Muslim sentiment affects us—including the military interventions against "terrorism," as defined by governments, and the routine violence directed against Black and brown bodies. The Qur'an reminds us there has always been injustice among humans, and it is always our responsibility to challenge this.

The category "Muslim" has become homogenized and fraught amidst concerns over security and terrorism, as in the aftermath of the London terrorist bombings of July 7, 2005. Counterterrorism measures curtail civil and individual liberties; Muslims are framed as enemies of democratic states, resulting in discrimination against us and those who "look" Muslim. Islamophobia and anti-Muslim violence have become routine in our lives in the West. Bodies and populations seen and defined as Muslim are singled out for blame of sexism, homophobia, and anti-Semitism, and consequently, if ironically, anti-Muslim violence is normalized—whether from the police, airport officials, or other communities.

These sociopolitical scripts affect where and how we may travel and pass through airports and borders, how we behave in public spaces, how many of us gather, and whether we pray in certain places. It prescribes what we may wear and how we should believe, including how to practice our beliefs in public, whether at schools, universities, mosques, or community centers. It determines how we must act so as not to appear suspicious, and how we use technology (and how technology is used against us). It tells us who we should have as family, how we should treat them, what we should teach our children, and which words to use to explain Islam to them.

We are prevented from resisting those in power and told what we should vote for and against, and what we may or may not protest against. Increased state powers to curtail civil liberties means there is no legal accountability for those who prejudice us in these ways. This climate affects our families, with those most vulnerable being children, young adult men, and elders. The authorities increasingly direct vicious accusations at us without evidence, and police and social services may even separate parents and children, spouses and partners, and break up extended families. Many Muslim children have been placed in foster care; their foster families, however well-meaning, cannot affirm the Muslim identity of these children or empower them to resist racism and anti-Muslim prejudice, because they lack experience of Islam and life stories as Muslims.

Indeed, we must challenge the discursive binaries created about us, positioning us as foreign Muslim or British Muslim, "good Muslim" or "bad Muslim." Political scripts view our mosques as sites producing terror; the government of the United Kingdom, at one point, discussed closing down mosques. The result is super-surveillance that increasingly and arbitrarily targets Muslims. Since 9/11, arson, vandalism, violence, and intimidation at mosques, Islamic institutions, and Muslim organizations have become commonplace. The threat of death has become a very real anxiety since the violent incidents in New Zealand in 2019.

Many of us ask how we should respond toward peace when faced with such injustice. A spiritual response could be to reflect deeply on the Qur'anic verses linked to compassion, patience, and mercy. Let us be clear, though: justice and peace cannot be achieved through further injustice. Allah sent Prophet Musa to Pharaoh, whose cruelty and arrogance before God were unparalleled, commanding his prophet to

> Speak to him with gentle speech;
> Perhaps he may take heed of the reminder
> Or become God-conscious. (Q. 20:44)

Further, Surah al-Maidah states:

> Believers, stand out firmly for God, as witnesses to fair-dealing
> And let not the hatred of others toward you make you
> Swerve to wrong and depart from justice
> Be just, for that is next to piety
> Be God-Conscious, God is well-acquainted with all that you do. (Q. 5:8)

This *surah* was revealed soon after the first Muslims returned to Mecca, from which they had exiled themselves following persecution and torture.

As I write this, the world is mourning for the Muslims murdered during *Jumu'ah* prayers in New Zealand. I too mourn, but I am also furious, because systematic and structural injustices are root causes of such attacks. I stand against the social, political, and economic conditions that foment such violence and pray we can contribute a solution that also heeds the wisdom of Allah in Surah al-Maidah, which teaches that even while faced with injustice, we *must* be just to others. There is no justice without peace, but the route to this must be a clear one.

God is clear in Surah al-Shura:

> The recompense of an evil deed is an evil equal to it
> But whoever pardons and makes reconciliation
> His reward is due from God.
> Surely She does not love the wrongdoers. (Q. 42:40)

I offer the following suggestions as practical peace-building strategies toward social justice:

—Get involved, be part of the solution, make yourself aware of various sources and perspectives.
—Lobby your elected representatives for justice and proportionality.
—Donate your time, energy, skills, and surplus wealth to social justice efforts.
—Consider fostering children if you have the means, especially Muslim teenagers and children with unique learning, health, or physical needs.
—Empathetically and nonjudgmentally support community members who are being harassed.

And always remember, Allah is the ultimate judge and dispenser of justice:

> The Word of your Lord has been fulfilled in truth and in justice. None can alter His Words. (Q. 6:115)[86]

Tamsila's Journey to the Minbar:
"Establishing Mosques Is Something of a Family Tradition"

I HAVE BEEN INVOLVED with social justice efforts as an activist for nearly twenty-five years, because I see a disconnection between the ideals of Islam and the lived realities on the ground. Injustice thrives within our communities, working against the well-being of all of us. It is thus a primary focus in my role as a *khatibah* to address, in particular, the anti-Muslim trends in contemporary Britain, where I live. Our community needs stronger and clearer strategies and responses to these challenges. Both my activism in the Inclusive Mosque Initiative (IMI), for example, and my spirituality provide the route to navigate this journey.

In taking up the challenge to cofound the IMI in 2012, I accepted the responsibility to lead by example. If I expect others to take on the various roles an organization needs to operate successfully, I must also do so. I wrote and presented my first khutbah out of that necessity. Fortunately, I could call upon the experience of decades of activism in Islam and social justice from across the globe, education in Islamic theology, and expertise in policy writing and account keeping.

Leading the IMI community in religious services required I learn khutbah-writing skills. The work of the IMI is firmly grounded in grassroots efforts to challenge social injustice wherever we find it, and to change the structural conditions that enable prejudice and exclusion of all kinds. The organization is concerned about the future of our children, inspiring us to work harder against systemic injustice in all its forms. That said, the current political climate of Islamophobia affects the IMI, and similar organizations, in very particular ways. The threads of a globally mobilized "terrorist assemblage" affect the everyday life of British Muslims individually and in our cultural institutions.

Inspiration for preparing a khutbah derives from a sense of compulsion within me that something needs to be said and shared while also being relevant to the *jama'ah* (congregation) in its particular location and setting. I am motivated to write khutbahs that reflect my leftist, social justice politics and values.

When I first wrote this khutbah, the police and social services had laid false charges against my brother, resulting in the real threat that his sons, my nephews, would be taken into state care. After two years of legal battle, all charges against him were dropped; the authorities eventually admitted there was no evidence of his supposed crime. The stigma and harassment of this event remain, and the long-term impact on our family's mental and physical health is still felt today. The authorities were not only unaccountable for their power over our lives but also over the lives of other Muslim families. I thus felt compelled to voice not only my situation but theirs too—all whose lives were being thrown into chaos due to right-wing public policy and Islamophobia.

Raising a voice for justice and utilizing one's spiritual knowledge and convictions against oppressors is a family tradition. I remember stories of my grandfathers, who were both vociferous public opponents of colonial rule before India's partition; one of them was imprisoned a number of times for speaking publicly against colonialism. After independence, that same grandfather, who had a conservative Islamic education (including spending time in Saudi Arabia), established an Islamic school and a mosque in the Punjab, where I myself would study. Additionally, my cousin living in the United States has established a traditional mosque there. So it can be said that establishing mosques is something of a family tradition, which I often share satirically with family members who feel I have no place being in a mosque because I am a woman.

I am fortunate to have experienced a traditional Islamic background, with a commitment to maintaining familial and community bonds. Real change does not happen in an echo chamber. The challenge I take in writing a khutbah is to write one that does not disenfranchise our communities but exposes them to our journey in an accessible way. I appreciate feedback from others who differ from me or who are more knowledgeable. I am concerned with the political and spiritual essence that envelopes the space at the *Jumu'ah* congregation and the animated conversations that follow.

I am humbled by my role as a *khatibah,* a position of authority entrusted to me by the IMI community. I do indeed stand on the shoulders of giants—theologians and activists, in multiple Muslim contexts of history and location, who produced the environment for the IMI to be formed and where my contributions have meaning.

Resisting Injustice
Ummah and *Ubuntu*

Our People First:
Reclaiming the Spirit of June 16, 1976
TSHEGOFATSO MASIBI
(South Africa)

Greetings of peace, beloved elders, leaders, activists, brothers, and sisters in Islam! *Assalamu alaykum.* It is the grace and mercy of Allah that gives us the opportunity to celebrate Eid al-Fitr every year, as is our Islamic tradition. I take the opportunity to mark the generosity of Allah's revelation through the Prophet Muhammad, peace be upon him. In doing so, I commemorate in these times of intense social strife and efforts for social justice the student-led Soweto uprising of 1976 that spread across South Africa.[87] You may ask yourself what a historic event that began in Soweto on that day during the apartheid regime has to do with Ramadan or its closing in the feast of Eid al-Fitr.

The connection between Eid al-Fitr and the commemoration of the 1976 Soweto uprising is first and foremost symbolic; both are celebrations of the ability of human beings to individually and collectively, metaphorically and literally, exert themselves beyond their comfort zones to question established routines that unwittingly lead to conformity with social injustice, causing pain and suffering in spiritual and material ways. Second is the powerful connection between the spiritual and the political. Both events point to the significance and power of self-mastery and selflessness as weapons of resistance against unjust social practices that prevent the growth and fulfillment of our highest human potential.

The Ramadan reawakening, evoked by the spirit of *taqwa* or Allah-consciousness, has the effect of subduing human cravings and desires of the flesh. The 1976 reawakening, sparked by the wave of Black consciousness, had the effect of subduing the fear, self-doubt, and inferiority complex instilled in people by colonialism and apartheid, declaring instead, with Steve Biko and Aimé Césaire, that "no race possesses the monopoly of beauty, intelligence and force . . . [and that] there is room for all humanity at the rendezvous of victory."[88] The selfless spirit that moved the 1970s activists of the Black consciousness movement finds expression in the words of a student leader of the time, Tsietsi Mashinini: "My people first!"[89] With this rallying call, Mashinini became the face and voice of the 1976 student uprisings, a year before the death of Biko at the brutal hands of the apartheid police.

The rallying call "my people first" resonates with the example of our Prophet, who was preoccupied with the spiritual and material well-being of humanity over personal needs. The hadith tradition tells us that on the day of judgment, when all people will try to save their own individual souls, saying *"nafsi, nafsi"* (myself, myself), our Prophet's call to God for Mercy will be for his community: *"ummati, ummati"* (my community, my community).[90] Similarly, at Hudaybiyyah, despite opposition among his followers, the Prophet preferred the long-term benefits of a peace treaty, even if it required personal sacrifice. Another time at the city of Ta'if, the Prophet prioritized his care for future generations rather than seek retribution for the torture he suffered at the hands of that community.

The Prophet's choices at Hudaybiyyah and Ta'if indicate a spiritual, social struggle and resistance to a culture that promotes worship of the self in favor of a culture of care and communal concern. The choice to prioritize the people over the individual is an ethical and political choice that exemplifies the intersection between the inner self as consciousness and outer struggles, also as consciousness. Subjecting individual interests to collective interests and putting public interests before personal interests maintains the integrity of values in the course of struggle. Being guided by a higher conscience, social dialogue, consensus building, and collective action enables us to keep the integrity of our values even in difficult times of struggle.

The key challenge, which is also an opportunity for our spiritual and social growth, is to internalize and live the resilience of the human spirit reflected in Ramadan and on June 16, 1976, every day and in all facets of life. How do we ensure that our personal, social, political, and economic conduct is characterized by the virtues of selflessness and regard for human agency against those forces that denigrate human dignity? As human beings we are prone to forgetfulness and need reminders to reinvigorate our struggles for justice.

Perhaps the best way to answer that question starts with reflections on how we celebrate these days. It is instructive to look at how those who initiated the original uprising subsequently commemorated it. Just after they had buried their beloved brothers, sisters, and fellow comrades, while shocked and traumatized, still nursing deep psychological and physical wounds, the children of 1976 were clear about how to remember that day. In pamphlets that year, they called for a Black Christmas, seeking to commemorate June 16 through solemn occasions of prayer, reflection, and social dialogue, providing detailed time frames for moments of silence and the duration of prayer meetings.

They requested all activity be brought to a standstill, except for the transportation of people to hospitals, indicating their respect for life even in the midst of a resistance campaign. The pamphlets show that students recognized the importance of notifying and educating the broader community about their actions and securing the participation of the community through rational argument rather than coercion; they did not subscribe to a culture of infinite boycotts or protest action without a clear and reasonable time frame. Their actions were clear, precise, and directed.

This is a far cry from the late 1980s when you might wake in the morning, go to work, and find yourself in the middle of a consumer boycott, bus boycott, or strike action you did not know about; when you could find yourself forced to drink bleach, or worse, necklaced, for breaching a consumer boycott you didn't know existed. I am not suggesting that no excesses were committed during the struggles of the 1970s, but rather that activists of the time reflected dignity, discipline, and integrity in their struggle—demonstrating the integrity of the agents of the struggle and the dignity of the people in whose name the struggle was waged.

What we learn worth reclaiming is that in the struggle for justice, we should strike hard at the system but never lose our humanity and the core principle of respecting human life and dignity. The tradition of keeping the sobriety of the day continued in 1978, with the Soweto Action Committee and the Soweto Students League making the call:

> All shops and business centres shall be closed on the 16th and opened on the 17th for half a day.
> All shebeens should be closed on the 13th of June to 19th on Sunday.
> The NPSL [National Professional Soccer League] together with its multi-racial Football League should suspend games.
> Discos and cinemas shall not operate too during this period 16th June to the 19th Sunday.[91]

The 1970s generation of youth activists commemorated these days not only with mourning but also with reflection and consciousness-raising. Funerals and night vigils for victims of police shootings became schools for social awareness, political consciousness, community organizing, and mass mobilization. A nineteen-year-old activist aptly recollects:

> The night vigils were very significant. After June 16 until 1978, virtually every weekend there was a political funeral. At that time, we did not only attend political funerals, we also went to night vigils. Night vigils were a place where we met leaders of the Black Con-

sciousness Movement who knew about these particular things. And they would come to give a perspective to us.[92]

The practice of anti-apartheid night vigils highlights the wisdom of connecting communities in prayer and reflection during times of darkness, silence, and fatigue. The similitude of this in Islam is the practice of *qiyam al-layl*, the voluntary night prayer, especially encouraged during Ramadan. In addition to gaining closeness to Allah, *qiyam al-layl*, performed late at night and before dawn, serves to instill discipline, self-control, and willpower, subduing the ego and personal desires and thereby helping one gain clarity of moral purpose, internal purity, and excellence.

We learn from this to reclaim innovative and imaginative uses of space, to create new languages and cultures of liberation, human solidarity, and resistance against injustice. This emerges from a keen awareness of our own humanity and the humanity of others and encourages us to refuse to be silenced or to be parrots that merely mimic what the academy, media, government, priest, imam, or *mawlana* tell us.

Listening to the inner voice tells us that we are more than what the environment, the society, or our carnal desires dictate. The spirit of Black consciousness refutes the lie that we are just bodies and rejects the false idea that we are all exterior and lack interiority. Reclaiming the spirit of Black consciousness that propelled the 1970s activists and the spirit of Ramadan, we should fight for the right to intentionally take care of our own souls and consciousness. We should not imbibe forms of culture and mass media that feed people false consciousness based on consumerism, crass materialism, greed, and individualism. Like the June 16th generation, we should not be cajoled by the White Christmas of new deals that promise us a better life depending on foreign investments, bail-outs of big corporations in many disguises, tax cuts for the rich, and tax increases for the poor. In the spirit of activism and solidarity evoked by the students, we would be at the center of the struggles for quality social services for all, and at the forefront of all radical acts of civil disobedience and protest action aimed at subjecting the people in power to the power of the people. We should loudly and actively demonstrate our solidarity with all the exploited and oppressed poor people of the world.

With these words, may every day be Ramadan, a moment of reflection, self-realization, selflessness, and self-mastery. May every day be June 16, 1976, a moment of reawakening, self-realization, selflessness, and self-mastery! May our motto be, Our people first! People first!

Tshegofatso's Journey to the Minbar:
"The Path to Myself and Search for My Creator Unfolded"

I AM A GENDER ACTIVIST working in the area of women's empowerment in entrepreneurship and leadership. My experiences as a child growing up in a peri-urban setting in the former homeland of Bophuthatswana inform my activism. So do my experiences in apartheid and post-apartheid South Africa, which have taught me that racial and gender inequalities are facilitated by exclusion and marginalization in all areas of life. This is the case in all areas of leadership—economic, political, social, and religious. Believing that these racial and gender exclusions must be challenged, I am involved in several Islamic feminist initiatives to combat the social subordination of Muslim women by dominant Islamic social structures.

Looking back, I see how my expanding sociopolitical consciousness as a teenager has been pivotal to the spiritual path of Islam I have pursued. I was born into a family of Methodists; however, I attended a Catholic school, St. Mary's, in my little village of Lomanyaneng, until senior high school. My parents were not particularly religious, so they did not mind my attending a school with a different Christian curriculum. Having eagerly learned the practices and teachings of Catholicism in my formative years of schooling, it became natural for me to join the Catholic Church at the age of eight with no objections from my family. I assisted faithfully as an altar server from the ages of ten to fourteen.

I love books and read a lot. Yet my home had few books because my parents were not readers; the only ones available were my siblings' school books. Also, my brothers were Muslims and had Islamic literature at home, which I also stumbled across. I learned a bit about Islam from biblical studies at school but encountered a different Islam in my brothers' books; I began to question and seek more information. Today, I still seek more knowledge, inspired by the Prophet Muhammad's teaching that believers should seek knowledge from the cradle to the grave. I am a seeker, and time and age have taught me to doubt and always question, and to seek new knowledge.

Early in 1997, I decided to leave the Catholic Church, to the consternation of Sister Beata Maria, a nun who loved me dearly. Pained, she warned me that denouncing the Catholic faith was like throwing away a piece of gold in exchange for dirt. Her words haunted me for a long time, and they still do, especially as a Black African woman who experiences the misogyny, sexism, racism, and classism integral to the politics of Islam and being a Muslim in

South Africa today. The truth is, what I had read about Islam was totally different from the realities of my experiences within the Muslim community. Drawn to Islam, I left the Catholic Church; yet from the very beginning, as a curious and spiritually yearning fifteen-year-old, it was difficult for me to understand both my inclinations to follow the path of Islam and some of the unexpected, painful challenges I confronted as a Black African woman in the Muslim community.

At the time in most mosques there were either no prayer facilities for women or we were confined to a tiny, dingy part at the back where we were unable to properly see or hear the imam or *khatib*. With dismay and deep disappointment, I discovered that Muslim women are not allowed to deliver sermons, let alone lead a prayer or serve on a mosque committee. This was a far cry from my Catholic experience, where Christian women are allowed to have a voice and are given the podium. Again, Sister Maria's warnings reverberated and haunted me. To my enormous relief, I soon discovered and joined activist Muslim organizations fighting against racism and patriarchy. Ironically, however, in most of these organizations, the leadership and authority were still dominated by men. Nonetheless, some of them enabled a space for women to undertake critical engagement with the message of Islam, encouraging me to expand my reading and study of Islam.

Slowly, the path to myself and the search for my Creator unfolded. This critical journey of self-discovery and robust contemplation of the deeper religio-spiritual and sociopolitical aspects of the message of Islam led me to find spiritual community or a home in the Qadri Rifai Ansari *tariqah* under the guidance of *murshid* Taner Ansari. Here, I learned of the spirit of love, peace, and togetherness. *Ya Wadud, Ya Salam, Ya Jami.* This is the God I want to serve and live for.

Through my activist work, I eventually found my way to the minbar as *khatibah*, addressing a sizable and spiritually receptive Muslim congregation at two annual Family Eidgahs organized by the group Taking Islam to the People (TIP). I still have concerns that at this and similar alternative platforms, women do not offer the Arabic khutbah but only the pre-khutbah talk. Yet I continue to consider these important spaces of reprieve where I can engage and share my thinking and lived experiences with men and women in the South African Muslim society. To be sure, some Muslim societies still believe a woman's voice is part of her *awrah* (a part of the self that requires covering) and that her space of worship is her home. Yet we live in a country where many women live in extreme poverty and squalor, in shelters, and on the street and are subjected to undignified practices by *zakah* (alms-giving) organizations in the name of Islamic charity.

The mosque can and should be a place of peace and tranquility for women and provide spaces for our active community participation. However, because of male-centered and patriarchal expressions of Islam, this is seldom the case. This reality deepens my appreciation and gratitude for the alternative spaces that provide me and other women with empowering and liberating experiences. We must not take for granted the intense struggles involved in creating such gender-inclusive spaces, particularly the community ruptures, pain, struggles, and sacrifices involved in these initiatives. My vision as a Muslim woman is the creation of a society where gender equality and equal access to and full participation of women in spaces, services, and resources permeate all facets of our social fabric.

ﻬ

Black Consciousness and Intersectionality: Toward Social Justice and Spiritual Growth
LEILA KHAN
(South Africa)

Assalamu alaykum.

> Believers! Be upholders of justice, bearing witness for Allah,
> Even if it means testifying against yourselves, or your parents and relatives
> Whether it is against the rich or the poor
> Allah is nearer to all of them in compassion.
> Do not follow your own desires lest you distort or decline to do justice.
> If you twist or turn away, Allah is all-aware of what you do. (Q. 4:135)

For young South African Muslims, the Qur'anic call to justice resonates strongly as we grapple with many social injustice challenges. Since 2015, student-worker uprisings across our tertiary institutions have highlighted the ongoing legacy of apartheid inequality. In this khutbah, I reflect on the importance of youth activism against multiple forms of oppression from my experience as a member of the Rhodes Must Fall (RMF) and Fees Must Fall (FMF) social movements. Both have ignited urgent public debate about the slow pace of change and absence of meaningful justice two decades into South Africa's democracy.

RMF formed in March 2015 among Black students, workers, and staff at the University of Cape Town (UCT) who were calling for the removal of a statue of Cecil John Rhodes, a colonial icon, from campus grounds, condemning it as an embodiment of South Africa's history of Black alienation and dispossession.[93] The statue, centrally positioned on UCT's campus on the slopes of Table Mountain, commemorated Rhodes's "generosity" in gifting land from his vast estate as a site for South Africa's first university. How can land acquired through plunder in Africa by the British Empire, RMF challenged, be "gifted" to the very people from whom it had been stolen? To Black people on campus, the statue glorified a racist who was indispensable to the project of settler colonialism and Africa's underdevelopment. Rhodes's statue was a constant reminder of the institutionalization and normalization of white supremacist, patriarchal, and capitalist power.

However, RMF was never simply about a statue; it was a declaration of young South Africans' unwillingness to accept the post-apartheid myth of a nonracial "rainbow nation" and false promises of transformation. It criticized slow reform and the endurance of apartheid legacies. Although formal apartheid ended in 1994, socioeconomic inequality persists, and except for a small ruling and economic elite and Black middle class, the Black majority remains poor and landless. The white minority still controls much of the land and resources with astounding arrogance and entitlement.

Student activists, who came to be known as "Fallists," began fearlessly calling for radical decolonization through the dismantling of colonial structures that maintain inequality. The uprisings exposed the myth of the rainbow nation and the idea of a multicultural post-apartheid society used to promote superficial nation-building, despite the lack of reparations and continued economic apartheid. Disillusioned with the lack of substantial change two decades after the first democratic elections, Fallists demanded free education for all and the abolition of exploitative labor outsourcing at universities. New Fallist formations emerged at many universities under the banner of #FeesMustFall and #EndOutsourcing.

The Fallist language of struggle spread beyond the ivory tower, as seen in the "grave fees must fall" campaign against the high cost of burials and privatized basic services in Gauteng[94] and in demands by protestors occupying a supermarket in Khayelitsha township in Cape Town that the "bread price must fall."[95] The promising connections between struggles reflect the potency of that moment and the crisis beneath the rainbow's surface.

A New Language of Struggle

In calling for decolonization, young people adopted the language of Black consciousness (BC) and intersectionality. The political philosophy advocated by the BC movement during the anti-apartheid struggle in the 1960s and 1970s promotes the message of solidarity among racially oppressed peoples, resisting the divide-and-rule tactics of apartheid and colonialism. Intersectionality, a term coined by Kimberlé Crenshaw in the United States in 1989, allows for analysis of the systemic and overlapping nature of oppression. Both ideologies emphasize a unified effort against ongoing oppression rooted in colonialism.

Thus, when I speak of "Blackness," I draw on Steve Biko, who defines it to include all racially oppressed people categorized and separated by the apartheid regime as Africans, Coloureds, and Indians. The sociopolitical purpose of this definition is to reconfigure the term from the colonial lexicon of a supposed phenotypical descriptor used to construct a racist hierarchy to support the goals of resistance, self-determination, and unification against racial domination. BC is a necessary philosophy and tool to rid ourselves of the racism and antagonism between Black "Africans," "Coloureds," and "Indians," the result of colonialism's divisive tactics. Biko argued that "we are all oppressed by the same system," and the fact "that we are oppressed to varying degrees is a deliberate design to stratify us."[96] RMF claimed a BC political identity because Black pain and Black voices continue to be ignored and silenced in post-apartheid times.

Adopting intersectionality as another analytical lens recognizes that people are not oppressed only through one system, but that different systems of oppression, such as racism, sexism, classism, and xenophobia, overlap to compound experiences of oppression. Intersectionality compels us to differentiate and enunciate our various experiences of oppression and disadvantage. Past movements fail in their treatment of women; their exclusion of and antagonism toward queer, trans, and other nonheteronormative peoples; and their inaccessibility to the poor and disabled. Intersectionality can maintain a political perspective attentive to *all* voices and groups suffering oppression rooted in colonialism and apartheid. We should not choose between our struggles but unite in the fight for decolonization.

I began my khutbah with the Qur'anic verse 4:135. This verse is meaningful to me as a young Muslim woman who draws inspiration and impetus for my activism from my faith, emphasizing the level of commitment to justice that Islam requires. Its message and spirit are consistent with the principles of BC and intersectionality, demanding we fight against injustice wherever we find it, including within ourselves, our families, and our communities and despite the discomfort we may face. This requires we confront the spiritually polluting presence of anti-Blackness among South African Muslims. It demands we deeply interrogate the queer and trans antagonism and misogyny in mainstream interpretations of Islam. The pure message of Allah that "we have honored (all) the children of Adam with innate dignity" (Q. 17:70)[97] has been so disfigured by colonial morality and patriarchy that it is not only ignored but actively defied by Muslims who exclude particular groups and refuse to recognize their humanity.

Fighting injustice within means steadfastly performing *jihad al-nafs;* this is the struggle against the "lower" self—egotistical qualities and selfish impulses like self-aggrandizement, conceit, and narcissistic instincts blinding us to the equal value of each human life. This resonates with the challenge of BC to develop a truer understanding of our human identity, demanding that we look inward to unlearn our prejudices and privileges in relation to others and to align our beliefs and actions with a principled commitment to justice. The importance of this jihad is made clear by the Prophet Muhammad, who observed the struggle against the self as more important than physical warfare.[98]

Thus Q. 4:135 is an injunction for radical social equality, requiring justice be upheld "whether it is against the rich or the poor," making clear that even the oppressed can perpetuate injustice, and this requires constant internal vigilance in our living and organizing spaces. The Qur'an highlights unwavering commitment in the fight for justice and teaches lessons about building and sustaining communities to become safe, dignified, and caring spaces in which we may all thrive. As with intersectionality, this verse shows we must truthfully recognize our own capacity to harm and dehumanize others even in the fight for justice. In the words of *Imamah* amina wadud, "Doing right actions for justice means resisting all attempts to be limited by or to limit someone else because of race, gender, sexuality, or ability. Our resistance is based on love and inclusivity."[99] Struggle must be fully inclusive for it to be revolutionary.

Spiritual Growth through Radical Decolonial Action

Beyond the political and spiritual lessons, the unapologetic methods of resistance and understandings of violence demonstrated through the student movement are instructive. We are told that people who resist outside of the law are violent, that communities that burn tires to protest a lack of service delivery are violent, that mineworkers protesting for a living wage are violent, that students burning the artwork of colonialists who dispossessed their ancestors of their land, resources, and dignity are violent. Yet denying people basic needs such as health care, food, quality education, or decent shelter because they cannot afford to pay for them is never similarly conceptualized as violent.

We reject this attitude. To resist power through disobedience has always been a necessary means toward a just society. This was the case during slavery, colonialism, and apartheid and must continue to be so today, especially if laws serve only to protect a privileged few and maintain a vastly unequal status quo. Young people in RMF and FMF have argued that true violence is the structural and systemic violence underlying the oppressive system that reproduces poverty, inequality, and discrimination. We have argued that the supposedly violent actions of oppressed people against oppressive systems are acts of self-defense against enduring systemic violence.

Subjecting Black people at UCT to the public display of a statue of a man responsible for millions of deaths on the African continent, in the context of ongoing oppression of Black people under the illusion of rainbowism, is deeply, psychologically violent. Violence happens when workers are not paid enough to attend or send their children to the universities they sustain with their labor. Violence is the deployment of police and private security by state and university management against unarmed student activists demanding a better society for all.

The supposedly violent and irrational responses by marginalized people to rampant structural and systemic violence are in fact rational reactions. Angela Davis captured this well when she said: "Because of the way this society is organized, because of the violence that exists on the surface everywhere, you have to expect that there are going to be such explosions. You have to expect things like that as reactions."[100] We cannot be limited by the law in how we resist and protest.

Justice and the pursuit of justice by any means necessary are inextricable components of our faith. The Qur'anic verse 8:39 calls on Muslims to fight "until there is no more oppression," as does Q. 4:135. Read with the overarching message of compassion that permeates the Qur'an, these verses reveal revolutionary violence and sociopolitical struggles to be also spiritual. Student protests adopting BC, intersectionality, and other forms of resistance cannot be viewed separately from our daily Islamic lives and should not be met with antagonism. Student protests are a valuable opportunity for older and younger generations of Muslims to learn from each other and to struggle together toward a truly postconquest, nonviolent society in which domination and subjugation may not persist.[101]

Leila's Journey to the Minbar: "The Nation's Imagination . . . Reignited"

THIS KHUTBAH WAS ADAPTED from a post-*tarawih* talk I gave in 2015 at the Claremont Main Road Mosque in Cape Town. I was invited to speak on "youth," by a friend who arranged the mosque's Ramadan program. The voices of young people were prioritized at the mosque that year, given the national shutdown of university campuses by Black students, workers, and some academics. The nation's imagination and debates about what a post-apartheid South Africa should look like were reignited.

Claremont Mosque, led by Imam Rashied Omar, has consistently incorporated social justice issues and current affairs into its khutbahs, *halaqahs* (religious study gatherings), and statements. It practices its politics through activist campaigns, including resisting the exclusion of women in the mosque space. At Claremont Mosque, men and women pray together alongside one another in the main section of the masjid, and women frequently speak at the minbar. *Imamah* amina wadud paved the way for this when she delivered a khutbah there in 1994, despite the vitriol and death threats hurled at her and Imam Rashied Omar. This radical moment began the normalization of meaningful engagement by women members of the congregation. I thus readily accepted the invitation to speak, which came with my share of backlash from men on Facebook proclaiming that I should be stoned to death and that "Rasulullah *SAW* would cry at the sight of this."

Unfortunately, such access for women to the mosque is not the norm in South Africa, with most women relegated to basements, balconies, or behind opaque screens without a view of the *khatib* or a chance to play that role. There is hardly replication of the Prophet Muhammad's mosque as a space for *everyone* to engage and participate equally. Even Claremont Mosque has its glass ceiling: a few rows of men still separate women from the minbar, and women deliver only a pre-khutbah, never the actual Arabic khutbah. Nevertheless, the space has been encouraging for me as a young Muslim woman developing my relationship with Islam as deeply spiritual *and* political.

My activism emerges inextricable from my faith because my parents raised their children to talk openly with them, to ask questions about our religion, and to share our concerns about mainstream interpretations of Islam. Growing up in South Africa, with a history of Muslim resistance to slavery and apartheid, also informed my understanding of social justice through the lens of Islam. From slaves who practiced and taught Islam despite this being forbidden by settlers, to prominent anti-apartheid leaders like Imam Haron, and on to Islamic feminists like Shamima Shaikh who found inspiration in Islam to struggle against apartheid as Black consciousness activists, the connection between Islam and resistance has always been clear. And so in 2015 I and other young people formed at the University of Cape Town a branch of the Muslim Youth Movement, which had first emerged in 1970 responding to the Qur'anic call:

> Let there arise out of you a group of people
> inviting to all that is good,
> enjoining what is right and forbidding what is evil;
> they are the ones to attain success. (Q. 3:104)[102]

Our aim was to promote a humane interpretation of Islam toward authentic inclusion of marginalized groups and a progressive critique of social issues. We were one of the first student organizations to issue a statement supporting Chumani Maxwele's protest against the Rhodes statue on March 9, 2015. Our declaration:

> As conscious Muslims, we are against the unjust accumulation of wealth, and indulgence in excessive luxury. We are commanded by our faith and understanding of Islam to promote all forms of socio-economic justice, and to firmly resist and demolish systems, institutions, and symbols of injustice and oppression. It is our faith in Islam that compels us to support radical transformation and stand firmly against racism and colonialism.[103]

The khutbah I delivered at Claremont Mosque explained the radical approach of the student movement from an insider's perspective, in response to the dogmatic view that democracy had already been won and that the youth were "born-free," with nothing to complain about or fight for.[104] I also wanted to challenge the *ummah* to take seriously the principles of solidarity and inclusion that the students were promoting. Despite an overwhelming spiritual impetus within Islam to resist oppression, patriarchal interpretations and colonial tactics persist; apathy toward politics, attitudes of racial superiority, and queer-antagonism are rife among South African Muslims. So prevalent are these narrow-minded attitudes in the Cape that it is termed a *koeksuster* mentality. Imam Davids of the Gatesville Masjid in 1990 dismissed this mentality as insular and unengaged and contrary to the duty of Muslims to eradicate oppressive laws.[105] This shows the ongoing and necessary task of connecting social justice and Islam.

In the five years since I delivered that khutbah, the student movement has largely disintegrated because of internal conflict and factionalism, disciplinary and legal action by universities, and severe state repression. Patriarchal tendencies within Rhodes Must Fall led to tensions and silos within the movement. Short-term goals such as fee decreases overtook broader decolonial aims for providing free education and ending labor brokerage. Opportunistic political parties and academics extracted benefits for themselves. Student formations became unsustainable, burdened by legal fees and traumatized by violence from police and private security. Despite what I view as a heartbreaking defeat at a powerful and necessary turning point in post-apartheid South Africa, I take comfort in Islamic values and teachings that encourage continued resistance against injustice.

ꙏꙮꙏ

A Self-Reflexive Response to Gender-Based Violence in Our Communities
NAFISA PATEL
(South Africa)

In the Name of Allah, the Sublime, the Loving, the Embracing.

In Surah al-Takwir, The Darkening, Allah *subhanahu wa ta'ala* draws our attention to signs that depict a slow yet violent decay of the world. The opening verses mention a darkening sky, from which stars have fallen and dispersed, no longer illuminating the world, and mountains no longer stabilizing the earth. The *surah* rhetorically asks:

Wa idha al-maw'udatu su' ilat
bi ayyi dhambin qutilat

When the female child is buried alive
And man is questioned
For what sin was she killed? (Q. 81:8)

Here, Allah points out one of the most ominous of these signs—when human life is valued unequally or devalued on the basis of gender and social vulnerability. In his commentary on Surah al-Takwir, Egyptian scholar Sayyid Qutb suggests that the violent rhythm in the opening verses of the *surah*— where everything that is known or familiar is thrown, smashed, or scattered— illustrates the effects of the human heart being pulled from everything it associates with safety, security, and protection. This verse highlights the plight of the girl-child and the moral impetus toward social justice; it describes the devastating social effects of gender injustices in terms of humanity uprooted from its moral core and spiritual center. The forceful articulation of this *surah* demands action to counter the injustice against those made vulnerable through gender.

Thus I call our attention to the conditions of the girl-child in our midst, to the current scourge of rape and other forms of gender-based violence crippling our communities. I call on us to collectively reflect on the condition of our hearts and consciousness reflected in our societies.

We live in a world darkened by the dimming of our ethical perspectives; let me mention some recent darkenings. A sixteen-year-old girl from Kenya is brutally gang-raped, her battered and unconscious body thrown into a latrine. In Delft, South Africa, four girls, younger than ten years old, are sexually violated and murdered, their small bodies burned and discarded in their own neighborhood. In Delhi, India, a young woman student is abducted by intoxicated men and raped and tortured for hours on a moving bus.

Mass rape, sexual slavery, and human trafficking are routinely used as weapons *of* and rewards *for* war. A girl in Bangladesh is doused in kerosene and set alight after filing a complaint of sexual harassment against her school headmaster. Adolescent girls are forcefully cut, their sexual organs mutilated in the name of tradition and cultural practice. A child is made a bride and used as payment to settle family debts.

In this darkened world, sexual violators hold high offices of leadership— a U.S. presidential candidate says he can "grab" women by their genitals, and his utterances are dismissed as jovial locker room talk. Wealth and status are veneers of First World civility, hiding many forms of savagery and brutality. Rape is used as a "corrective" for those who do not conform to normative notions of sexuality and propriety. The threat of sexual violence is normalized; our experiences of being gendered people subjected to these forms of sexual violence are commonplace. Women live with an implicit default of sexual vulnerability and anxiety; not even our grandmothers or our babies are safe from these harms.

The societal pandemic devaluing the lives of child and adult females is clearly not a pre-Islamic *jahili* practice, not something purely historical mentioned in the Qur'an. This darkness *is* our present reality. These brutal occurrences are *ayaat*, or signs demanding our attention; they ought to tug at our hearts and call us to a deeper consciousness and action.

Sexual violence is not exclusive to women and young children, but they are more likely to be its victims rather than the perpetrators. Risk levels and vulnerability to sexual and gender-based violence are related to other social problems, yet the occurrence of sexual and gender-based violence appears to be indiscriminate. These forms of abuse persist across the whole range of socioeconomic and cultural contexts; they often go unreported, unacknowledged, and tacitly accepted, which indicates society's moral deficit. We are all deeply wounded as a result.

Reflecting on the current condition of our hearts, we must ask a number of questions. How do members of a faith community attend to these social wounds and fractures? To what extent are we part of those who wound and those being wounded? What conversations are we holding as a community of believers regarding gender-based and sexual violence; what conversations are we avoiding too? What actions are we undertaking to really deal with this scourge; what actions are we failing to take?

When we speak *about* and *against* gender-based and sexual violence in our communities, we are effectively asking what it means to be a human being in these contexts. We are also raising critical questions about what it means to be part of a faith tradition that holds its own historical patriarchal imprint in thought and practice, and highlighting how gendered roles and norms are formed and performed within our Muslim communities. Furthermore, we are challenging how deeply entrenched values and attitudes about gender unfairly prejudice Muslim women and girls, making them vulnerable to abuse and personal violation; these are often tacitly considered appropriately religious and normal.

All too often, the gatekeepers of religious institutions avoid meaningful discussion and withhold interventions about these issues, or they are willfully blind to how male privilege shapes understandings about gender-based violence and impacts how Muslims deal with it. We tend to engage the issue of gender-based and sexual violence—including rape—as *if* it exists outside the Muslim community, as *if* Muslims are immune to or protected from it or do not themselves perpetrate this violence.

Gender-based and sexual violence deeply challenges us religiously and spiritually. We often fail to engage the issue meaningfully; our default position is silence or distance. Yet do we consider how our silence and failure to act contribute to our social and spiritual wounding and fracturing as Muslims?

A report by the United Nations on gender-based violence shows that fifteen million adolescent girls (age fifteen to nineteen), worldwide, experience forced sex (forced sexual intercourse or other sexual acts) at some point in their lives.[106] Adolescent girls are most at risk of enduring forced sex by a current or former husband, partner, or boyfriend; only 1 percent reported having sought professional help.

Here are more darkening facts and figures.[107] It is estimated that 87,000 women were intentionally killed in 2017 globally, more than half by their intimate partners or family members. This means that 137 women across the world are killed by a member of their own family *every day*—more than a third by their current or former intimate partner. One in ten women in the European Union report having experienced cyber harassment from age fifteen, including unwanted, sexually explicit emails or text messages or inappropriate advances through social media sites. A study from the Middle East and North Africa shows between 40 and 60 percent of women report having experienced street-based sexual harassment (mainly sexual comments, stalking, being followed, stared at, or ogled).

Locally, a survey in South African schools by Human Rights Watch in 2001 reveals that eight of every ten young boys interviewed believe that *women are responsible for or are the cause of the sexual violence* they experience; three of every ten boys questioned thought female rape victims to be "asking for it." Statistics like these demand we pay closer attention to our parenting attitudes, our teaching and public values.

We have to ask the hard questions. Are we mindful of our own prejudices and gendered attitudes? Do we question how we might contribute to fostering unequal and unhealthy relationships within families and communities? Are we critically conscious that when we apply standards of modesty, shame, and honor to Muslim women's bodies and fail to speak up about toxic masculinities, it is *we* who are helping to create these standards? Do our attitudes and actions perpetuate gender stereotypes, such as weak, incompetent, and fragile females and strong, domineering males? Do we understand that such stereotypes rob and distort the humanity of both men and women?

Are we guilty of teaching our daughters to "avoid rape," unwittingly creating the impression that sexual violations are somehow related to dress codes or the spaces those daughters inhabit or their behavior? Do we uncritically use notions of *haya* (modesty) and hijab to teach them protection and prevention against sexual violation, yet fail to also teach our sons *not* to be violators, how *not* to wound or use their voices, bodies, and physical strength to intimidate and harass others? Do we teach our young boys a sense of entitlement to the female body and such prejudices as judging girls and women by their dress choices? Do we question assumptions about male privilege and marital hierarchy in Islam and how these are used to excuse marital rape and domestic abuse? Do we see how women are forced to endure violent relationships because of their financial dependence, lack of safe alternatives, and fear of stigmatization within our communities? Are we among those who encourage women to stay in toxic marriages, blindly following religious leaders and family members who entertain the warped views that a woman's patience with marital abuse somehow reflects her piety and that such marriages are acceptable as some divinely sanctioned social order that privileges male rights?

Let us ask boldly whether we conflate our understandings of *qiwamah*, or a husband's responsibility to financially protect and maintain his wife, with male authority, control, and sexual entitlement. Do we understand that such conflation serves to religiously support male abuse, making it difficult to recognize abuse in our homes? Are we letting ourselves off the hook, failing to recognize that such abuse makes it impossible for the victim and the abuser to repair or break from the cycle of violence and heal?

By failing to be self-reflexive, our collective heart remains wounded and fractured while we allow gender-based and sexual violence to continue, silently and unabated.

Allah reminds us in Surah al-Infitar:

> O humanity! What has caused you to forget the compassion
> That binds you to your Lord, the Generous? (Q. 82:6)

Human beings are called to remember their inner moral impulse, or *fitrah*. This verse reminds us that just as we are capable of inflicting pain, wounding and oppressing each other, we all hold within us the capacity for compassion and healing.

As we call into consciousness the wounded and fractured state of our collective heart, I return to Surah al-Takwir, in which Allah draws our attention to the following oath:

> Surely as there continues to be a new dawn
> After every nightfall
> Light after every darkness. (Q. 81:17–18)

There can be healing after fracturing. But we are also reminded:

> (Divine healing) is for those who rise up
> Choosing to walk a reparative, restorative, and humane path. (Q. 81:28)

Let us reflect and remind ourselves that as a community of believers, we not only submit to the moral imperative of ensuring social justice but also to being actors for social change, agents of mercy, love, and compassion.

So today, we extend our arms and offer support, healing, and comfort to each and every heart that has suffered abuse and been violated and wounded. On this sacred day of *yawm al-Jumu'ah,* a day of bearing witness, let us join hands in solidarity with thousands across the globe to raise awareness and speak out against gender-based and sexual violence—including rape—in our communities.

Nafisa's Journey to the Minbar:
"Addressing My Sixteen-Year-Old Self"

IN 2014, I was invited to deliver a pre-khutbah talk at the Claremont Main Road Masjid in its campaign against gender-based violence, after which congregants gathered outside to hold a silent vigil for the victims of such violence. We held up placards bearing the names and ages of the most recent victims—some were messages of support and others of outrage at the prevalence and silence regarding this scourge in our communities. We next held an interfaith prayer and poetry reading to share our grief and pain as a gesture of collective healing and hope for our deeply fractured community.

That day was especially meaningful and personally resonant for several reasons. It was the first time I addressed the congregants of a masjid from the minbar. Wrestling with my own insecurities and fears about occupying a space that many in my faith community consider a male-only domain, I had to navigate my uncertain inner voice that questioned my worthiness to bear the responsibility of occupying that space. The strain and stain of social conditioning provoked internal doubts about my authority to speak, rather than my ability to speak authoritatively as a female. Although the presence of a *khatibah* is not unusual at this masjid, the notion itself is exceptional in the broader landscape of South African masajid.

Counterpoising my inner voice of doubt was the louder voice of internal rage mixed with feelings of profound pain and sadness. These were caused by my own experience of gender-based violence and bearing witness to so many others. I recognized and appreciated the immense significance of the platform. I understood that my female voice, my own lived reality and gendered experiences of violence provided the knowledge base and authority from which to speak, and to speak from the minbar.

Reflecting on my thought processes as I prepared the talk, two points of motivation stand out. First, I imagined addressing my sixteen-year-old self; I thought about what it would have meant to her to have heard from the minbar a message of care, compassion, and outrage at the silent violence occurring in Muslim families and within the Muslim community. I thought of this message that not only acknowledged the reality of her abuse, but also put words to the experience, identified the particular violence instead of "sweeping it under the carpet," pretending it was "not a big deal" or that she was blameworthy.

Addressing the congregants about gendered violence validated my own experiences, which I had found the words to describe as abuse only in my adulthood. I understood the immense power and importance of calling out abusive behavior as a matter for collective action and an imperative of faith. My inability to do this as my younger self meant I had until this moment not engaged my faith and its divine message as a healing salve and call to stand for justice. My sixteen-year-old self had confronted barriers preventing her from even accessing the masjid space, let alone hearing messages of hope and healing from the minbar. Thus, the foremost motivation for my khutbah was ensuring that my voice would be a message of hope and support that acknowledged the violence and abuse that many endure in silence.

The second motivating factor was the knowledge that my two teenage sons would be at the *Jumu'ah* prayers. I thought about the significance for them—and all other young boys and male congregants—of hearing the divine message filtered through a female experience. Shifting the aesthetics of the masjid space offers children an enriching pedagogical tool to reflect different embodied leadership models. A woman occupying the minbar space symbolized and conveyed an important message of gender equality that resonated with my own convictions.

I chose verses from Surah al-Takwir, translated as "The Darkening," as the key message from which to unpack the complexities of gendered violence because the chapter evocatively captures the depth of internal despair manifested as external chaos. The inner-outer contrast depicted effectively captures the pain of gendered violence as both personal and collective wounds. South Africa, in particular the Western Cape, has one of the highest levels of sexual violence and "reported" rapes of women and girl children. In the weeks preceding my talk, I daily adjusted the statistics of these incidents, each new incident more gruesome in detail—the ages of each victim seemed so disparate and the social destruction encapsulated by the verses of the *surah* seemed even more relevant. The *surah* concludes with a reminder that summed up the objective of my talk—a call to individual and collective action.

The khutbah I present in this book was delivered more than five years ago; I have since had an opportunity to deliver a few more talks at the masjid on a variety of subjects. I note that the minbar continues to be regarded as a male space; the voice of the *khatibah* remains the exception in many masajid. Yet in my own experiences of teaching and learning in the community, I have noticed with pleasure the many creative ways that women and girls have begun to insert their authority, voice, and presence. As women create alternative spaces—Islamic symposia, workshops, and *dhikr* gatherings—they are marking and claiming the religious space as their own, an important intervention for the whole *ummah*.

Black Muslim Women Preserving Islam in Women-Headed Households
SINDILE AMINA NGUBANE
(South Africa)

I would like to discuss the struggles of widows, single mothers, and women who are divorced. Neither Muslim communities nor the general South African context appear to support them, despite the model provided by the Prophet Muhammad, peace be upon him, who designed a model of care for vulnerable members of society. The prophetic approach to women is enshrined in the shari'ah, which Muslims must engage in the context of a changing society to ensure the just application of Islamic law. Contemporary Muslims have an obligation to explore the shari'ah and derive pertinent laws that meet present-day needs and aspirations, as have previous generations. Change is occurring in many Muslim communities that previously would have been unimaginable, including in South Africa where new forms of family structure are now common.

South Africa has high poverty levels, and women bear the brunt of poverty, especially those heading households independently—as much as 58.6 percent. Widows, single mothers, and divorcees inadvertently develop self-help strategies to cope. I argue for greater justice to be shown to them, especially Black or African Muslim women who are among the poorest, left to raise children on their own and remain mostly invisible within the *ummah*.

Many women choose to stay single after being widowed or divorced. After divorce, separation is a hard transition, particularly as women assume the role of both parents. Some bring up children alone, and some with the help of their extended families or in-laws. Many who choose to remain on their own face ridicule and abuse by society, which also impacts children negatively. Single Muslim mothers battle prejudice and discrimination, from both the state and the Muslim community.

Black single Muslim women raising families by themselves is not a new phenomenon. Hajar was our first example; and apartheid, which historically forced Black men to provide migrant labor to white industry, left Black women in conditions of extreme poverty to tend to children and the elderly. These women have regularly found ways to survive, including informal farming and economic activities that they continue today. *Stokvels*, a local form of rotating credit and savings, enable women to organize savings outside formal financial structures. It is a self-help community-based initiative to improve people's economic and social well-being via fixed regular contributions of a number of individuals in a group. Money saved is used for funerals, investments, savings, or purchasing high-budget items such as children's schooling or household and work-related equipment. Communal farming, or *letsema* (in Sesotho), initiatives involve communities planting together, sharing the harvest, and breeding livestock for larger herds. Some women also undertake informal trading of small items or domestic work in middle-class homes.

Most Black Muslim women heading their households play a crucial role in raising Islamic families. They take ownership of and promote Islam in their homes and families in the absence of a father figure for their children. They take responsibility for their children's religious identity, sending their children to madrasah and teaching them *salah* and other Islamic activities, thus ensuring they develop their Muslim identity from an early age. Islam reinforces seeking knowledge from the cradle to the grave, and the South African experience shows that women do not rely on a male figure to impart Islamic knowledge to their children. Through formal and informal means, women acquire such knowledge and teach their children.

These independent women prove they are well able to provide a stable home for their children and teach them Islamic values. Children learn through imitation; the careful, loving Islam these women practice make them powerful role models for their children. Yet the same women are not allowed to sit on *shura* committees or to participate in decisions made to advance Muslim communities. As a result, imams and other community leaders remain uninformed about the challenges facing widows, single mothers, and divorcees in their communities. They must engage with vulnerable women to build informed and equitable social structures so as to ensure justice in the community.

Our *Nabi* (Prophet), peace be upon him, set up a prophetic model in which poorer members of our communities would not find themselves in vulnerable situations. Ideally, Muslim communities should be structured to support and shield those experiencing such vulnerability. In our tradition, Caliph Umar, hearing the cries of a poor woman unable to provide a meal for her family, immediately approached the *bayt al-mal,* or public treasury, for food to give to her. In this proactive, ideal community people took responsibility to look after the vulnerable. Today, the prophetic model is unheeded, and Muslim women-headed households are disadvantaged, without functional links to or support from the community.

Frequently, in the face of poverty, widows, divorced women, and single mothers are compelled to marry for financial and other forms of security, often exchanging their independence for abuse. In the struggle to care for their families they can end up courting even more vulnerability for themselves and their children at the hands of abusive new husbands. Muslim society's dereliction of responsibility toward these women must be recognized as an intrinsic part of the problem.

The laws of inheritance are clear in the Holy Qur'an:

> Allah instructs you regarding your children: A male receives the
> same as the share of two females. If there are more than two daugh-
> ters they receive two-thirds of what you leave. If she is one on her
> own she receives a half. (Q. 4:11)[108]

This verse reflects the Qur'anic wisdom in that, prior to Qur'anic revelation,
women had not been allowed an inheritance. Arab socioeconomic norms of
that time were such that men were financially responsible not only for their
wives but for their unmarried female relatives. That the Qur'an insisted on
inheritance rights for women in a premodern context where other women had
very little, if any, rights to inheritance reflects a deep gender-sensitive commitment to economic justice. Islam is firm in the economic empowerment of
women, ensuring Muslim women's financial rights, yet this is still not practiced in many Muslim communities.

Further, Islamic law grants women the right to independent ownership
and control of property, and to engage in activity outside the home. Yet these
rights are often withheld by domestic obligations, injunctions on obedience
in marriage, and segregation-based social practices such as purdah, thus limiting Muslim women's control over their own income. This especially affects
single women and those heading families independently.

All Muslim women are entitled to own their own wealth and to operate
their own businesses, as clearly stated in the Qur'an:

> Do not covet what Allah has given to some of you in preference to
> others—men have a portion of what they acquire and women have
> a portion of what they acquire; but ask Allah for His bounty. Allah
> has knowledge of all things. (Q. 4:32)[109]

The independent earnings of women are theirs to keep, and nobody may in-
terfere in their economic activities. Indeed, history and contemporary Islam
show many Muslim women devoting their lives to their families, including
through their own business activities.

The protection of the wealth and property of women is stipulated even
after divorce; economically, they are empowered through the obligatory
payment by former husbands during the period of *iddah* and for a time there-
after too:

> Divorced women should receive maintenance given with correct-
> ness and courtesy: a duty for all who have taqwa. (Q. 2:241)[110]

Scholars have called this payment *mat'ah,* and in some countries, such as Bahrain, it applies for one year after divorce. Correctly practiced, such provisions would empower and strengthen women who were previously prevented from work by their family responsibilities to also become financially independent.

After completion of the obligatory time period of three menstrual cycles for divorced women, husbands are guided by the Qur'an to either reconcile with their wives, if they agree, or to release the bond of *nikah.* At this juncture, Islam ensures the care and protection of divorced women, urging decent behavior from men:

> Once you divorce women, and they have reached the end of their waiting period, then either retain them in all decency or part from them decently. Do not retain them in order to harm them or wrong them. Whoever does this, wrongs his own soul. Do not make a mockery of God's revelations. Remember the favours God has bestowed upon you, and the Book and the wisdom He has revealed to exhort you. Fear God and know that God is aware of everything. (Q. 2:231)[111]

Allah warns against denigration of divorced women, paving the way for establishing the care and protection of them:

> O Prophet! When any of you divorce women, divorce them during their period of purity and calculate their 'idda carefully. And have taqwa of Allah, your Lord. Do not evict them from their homes, nor should they leave, unless they commit an outright indecency. Those are Allah's limits, and anyone who oversteps Allah's limits has wronged himself. You never know, it may well be that after that Allah will cause a new situation to develop. (Q. 65:1)[112]

Despite legal rights for women under shari'ah, in reality male-centered governing religious bodies do not grant women these rights within the community. Outside of the Muslim community, there are further problems of inaccessibility to courts and unsympathetic legal officials. Attention must be paid to these impediments to advocate for fair outcomes for divorced women.

Although not always on a par with men regarding income, a number of single Muslim mothers are increasingly occupying influential positions that can directly serve to educate their fellow Muslims, especially other women, about alternative, nonpatriarchal approaches to Islam. This provides a great source of hope and possibility.

Let us be heedful that the prophetic model, the sunnah, highlights the importance of caring for vulnerable members of our community. We pray that Allah *subhanahu wa ta'ala* grants us understanding in this matter so we may always strive to gain Allah's pleasure.

Amin

Sindile Amina's Journey to the Minbar:
"Walk toward Me, I Will Run toward You"

IT IS AN HONOR and a privilege to be granted a chance to share my journey to the minbar. Since I became a Muslim some years ago, I have been under the impression that my views as a Muslim woman can never be expressed through the minbar and that, instead, I will have to continue to address women and men in only non-Islamic circles on matters concerning Islam.

In my professional life, I serve as an academic who provides skills training to postgraduate students to improve their scholarship and help them publish and influence societal change through research. I also support academics with curriculum transformation skills in higher education and emerging scholars in their scholarly writing, community engagement, and professionalism. Further, I serve on various forums relating to women and disability in Africa, especially on matters of sustainable development.

My experiences as a Black Muslim woman are tied to my professional work. Islam is critiqued for sidelining women, including those in leadership positions, yet the *din* stresses the importance of taking responsibility regardless of gender. One aspect of Islam I truly love is the emphasis that all human beings are accountable for their own actions. This entrusts me with the responsibility of servant leadership. The Qur'an states:

> Remember Me—I will remember you.
> Give thanks to Me and do not be ungrateful. (Q. 2:152)[113]

Providing any kind of religious service enables me to remember Allah and encourage others to remember Allah; this is a vital form of worship.

How do I conceive of my authority in a religious space? Since I embraced Islam, I have always understood that worshipping Allah involves serving community, sharing knowledge, giving charity, performing acts of kindness, or offering monetary support. I choose to play a leadership role to promote goodness and excitement about being Muslim. I assist Black Muslim women with skills to sustain themselves and their families so that they can live independently. I believe this adds to their dignity as Muslims, reflecting Islam as an enabling way of life. To me, it is important to spread Islam as a way of life among local Black South Africans. Islam is beautiful; it enables us all to be leaders in calling others to Islam, just the revelation *La illaha illa Allah, Muhammad al-Rasulullah* (there is no deity except Allah, Muhammad is the messenger of Allah) charges us with propagating this message.

Sharing valuable religious knowledge and inspiration is an intrinsic part of my spiritual makeup, making it possible for me to contribute to the revival of the community of Black Muslim women through their love of Islam. I cannot claim to be in full possession of all Islamic knowledge, but I know my love for Allah and witnessing Allah's endless and indisputable *rahmah* in my life enable me to share sufficiently with humanity. Memorizing the Qur'an is commendable, but implementing its teachings is more important. The value of a community of practice informs my religious works; thus, I consult my sisters and brothers with more knowledge as I might require.

There are many ways in which we should seek Allah's favor and pleasure; pronouncing the greatness of Allah to humanity earns me this favor! When I share the contentment that closeness to Allah brings to me, I feel worthy of Allah's forgiveness and mercy. A hadith *qudsi* states that Allah says: "Take one step toward Me, I will take ten steps toward you. Walk toward Me, I will run toward you."[114]

In preparing this khutbah, I was inspired by the shelter and love Allah has given me throughout my difficulties and successes. I know that other Black Muslim women find themselves in difficult situations as they try to maneuver challenges in their lives. Unfortunately, these women are triply vulnerable as Black Muslim women. Even though Islam preaches equality and kindness toward humanity regardless of a person's social position, women are not treated well. A hadith states:

> The believers in their mutual kindness, compassion and sympathy are just like one body. When one of the limbs suffers, the whole body responds to it with wakefulness and fever.[115]

This hadith emphasizes the need for fellow Muslims, especially men, to ensure mercy, justice, and compassion for women and children. Our life and *rizq* (provision) are in Allah's hands, as women submitting completely to Allah; this is reflected in the way we undertake our religious duties, or *ibadah*.

Our responsibility and relationship to the Creator are reflected in the Qur'an:

> Hold fast to the rope of Allah all together, and do not separate. Remember Allah's blessing to you when you were enemies and He joined your hearts together so that you became siblings by His blessing. You were on the very brink of a pit of the Fire and He rescued you from it. In this way Allah makes His Signs clear to you, so that hopefully you will be guided. (Q. 3:103)[116]

Providing support to vulnerable women in the *ummah* comes with its joys and tribulations, including my satisfaction in knowing I am constantly seeking closeness to Allah. I feel grateful when other women are motivated by my words of hope. My quest is to encourage Black women, especially young ones, to adopt education as a means of emancipation. Having a qualification enables them to care for themselves regardless of a generous partner. It sustains me to know that other women see me as a symbol of resilience and hope.

Of course, there are people who think women should not speak publicly, condemning those of us who call out social injustice; they call us "feminists," "*shaytans*," "modern and misguided" women seeking male attention through public speaking. They believe we do not deserve to share our Islamic knowledge because we are divorced or single mothers, and for them we are lesser human beings. Indeed, choosing to proclaim Allah's greatness publicly requires we develop a thick skin and understand that perceptions differ. I will never be discouraged; I accept that we have different ways of worship, and the way that demands justice within Islam is my favorite.

I pray that Allah rewards us for each and every step we take toward Him. I pray that Allah forgives us for the wrongs we commit, intentionally and unintentionally. I pray that Allah does not take us until Allah is pleased with us. Thank you for the opportunity to share with humanity my love for Allah.

Knowing God, Seeking Justice
ZAINAH ANWAR
(Malaysia)

> Indeed, the Muslim men and the Muslim women, and the believing men
> and the believing women, and the obedient men and the obedient women,
> and the truthful men and the truthful women, and the patient men and
> the patient women, and the humble men and the humble women, and the
> men who give charity and the women who give charity and the men who
> fast and the women who fast, and the men who guard their chastity and
> the women who guard their chastity, and the men who remember Allah
> much and the women who remember Allah much, for (all of) them
> Allah has prepared forgiveness and a reward great.
> —Q. 33:35[117]

My friends, when I began to speak publicly more than twenty-five years ago
of finding gender equality and gender justice in Islam, I was often asked,
"Why bother?" Feminists would tell me I was wasting my time fighting a
losing battle because Islam is, in fact all religions are, inherently unjust and
patriarchal. They would say for every alternative interpretation I offered to
justify equality, the *ulama* would counter with a hundred others. And, to be
sure, it is indeed the patriarchy of the *ulama* that is recognized as the voice of
authority on matters of faith, not mine.

The secularists would tell me it was a dangerous enterprise, that I was
giving legitimacy to religion in the public sphere, that religion should be
private between me and God and should play no role in public life, let alone
public law and policy. Even if I argued for religion as a source of good and
justice, for them I was giving undue legitimacy to religion in public life. According to them religion must always remain personal and have no role in the
public sphere.

The human rights activists would tell me it was wrong to engage religion because the fight for justice and equality should be through only a human
rights framework, according to United Nations conventions and the principles of the Universal Declaration of Human Rights. They argued that human
rights is our strength, the *ulama* and Islamists lack such analytical tools, and
we should thus focus our struggle on this international and secular framework.

There are merits in all these arguments, of course, but I do not believe they are strategic arguments. Religion has not disappeared from public life. Most Muslims live in countries with no separation between religion and the state, let alone religion and politics. I live in Malaysia where Islam is a source of law and public policy. Thus, to willfully ignore religion and its importance to the women feminists claim to help is both irresponsible and self-defeating. Instead, we should challenge the harm and injustice caused to women, family, and society through the abuse of religion and magnify the message of justice insistently enjoined by the Qur'an.

For too long, ordinary Muslims have left the field of religion and public policy to the monopoly of the most conservative, authoritarian forces within Islam to define. They decide what defines a good or bad Muslim, dictating norms for a good Muslim woman, wife, or daughter and prescribing laws and policies to keep us as second-class Muslims. When we protest, they shut us up, saying we have no authority to speak on Islam.

Yet Islam, in their very words, is a "way of life," Islam "has all the answers," Islam "is the solution." But how can Islam be our way of life with all the answers to the wrongs in our lives and our society when those of us directly affected by Islamic laws and practices have no say in it? How can we know what Islam means to us if we are supposed to just listen and obey others? How can it be relevant to our lives when those of us questioning certain orthodoxies are intimidated into silence? How can it be a tenable solution when so many of us are persecuted in the name of Islam and in some countries maimed or even killed?

As a Muslim woman who believes in a just Islam and a God of justice, I am outraged that the religion and God I love have been hijacked by forces that have turned faith into a set of laws and practices I cannot recognize. An authoritative God and an authoritative text are abused for those forces to hold power and dominance over us. What are the choices before me? I could turn my back on my religion, as so many Muslim feminists and human rights activists have done the world over, forgetting about Islam, and focus my struggle for equality and justice within the human rights framework.

But I am a believer, and turning my back on God is simply not an option. I am compelled to better understand my religion, ask questions, and search for answers to reconcile the disconnection between my faith and the realities I experience as a Muslim woman. Why must I choose between being a Muslim or a feminist, or being a Muslim or a human rights activist? For that matter, why must we choose being either Muslim or gay, or lesbian, or bisexual, or transsexual, or queer? These choices are set up as false binaries and are constructed to divide us for political purposes, for an ideological project whose binaries are not about Islam. They are not Islam. These false binaries are about politics, privilege, and the power of some to dominate others.

More than thirty years ago, in 1987, a group of us felt compelled to turn to the Qur'an directly to better understand its knowledge and teachings about women and spiritual equality. "Read" (*iqra*), the first word God spoke to the Prophet Muhammad, peace be upon him, was both the first revelation and the first command. For us, opening the Qur'an with feminist eyes was a revelation. Our need evoked the command to read the revelations as they had been sent to the Prophet. It was a liberating experience to discover the many verses that reveal the ethical vision of Islam advocating unequivocally the moral, spiritual, social, physical, and corporeal equality of women and men.

I was inspired by verse Q. 33:35, with which I began this khutbah, which revealed the common and identical spiritual and moral obligations placed on all individuals, regardless of sex. Additionally, I read in Q. 3:195 the clear divine declaration that men and women are members, one of another. The verse Q. 2:187 evocatively describes men and women as each other's garments. Yet another verse, Q. 9:71, depicts the relationship between men and women as *awliya*—protecting friends and guardians with their mutual obligations, and directing both women and men to enjoin what is just and forbid evil, to observe regular prayers, to pay the *zakah,* and to obey Allah and the Messenger so they may be *equally* rewarded. These verses are unambiguously egalitarian in spirit and substance and reflect the highest Qur'anic view on the status of the relationship between men and women.

This egalitarian vision extends to the verses on creation that reveal the characteristic of pairs in creation (Q. 22:5, 36:36, 50:7, 51:49, 53:45, 78:8). Since everything created is of a pair, the male and female are both necessary and must both exist by the definition of createdness. Neither comes before the other or from the other; one is not superior to the other or a derivative of the other. This means that in Allah's creation of human beings, no priority or superiority is accorded to either man or woman. As a cis-gendered woman, I found the revelations in these verses to be incredibly empowering.

If we are equal in the eyes of God, why are we not equal in the eyes of men? What happened to the commanding voice of the Qur'an and its ethical vision, which insistently enjoins the equality of all individuals and enjoins justice—even if this goes against one's personal interest, parents, or relatives? How did this commanding voice and ethical vision become silent and obscured, absent in the body of political and legal thought of Islam? When we women decided to read the Qur'an for ourselves, we discovered, plainly, in the original words of God this message of equality and justice in Islam. We began to question why this message was omitted in the Friday sermons, in the teaching of Islam at schools and universities, in the codification of the teachings of the religion into public law.

Why were these egalitarian, ethical, and compassionate verses not being used to properly guide the laws governing marital relations in Islam? Who decided that other verses, interpreted in discriminatory ways, would be the source of law and public policy? In making these choices, whose interests were served, protected, and advanced, and whose were not? Is the view of these men in authority really related to living the will of God on earth, as they would like us to believe, or have they twisted the divine words to perpetrate patriarchy and dominance and to resist realities changing before their very eyes?

I believe one of the most profound challenges we Muslims face today is finding ways to live our faith in a world where democracy, human rights, and women's rights constitute the dominant ethical paradigms of the modern world. In the twenty-first century, there will not be justice without equality. It is that simple and indisputable.

How do we find solutions from within our faith if we do not exert our efforts in *ijtihad*, or independent reasoning, and produce new knowledge and new understandings about Islam, especially in the face of new problems, issues, challenges, realities, and contexts? How do we ensure that the eternal principle of justice in Islam remains at the core of Islamic law and practice?

Those of us who have decided to engage with religion to fight for our rights are fueled by our utter faith in a just God and a just Islam in this perilous but compelling struggle. Our struggle is for an understanding of Islam that ensures we are all treated equally as human beings, regardless of our gender identity or sexual orientation, and that we experience this reality of our equal worth and dignity in our lifetimes. Is this such a radical or unIslamic goal?

Let us summon the courage to tell the self-appointed soldiers of God roaming our streets, installed in our institutions, ensconced in our homes, families, and beds and treating us with contempt: Do not play God on this earth; you are merely deceiving yourselves.

And to help us build our courage and confidence, let us all seek Allah's guidance and mercy in our journey on the right path.

Zainah's Journey to the Minbar:
"I Said Yes, albeit with Trepidation"

IN 2016, Fatima Noordien, a friend and fellow feminist activist from the organization Positively Muslim, in Cape Town, asked me to give a khutbah at a *Jumu'ah* prayer at the Annual International Retreat held by the Inner Circle, a human rights organization that engages with gender and sexual diversity from an Islamic theological perspective.

I felt very honored by her invitation yet also thought I was not nearly qualified enough to be a *khatibah*. I was not a regular worshipper at the mosque, which I attended only for funerals, weddings, Ramadan, and Eid. My neighborhood mosque was not a place of solace; I resented that I had to enter via the narrow back entrance and climb two flights of stairs to stand cramped in the women's section while the men communed with God comfortably in the spacious ground floor below.

Eid prayers were the worst; the mosque was so crowded that I could not help wondering what would happen if a fire broke out. Would we women be burned to ashes, crushed together in the narrow staircase trying to escape the fiery flames? The men would leave leisurely through the mosque's grand entrance and wide staircase. Routinely, the doors from the women's floor leading to the grand entrance would be firmly shut, lest straying eyes rest upon the forbidden—us, women.

So how could someone with such an uncomfortable relationship with a place of worship give a khutbah? But after a few days of deep thought, the appeal of rebelling against orthodoxy won me over. Here was an opportunity to claim my right as a believer, to speak and lead others in the spiritual domain. And there would not be many other Fatimas who believe that I possess the authority to deliver a khutbah. I said yes, albeit with trepidation, and warned Fatima that my khutbah would be more political than spiritual. She whole-heartedly agreed—we needed more political khutbahs, and from women, she proclaimed. Fatima had also asked Farah Zeb, another feminist activist/ scholar friend I had met earlier in Malaysia, to do the khutbah, and she too had agreed. We collectively decided that in the true spirit of sisterhood, we would share the platform—Farah and I shared the khutbah space and Fatima led prayers.

I grew up in Malaysia with parents who never missed their five daily prayers. I learned how to read the Qur'an at a young age. For five years, I attended religious school two hours a day after regular school. I grew up with faith in my heart and the utter belief in a kind, compassionate, and just

God. This was the 1960s, before the age of political Islam when being a good Muslim meant being ethical—being kind, respectful, honest, helpful, generous, clean, and giving of your best in everything. This Islam was taught and modeled to me: God will help those who help themselves, will reward you for the good you do, and knows if you have a bad *niyyah* (intent); therefore, always think and act with goodness.

In those early years, I had an uncomplicated relationship with God, secure in a God of love and compassion. By the time I graduated and became a journalist in the late 1970s, my country had changed greatly, torn apart by political Islam. As a political reporter covering the growing hostility between the nationalist ruling party and the Islamist opposition party, I saw my beloved God abused to serve the greed and lust of politicians. For their own ends, they waged a battle, each side trying to prove they were holier and more authentic than the other.

By the mid-1980s, my ears were burning with the patriarchal messages reiterated in the media, in religious schools, and in private homes: men have authority over women; women must obey men; a man has a right to four wives; he has the right to beat his wife; the wife cannot refuse him sex under any circumstance; a woman's testimony is worth half of a man's; a woman demanding a divorce is equivalent to her destroying a whole mosque. And these pronouncements were being made in the name of God!

I was outraged at these statements broadcast from the bullying pulpit. I had grown up knowing discrimination against women was because of culture and tradition, not Islam. When I protested that I had to do housework while my brother did not, my mother did not use Islam as her defense. It was tradition. None of my teachers had ever said anything to us about women being inferior to men in Islam. We were all equal in the eyes of God, enjoined to do good and forbidden to do evil, and we would all be equally rewarded, punished, or forgiven.

Confronted in my early adulthood with such misogyny justified in the name of Allah was an affront to my faith in a just God. To me, it was—still is and will always be—simply impossible for God to be God if God is unjust. It is this faith that led me to turn directly to the Qur'an. The words jumped up at me through my feminist eyes:

> If you fear that you will not be able to do justice . . . then (marry) one. . . . That (is) more appropriate that you (may) not oppress. (Q. 4:3)[118]

And among His Signs (is) that He created for you from yourselves mates that you may find tranquility in them; and He placed between you love and mercy. (Q. 30:21)[119]

. . . male or female: you are members, one of another. (Q. 3:195)[120]

. . . men and women, are protectors one of another. (Q. 9:71)[121]

These are some of the spiritually uplifting messages in the Qur'an that have inspired my feminist mission toward equality and justice for women. This struggle still matters in the growing conservative context that demonizes those who differ with the patriarchs within traditional Islam and the political Islamists.

I believe in and continue to struggle for a country and a world where Islam, as a source of law, policy, and practice, upholds equality and justice and empowers everyone. Islam cannot be a complete way of life or have all the solutions to the problems that beset society, as the Islamists claim, if so many of us are harmed and silenced by sexist interpretations. Those of us impacted by the misuse of Islam to harm us must stand up and have our voices heard.

Giving that khutbah in October 2016, having my voice heard in a religious space, from the minbar, was spiritually rejuvenating. I could not have felt closer to God.

ꙮ

Knowing God, Opening the Heart
FARAH ZEB
(United Kingdom)

Bismillah al-Rahman al-Rahim.

I begin in the name of the Allah, the most Gracious, the most Merciful.

I continue from the first offering of this khutbah, presented by Zainah Anwar: "Knowing God, Seeking Justice." In the second part of this joint khutbah, I would like us to reflect on the ways in which we can meet the challenges we encounter when faced with concerns that disagree with our hearts and spirits on the personal, spiritual, social, and political levels. So for this part of our journey, our starting point is to find a way from within our religious tradition to meet and overcome challenges, pain, and hardship.

One light of guidance that I find helpful, and use here as an initial point of reflection, is a hadith *qudsi* in which Allah says, "I was a hidden Treasure, and desired to be known; thus I brought forth creation, that I may be known."[122] This hadith *qudsi* is a way to think about how we can honor and replicate that same desire to know the Divine in our relationship with the Divine. How do we come to know God both in our hearts (that gives us a particular kind of wisdom) and in our minds (that provides us with another kind of wisdom). Combining head and heart is how I would like to take us through a sacred *du'a*, or supplication of Musa (peace be upon him). It is a supplication in which Musa calls to his Creator for help at a time of hardship, and it is mentioned in the Qur'an, in Surah Taha. Let us look at this *du'a* deeply in ways that can also help diverse and marginalized communities to overcome their trials and hardships.

Qala Rabbi ishrah li sadri

O my *Rabb!* Expand for me my breast. (Q. 20:25)

"Open my heart, broaden it," Musa calls to the Divine. Likewise, in our moments of despair, we too must remember to reach out to the Divine. In these sincere attempts, we will, *insha Allah*, find the Divine present. Remember Allah so that Allah remembers you.

Wa yassir li amri

Ease for me my task for me. (Q. 20:26)

"Ease for me my matter," whatever it is that we are engaged in, our hardship, our struggle, whether on a personal level or a collective community and solidarity level. How can we, from our diverse and unique backgrounds, raise and support each other in community-building so that Allah may ease our respective struggles? And as we seek ease, we must also invest in creating ease; in offering support and solidarity to be of service to one another in order to lift and be lifted by one another, we strive so the collective heart of our various communities can, by Allah's grace, expand to transcend tests that are sent our way.

Wahlul uqdatam min lisani

And resolve for me the impediment in my speech. (Q. 20:27)

Remove this knot in my throat or tongue, Musa says to God. Musa is saying, Help me, I have this impediment; I am finding it difficult to speak. So what is going on here? We have Musa, a beautiful, sublime Prophet, who gave us the example of taking off our shoes when we enter sacred ground, Musa the friend of God; and yet Musa in his humility says, "I have an impediment, help me dear God, help me, take away this difficulty." Despite Musa having many beautiful gifts, in this moment of need, humility enables him to ask for support to overcome his impediment.

An impediment is something that gets in the way of our ability to do something. Physical, visible, or invisible impediments, disabilities, and abilities are what Musa is pointing us to. Let us not forget that what others may see as an accomplishment may at times also feel like an impediment for some. So we need to look at how impediments arise in different contexts. We need to ask ourselves how we can support one another, and in so doing, we need to constantly check the needle on our own compass of humility.

> *Yafqahu qawli*
>
> So that they may discern my meaning. (Q. 20:28)

"Untie this knot so that they may understand me." Who does Musa refer to when saying "they"? Musa was confronted by those who did not agree with him or with his message; they could not understand him and, presumably, also did not want to understand him.

So when we speak to one another in community, we need to remember to speak in a language that embraces everybody. In addition to physical speech impediments, the manner and language we use can also be impediments. To overcome this, we need to remain attentive to how we use language, and how we make it accessible to those we address so that we, in turn, can be understood. Essentially, we must pay attention to making the language in our minds, with our various perspectives, cohere with the language of our hearts. Likewise, when we ask for clarity from somebody, our hearts must remain open to their feedback; we must be attentive to the humility in our hearts in the way that we present our protest or our request so that it is softer on the soul of the one who receives the protest or the request. In our current day and age, we must extend this attentiveness to all our other forms of communication, such as writing in blogs and tweets and communicating via various social media formats.

> *Waj'al li waziram min ahli*
> *Haroona akhi*
> *Ushdud bihi azri*
> *Wa ashrik hu fi amri*

And appoint for me a vizier from my family
Haroun, my brother.
Increase my strength through him
and let him share my task. (Q. 20:29–32)

The beauty of Musa's humility in this act of recognizing and then seeking support by asking for assistance to overcome his speech impediment provides us with a powerful tool to overcome the challenges posed by our own impediments. It is a compelling example of the guidance we seek in order to overcome different challenges in our own interactions, partnerships, and relationships.

In any situation, it is necessary to reflect on what is healthy for us, and why we hang on to things that may be unhealthy. Through this process we can begin to confront our struggles and learn how to move beyond them, who to ask for support, and to whom we should offer our support and when. In this vein, we can apply this principle to our networks, to concepts of solidarity, and to community-building. Communities are forms of families. Through sharing of responsibilities and strength, one's individual vulnerabilities can be overcome. Both private and public domains of community-building can open spaces of safety, of understanding, and of strength.

Kay nusabbihaka kathiran Wa nazkuraka kathiran

So that we may glorify you abundantly, and remember you abundantly.
  (Q. 20:33)

Ultimately, what Musa says in his direct conversation with Allah is that this is why I am asking you for help, so remove the impediment; appoint a vizier; allow my community to understand me so it can share my responsibilities so that ultimately, we may all praise you collectively and in solidarity.

Connecting this with:

Sabbihisma Rabbika al-A'la

Glorify the name of your Sustainer, Most High. (Q. 87:1)

The lesson for us as members of humanity is that our focus in all we do, with every breath and action, in our various forms of community and community-building, is for our hearts to submit to the Divine in worship. In so doing, we aim to raise our individual and collective awareness of our consciousness of Allah.

Let us remind ourselves as a community, as we go into prayer and into the sacred humble position of *sujud,* prostration, that our hearts will be held higher than our heads.

Salawat

Farah's Journey to the Minbar:
"A Pause Could Serve as a Bridge of Faith"

I WAS BORN in the United Kingdom to Pakistani Muslim, Sufi parents, and faith has been an integral part of my life. As I was growing up, I regularly traveled to Pakistan and I was introduced to mesmerizing renditions of devotional music and spiritual poetry—known as the *qawwalis*—of the Sabri brothers, Nusrat Fatah Ali Khan, Abida Parveen, and Aziz Mian; the *naats* of Wahid Zafar and Umme Habiba; and the sacred poems of Baba Buleh Shah and Allama Muhammad Iqbal. Sacred poetry and music are infused with the earth and scent of South Asia, a land I experienced as teeming with saints, generous people, and inspirational teachers.

My love for Islamic studies took root in Pakistan, a nation-state that came into existence after fighting for freedom from its colonial occupiers. While in college there, I was fortunate to be taught Islamic studies by a wonderful woman who brought the subject alive with her deep humility, perfect grace, and love for the subject. She belonged to a generation of scholars who, like my parents, were children at the time of Pakistan's formation in 1947 and now were inspirational adults. They instilled in many of us a sense of personal responsibility to stand up for truth, to stand firm against oppression, to fight for justice, to take pride in our identity, and to create unity and solidarity among those with whom we lived.

I have taken these principles into every one of my jobs, both within the statutory and the nonprofit or voluntary sectors and across different ethnic, cultural, gender, disability, and religious spaces. Many years of service working with marginalized members of British society have provided me with a grounded knowledge of organizations that struggle against immense odds to promote the welfare and well-being of the vulnerable, those facing, among other things, homelessness, mental ill health, and domestic violence.

Witnessing firsthand the levels of discrimination still rife in our midst, I took to more deeply studying these social realities, pursuing a master's degree in gender and social policy. I wanted to know more about the root causes of gender inequality in society and understand the legal, political, societal, and religious machinery and how these are misused to justify discrimination. This course was an eye-opener, to say the least! I went on to study for a master's in Islamic studies to equip myself with much-needed tools to question inequalities and injustices I experienced in my religious sphere.

I have intermittently worked and saved up to study, always basing my academic template on the real experiences I encountered on the ground. The master's in Islamic studies was just the beginning, a dipping of my toes in the water of knowledge. I went on to gain a doctorate in Islamic studies that focused on marginalized communities. One would assume that my qualifications and hard work would enable me to legitimately pose questions and offer perspectives about gender discrimination and other social injustices in my Muslim community. Yet truth be told, being a scholar of Islam holds little weight among those minds closed to challenging views, whether these pertain to gender, sexuality, or other types of knowledge. An argument I encountered, mainly from those who uphold a patriarchal perspective, is that unless one has a thorough command of the Arabic language or has studied at an Islamic university, one is not qualified to speak about Islam. Different avenues of education and sources of knowledge are simply discounted. This gate-keeping must change.

I had unconsciously so internalized this limited, biased view of leadership that when I was first asked to offer a khutbah and lead a congregational prayer about ten years ago, I refused. I thought I was not qualified enough. Now, I hold a different perspective, not only because I feel grounded as I have grown older in my own knowledge about Islam, my interests, and my work, but also because I realize that those questioning my academic credentials will always find something with which to reject my religious authority. That is their prerogative, but I will not allow it to stop me from speaking in my community again.

Dominating, loud, and objecting voices do not have the right to appropriate religious discourse, prayer spaces, mosque havens, and minbars. Disagreement is perfectly fine, but discrimination and abuse, however thinly veiled, patronizingly conveyed, or blatantly voiced, are not. Each human experience lends a different perspective to life, and each person's applied lens provides a different vision. This is what sharing in community means.

When I was asked to offer this *Jumu'ah* khutbah during a retreat focusing on gender and sexual justice in Islam in South Africa, where I was an invited speaker, the process of being asked and then the subsequent active involvement of how it unfolded were simply wonderful. An amazing woman activist, Fatima, for whom I have immense regard, asked me whether I would consider offering the *Jumu'ah* khutbah. I agreed. Not known to me at the time, and as with all good strategists, Fatima had been determined to find a woman for this task and had also asked another activist and dear friend, Zainah Anwar, to offer the khutbah, who had also accepted. So a decision had to be made about which of us would do it. Fatima felt we both should do it, but I struggled to see how two women could offer the khutbah at the *Jumu'ah* without feeding into that broader traditional paradigm that "two women equal one man," which we Muslim feminists have worked hard to subvert.

I paused and reflected on this, and it dawned on me that two women could easily immerse themselves into the traditional khutbah format with a pause between them, a pause that could serve as a bridge of faith.

Zainah and I supported each other in this idea and made our solidarity clear at the outset so there would be no misunderstanding that we were co-*khatibahs*. I asked Fatima to search for *muadhins* representing diverse marginalized groups, and to lead the *Jumu'ah* prayer, both of which she did. This was a collective and inclusive *Jumu'ah* from inception to conclusion, from its *muadhins*, to its *khatibahs* and *imamahs*. By Allah's grace, that *Jumu'ah*—its gathering of the faithful, the call to prayer, the khutbah, and the prayer—unfolded organically, beautifully.

Marriage
Mawaddah and *Mithaq*

ꙮ

Marriage:
Foundation for a Peaceful Society
MUSDAH MULIA
(Indonesia)

Many Muslims understand marriage as one of the fundamental requirements of an Islamic way of life, as the foundation for a peaceful society. The core of Islamic teaching is the concept of *tawhid*, the oneness and unity of God and the basis for devotion to God, guiding Muslims on how to establish harmonious relationships among people. Understanding *tawhid* helps us better understand the roles we play in different relationships, including marriage. The principle of *tawhid* produces three principles in the community: mutuality, equality, and freedom.

First: the principle of mutuality. Islam explicitly teaches that human beings are sisters and brothers (Q. 49:10). Faith and piety are not regarded as complete unless one loves fellow humans in the ways one loves oneself. Mutual care creates a nourishing community and a spirit of generosity that sustain social relations.

Second: the principle of equality. A number of verses in the Qur'an stipulate human equality. The Qur'an tells us that all human beings are created from a single pair and so human beings are of one family, principally created as equals. No single human must be feared, worshipped, or regarded as unconditionally correct. A king is not god to his subjects, a husband is not god to his wife, a well-to-do person is not god to the poor. And because they are absolutely not gods, the people of a state must not idolize a ruler and a wife may not worship her husband as god. Unconditional fear and obedience to a leader or partner over the fear of God is absolutely a negation of *tawhid*—and thereby a great insult to Islam.

Third: the principle of liberty or human freedom. This principle is the consequence of a proper understanding of *tawhid*. Human freedom must be put into practice in real, daily life, especially in the context of the nation-state, to ensure the undamaged sustainability of a plural society. Islam teaches that freedom itself is not the objective but only a means to enable conscious, willful surrender to God. The main objective of Islam is to set human beings free in order that they recognize their dignity as God's creation and for God's worship.

Tawhid liberates human beings from all false beliefs and despotisms. The Qur'an condemns all forms of worship, loyalty, or obedience to any but God and enjoins believers to forsake everything that distracts from submission to God alone (Q. 51:56). The Qur'anic condemnation of *shirk* (idolatry) applies not only to worship but to every facet of human existence. In the context of social relations, the prohibition against *shirk* implies that no individual or group may exalt themselves over any other individual or group. Unjust social hierarchies thus reflect a form of idolatry.

Tawhid requires obedience to God over every other allegiance. Rulers may not dominate their people; the strong may not oppress the weak; white-skinned races may not raise themselves above people of color; men cannot consider themselves proprietors of women. People belonging to socially disadvantaged groups should not acquiesce to the domination of others since this taints the purity of *tawhid*.

On a social level, the power of the principle of *tawhid* gives us courage to defend oppressed people and those rendered structurally and systematically powerless, such as women, the poor, and children and those abused by leaders who hold positions of power while hiding their cruelty behind the name of God.

It is apparent, therefore, that *tawhid* is not simply a static religious doctrine. *Tawhid* is an active force that enables us to recognize God as God, and humans as humans. A genuine understanding of it brings salvation and prosperity to individuals while also forming the basis for a society that is moral, civil, humanitarian, and free of discrimination, injustice, cruelty, fear, and oppression.

The Qur'an discusses marriage in detail in no fewer than 105 verses, using the word *al-nikah* (meaning "union") twenty-three times, the word *zawj* (spouse) eighty times, or the word *wahaba* (sacrifice) twice. Approaching the real meaning of marriage thus requires unraveling all these verses by theme and understanding them as a whole to form conclusions about their essence and overall meanings. Marriage as a source of peace within society is essential to the collective Qur'anic message.

In Islam, married life, like all things, should be based on *tawhid*. Based on the principle of *tawhid*, wife and husband are entreated to build a peaceful, loving, and caring family drawing on the related Qur'anic virtues of *sakinah* (contentment), *mawaddah* (love), and *rahmah* (compassion). Living and embodying these virtues will have a positive impact not only on their own family members, but also on other families around them. A deeper analysis of the specific Qur'anic verses regarding marriage has allowed me to extract five basic principles to guide relationships.

First, marriage is a contract in Islam—the Qur'an calls it a "strong covenant" (*mithaqan ghalidhan*) (Q. 4:21), producing the principle of marriage as a strong commitment between spouses. The logical consequences of this principle are that each spouse must observe his or her respective rights and obligations. Islam regulates in great detail the rights and obligations of a husband and wife, parents and children, as well as relationships between families. Accordingly, it is logical to conclude that such a covenant cannot be entered into by children or people who cannot understand what constitutes a covenant. A meaningful covenant requires that people have the necessary capacity to enter it consciously, maturely, and with awareness of what such commitment entails. Even though divorce is permitted, marriage is ideally intended to be a lifelong partnership—a child cannot be expected to have the necessary experience or intellectual ability to choose a life partner. Thus, child marriage cannot meaningfully be Islamic.

Second, marriage is to rest on the principle of *al-musawah*, gender equality and justice (Q. 2:187). Equality can be built through efforts to end discriminatory acts that position men and women socioculturally, psychologically, and politically in a disharmonious state of hierarchy. Such hierarchy prevents them from playing their parts as husband-father and wife-mother, the duties for which should be fairly distributed. Fair does not necessarily mean that the duties and obligations are of exactly the same nature and quantity; rather, they are proportionally distributed on the basis of mutual agreement. The distribution of work, both in the home and outside of it, should pay due attention to the safety and function of women's reproductive acts.

Third, a prosperous marriage is built upon the principle of *mawaddah wa rahmah*, love and compassion (Q. 30:21); this enables a family that has a loving and compassionate atmosphere between a husband and wife. Affection and compassion develop when each spouse sincerely accepts their partner the way they are, demanding no more than that. A true sense of *mawaddah wa rahmah* prevents various forms of domestic violence, whether physical, psychological, or sexual or violence in the form of economic abandonment.

Fourth, in marriage the principle of *al-mu'ashara bil-ma'ruf* (living together with goodness) (Q. 4:19) points to the importance of good, humane behavior in the relationship between husband and wife. The word *ma'ruf* doesn't simply mean goodness, but goodness with attention to particularity and locality. So in the relationship between spouses, mutual protection and care attentive to each situation is needed. Married couples should be fully aware that as human beings they each have strengths and weaknesses; no human is perfect. Therefore, the couple should safeguard and complement each other's strengths and help one another to overcome weaknesses.

Fifth is the principle of monogamy drawn from Surah al-Nisa (Q. 4:3). A truly happy marriage can only be built on the principle of monogamy, namely, one husband and one wife. It should not be construed as such on paper only, but rather in reality. By this, I mean that neither a husband nor a wife has more than one partner, at home or outside the home, publicly or privately. Husbands and wives should not be allowed to violate the principle of monogamy. The social reality illustrates that a breach of monogamy leads to enormous pain and suffering and ultimately to the breakup and ruin of the family.

Collectively, these Islamic teachings on marriage reflect the goals of *tawhid* that strive to eliminate all forms of domination, discrimination, exploitation, and violence within marriage by anyone for any reason. From these five principles we also conclude that the main purpose of marriage in Islam is to create a family life built on the foundations of peace and compassion (*mawaddah*), bliss or happiness (*sa'adah*), and contentment (*sakinah*). Grounded in *tawhid* they help to establish a happy married life and provide guidance for peace of heart and mind and well-being to everyone.

An Islamic approach to human rights focuses on the fundamental principle that women and men are equally and fully human and in their essence are no different. In the Qur'an (Q. 4:1) there are no evaluative distinctions between the creation of man and woman, who each emerges from the same origin, Allah, and who each returns to that same Divine Source. By aspiring to mutuality, equality, and freedom in our relationships with our spouses, may our marriages be part of our devotion and commitment to a life based on *tawhid*.

Musdah's Journey to the Minbar:
"I Dare to Accept the Consequences"

IT IS STILL FRESH in my memory, the day my friend Aminah asked me to give the marriage sermon at her daughter's wedding. Her reason: "I don't want my daughter to receive a sermon that demeans women as sexual objects and reproductive machines." Before I could answer, she continued, "I realize this isn't an easy request—many will reject a marriage sermon from a woman, especially a feminist like you."

Aminah is my best friend and a prominent human rights activist in Indonesia who aspires for change, beginning with her own family, that some, including her husband, resist. Her older brother threatened to stay away from her daughter's wedding if a woman gave the khutbah. Aminah's response was, "I dare to accept the consequences; it isn't easy bringing about change, but there is no time to waste." I accepted.

I prepared the sermon meticulously. It was a new experience and I was anxious; I didn't have a role model at hand. I had never experienced a woman giving a marriage sermon. It was a first for everyone present too.

Al-hamdu lillah, I did it successfully. Aminah was happy and her family had followed the sermon solemnly. The sermon was considered remarkable and educational; it explained the important Islamic values of love and equality and the couple's related responsibilities.

Since then, I've presented marriage khutbahs in many places, even for people I've never met. Not everybody will accept a woman presenting a sermon, especially women with progressive gender views of Islam. I have been accused of being an apostate (*murtad*) and infidel (*kafir*), even a foreign collaborator. I choose not to respond to such accusations on principle—why waste energy on foolishness!

That first marriage sermon took place twenty years ago, yet even today hardly any women deliver marriage khutbahs in Indonesian society, which is still dominated by men. Clearly, we need more women giving sermons, those with clear gender equality perspectives who dare to voice a humane and dignifying view of Islam.

As a girl, I was fortunate to attend one of the oldest Islamic boarding schools in Indonesia, the Pesantren As'adiyah in South Sulawesi. Not many females have such a chance for a systematic Islamic education. I grew up in a highly educated family, loyal to Islamic traditions. My paternal grandfather was a venerated *tariqa* scholar; my maternal grandfather, a respected *fiqh* scholar; and my mother, the first girl in her village to graduate from a *pesantren.* I married a broad-minded man with deep humanitarian values. All this has supported my *da'wah* activities, which promote Islamic teachings that accord with human rights and gender equality, and progressive Islamic views.

At the *pesantren,* I learned about delivering sermons. Every Ramadan the senior students, as part of their community service, delivered sermons in their villages. *Pesantrens,* though, are steeped in conservative Islamic values;

it was no surprise, then, that these sermons supported patriarchal values, such as men dominating women, complete obedience by wives, and dismissiveness toward other faiths.

Indonesian women still may not deliver Friday, Eid, or marriage khutbahs (some people even believe that a marriage is not valid if the sermon is given by a woman). Women can give celebration sermons during *mawlid al-nabi, isra wa'l mi'raj*, Muharram, *majlis al-ta'lims* (study groups), and Ramadan, before and after *tarawih*.

At the Islamic State University, I majored in Arabic language and literature and studied *da'wah*. I was active in women's community organizations, like Fatayat National Union, for young women of Nahdlatul Ulama, the country's biggest Islamic organization. My *da'wah* activities included giving sermons at *tarawih* during Ramadan and *majlis al-ta'lims*. Sermons are for transformation and deepening our humanity through worship, for *amr bi'l ma'ruf wa nahy an al-munkar* (enjoining good and forbidding evil), which includes efforts such as education, advocacy, and writing, beginning with ourselves in the home and family. *Da'wah* prioritizes courteous behavior and noble morals over harshness, insults, and lies.

Thus my Islamic practice is critical and humane, deepened by engagement with vocal Islamic figures, feminists, and human rights activists locally and from elsewhere. I take an active role in advocacy movements focused on protecting vulnerable peoples, including victims of violence, discrimination, and human rights violations.

My human rights work influences my sermons, which are sharply critical of gender gaps in government policies that are also tyrannical toward street children, poor women, domestic workers, the disabled, the elderly, and religious, racial, indigenous, and other minority groups.

Social transformation is slow because moderate Muslims are not vigorous in advocating for the revitalization of ideas. Many remain silent and in their comfort zones—a dead end—afraid of being labeled liberals, infidels, or apostates. Meanwhile, militant Islamists spread aggressive ideas that prevent the enlightenment of Muslim congregations. It is no surprise, therefore, that narrow-minded views predominate socially.

For me, Islam offers peace and well-being to all people—it rejects hostility and hatred. Islam teaches equality, responsible freedom, brotherhood, and sisterhood. Ali ibn Abi Talib reminds us that human beings are brothers and sisters, if not in faith, then in their common humanity.

The threats I face, even against my life, serve to strengthen my *da'wah* and humane understanding of Islamic teachings, which I believe to be filled at their very core with love and peace.

In my personal work and living of Islam I have conceptualized *da'wah* as *da'wah bil hal,* or *da'wah* accompanied by concrete actions, such as fighting tyrannical governments; eliminating poverty, corruption, and violence against women and other vulnerable groups; and exploitation of the environment.

Therefore, my sermons invite Muslims to think critically, to practice Islam's moral message of peace for all human beings and creatures in the universe, and for us to love and care for nature too. I encourage Muslims to prioritize their humanity because Islam appeared in the world for the good of humankind. The Prophet said unequivocally: I came to improve human morality. This must occur in our daily interactions with all human beings, including family members, spouses too, without domination, violence, or exploitation but with care, *mawaddah wa rahmah,* and mutual respect.

As a Muslim woman, I am a *khalifah fi al-ard* (an agent of peace) working for a society that practices moral values; for indeed, *baldatun tayyibah wa rabbun ghafur,* this is a good place and our Lord is forgiving.

ᕑᕽᕒ

Two Wedding Khutbahs
SEEMI GHAZI
(Canada and the United States)

A Khutbah for Elena and Arian
The divine breath of Compassion
Taught the sacred recitation
Created the human being
Taught her, taught him, taught them, fluent expression
The sun and moon hold their orbits
And the grasses and trees bow down
The Divine raised the heavens, and established a balance
So do not exceed the balance.

—Q. 55:1–8

The cherishing Sustainer of the two easts
The cherishing Sustainer of the two wests

Caused to mingle the two seas flowing
Between them is a membrane they do not pass
Which of the blessings of your Sustainer would you two deny?

—Q. 55:17–20

These lines of the *surah* of *al-Rahman*, the breath of compassion, witness the divine presence in nature, in scripture, and in the human being, *insan*, which means, literally, the being that is capable of *uns*, or intimacy—intimacy with one's self, intimacy with a beloved, and intimacy with the Divine.

Divine unity pours out into the multiplicity of created forms, One becoming two; two, a multitude; and within the multitude everything turning, seeking a way to be whole and one—and the cycle begins again.

Arian and Elena, you come here with such rich multiplicities. Your families, histories, languages, and songs have converged and diverged from ancient times, long before Goethe, inspired by Hafez, composed his *West-östlicher Divan*. It was famously observed by Kipling that "East is East and West is West, and never the twain shall meet." But the Qur'anic passage invokes God as "The cherishing Sustainer of the two easts, / The cherishing Sustainer of the two wests" (Q. 55:17–20). This is an intriguing invocation to be sure. (Traditional commentators interpreted the dual in the passage as referring to the two realms of the humans and the jinn.) And yet, when I look at you, Arian and Elena, Elena and Arian, I see two easts, two wests, within each of you, both east and west, and also north and south. From southeastern Iran to west Germany, from the East Coast to the Pacific Northwest, like children puzzling over a globe, journeying east we find ourselves west, journeying west we come to the east, and our trajectories expand. You will find your orientation in multifocal relationships, from points of origin only you can define. "He caused the two seas to mingle, flowing. Between them is a membrane they do not pass" (Q. 55:19–20).

In the brief moments when we have conferred regarding this ceremony, in the grace with which you have balanced and brought to fruition so many aspirations for this day, I have already observed in you the deep self-possession, *khud-dari*, which permits you to surrender naturally and joyously to one another. As in the Qur'anic passage, the two seas of your hearts have mingled and become one, and yet that subtle membrane of your selfhood remains. Today you are eternally one but also more deeply each yourself. May you find each day a new understanding of the dance of intimacy and autonomy. And I close in reading to you words you have chosen from the German poet Rainer Maria Rilke: "Once the realization is accepted that even between the closest human beings infinite distances continue, a wonderful living side by side can grow, if they succeed in loving the distance between them which makes it possible for each to see the other whole against the sky."[123] May the *Rabb*—the Cherisher, the Sustainer, the Cultivator, and the Guide—of the two easts and the two wests and all points beyond, always cherish and sustain you both.

Elena and Arian, we gather together on this day, your family and friends, to bear joyful witness to your union in marriage. I invite you now to share the vows that you have prepared for this day.

Arian, in the spirit of the vows that you have shared, do you accept Elena as your wife, loving her for all the days of your life? . . .

Elena, in the spirit of the vows that you have shared, do you accept Arian as your husband, loving him for all the days of your life? . . .

We, your family and loving friends, those present in body, those present in spirit, witness you two, to be now one, in marriage, husband and wife.

In the name of Allah, the womb of creative compassion, the caring.

> O humanity we created you from a male and a female
> And raised you as nations and tribes
> That you may recognize one another. (Q. 49:13)

A Khutbah for Maimoenah

Janan, Dostan, Ashiqan, Soulmates, Friends, Lovers.

Salam! May Allah bless your path. May you walk in the light of the 124,000 prophets. May you always be one in the One.

That divine beauty which created you from one self, one soul, and one substance endowed us with its one breath, the ethereal medium, the ether of the Real, which animates and illumines us all. In your aspiration and articulation, in the newborn's cry and the lover's kiss and in the final exhalation of the dying you are offering and receiving the single divine life that is always sacred, surrendered, one.

Your eyes too are illumined by the one divine *nur*. In your glance there is mutual recognition, loving exchange, light upon light. Eyes meet, kindling an Abrahamic fire, purifying distinction and duality. These two powers within you, the breath and the light, form the subtle body of the sword of Zulfiqar. Wielded with reverence, mastery, and love they slay duality, envy, and rancor. The twin blades of the sword of our honored Ali, the son-in-law of the beloved Prophet, give rise to the One, to one being.

May your word and glance flow through one another like the ancient waters of Zam-Zam, healing every hidden sorrow, dissolving the crust of regret. May you be garments for one another as Khadija embraced her beloved, veiling fault, sheltering wounds, enfolding mystery, and adorning beauty. May your unity be the delight of your teachers, and may the long strings of your lineages, *silsilas*, resonate with the joy of your harmonious vibration.

This is the greatest tribute you can offer to the ones who have transmitted the *sirr*, the mysteries, to you through every human generation and in every corner of the world. How did they do this, transmitting *haqq*, reality, through their word and gaze? They walked from their ancestors toward their progeny with the water of divine life cupped in their hands of their heart, and did not spill a drop. They did this through love and unity, which preserve and transmit all things. Through love and unity may such beauty be accomplished, even now, through you.

If you grow impatient with one another, then remember the parable of your own hands. Their five fingers are not the same. Each has a different size and length, and yet when you bring them together in grasping, the five become one. They meet at the same point of unity. In their diversity, through this *shura*, consensus, they accomplish their intended task. It is the very difference in your fingers that allows their unified collaboration in building, cooking, writing, gesturing, and playing an instrument. Allah's myriad creative power expresses itself without mimicry or cloning. Allah could have made everything in uniformity, but this would not give rise to unity. Be patient with yourselves and with one another. Offer gratitude for the unique realities within yourselves, your communities, nature, and the cosmos. For your lord is Rabb al-'alamin, the one who cultivates, guides, and cherishes *all* worlds.

And hold fast together to the rope of Allah, and do not be divided (Q. 3:103).

With love and in service, your sister, Seemi.

Seemi's Journey to the Minbar:
"We Dwell in a Ghayborhood"

IF YOU ASK what authorizes me to be a *khatibah*, I might say: nothing. Nothing except the love and trust of those who have sought me out. I am a woman, after all, and our formal sermon was traditionally the remit of men. Or, I could say: everything. Everything that, even before I was born, filled the wellspring of my perception and expression, as if a hole dug out and abandoned by children on a beach were gradually filled from above by rising and receding tides, or from below by an aquifer. The pool remains contained until other children arrive to carve out a channel from its rim, and the water, drawn by gravity, flows into the empty spaces and interstices. This is the path of *ishq* and *irfan*, sacred love and spiritual knowledge, conferred through transmissions whether human or divine. They flow toward open channels and humble ground, toward receptive hearts and genuine thirst.

What was the source of this transmission? I was born with a love of words. My *Ammi* claims I sang before I spoke, and when I spoke I declared I wanted to be a poet. As far back as we can trace, women and men of my family were scholars, sufis, healers, and Chishti *pirs*. I imagine a *khatibah*, then, as one who speaks. She addresses her community in the path of her elders, offering reflections from the Qur'an and the Prophet, even if not in the formal khutbah of the Friday gathering, the wedding, or the festivals of sacrifice and breaking the fast. She speaks inspiration, consolation, and guidance to her *ummah*, a community originating from, and embodying, one *umm*, one mother. She might be Khadijah, steadying a messenger; A'ishah, transmitting half our traditions; Zaynab, speaking tragic truth to imperial power; or Rabi'ah, moving in reverie toward the Ka'bah, to find that the Ka'bah is moving toward her.

What is it, then, that I might bring to a khutbah? My parents, Drs. Tasneema and Abidullah Ghazi, were the visionaries of my early Islamic education. They taught me at home, in the pioneering Sunday schools they founded, and through their lifework, the IQRA Islamic curriculum. Western art song, Muslim hymn, and Qur'an recitation taught me mysteries of breath and phrasing across language and culture. In the academy I have pursued the study of languages (French, Arabic, Persian, Urdu) and religion (history, literature, mysticism, and law). All of my time as a student and pilgrim, living in Cairo and Jeddah and thrice performing hajj, has shaped the analysis and timbre of my words when I speak of Islam. For those who seek me out, it is this analysis, this timbre that resonates.

I have also been a student of Sufism since the age of eighteen. In the dervish community we learned to lead *dhikr* ceremony, to offer *suhbah* (spiritual discourse) and spiritual counsel, and to interpret dreams. Mostly we cultivated *khidmah*, service; *tawadu*, humility; and *rahmah*, the unconditional, outpouring compassion inspired by the womb, or *rahm*. We practiced love and fellowship in our *nazar*, glance, and with our *lisan*, word. It was in that Sufi community in the 1990s that I was asked to lead my first Friday prayer and offer my first khutbah. "This is for the company of dervishes," I was told. "There is no need to share it with those who will not understand. Remember our lady A'ishah, the Prophet's brilliant young wife, and the scandal of the necklace. How she suffered upon being falsely accused!" Among colleagues and friends, gender didn't matter; it was simply my turn. More than the light through Carolina windows, the fragrance of rose oil, and the feline vigilance of a dervish cat yawning in the corner, I remember our sense of siblinghood that autumn afternoon.

Like many trusted and caring Muslim women adept in Qur'anic knowledge and Sufi practice, I often serve as an unlicensed, unpaid pastor, invited to counsel courting couples, to sing old wedding songs, to recite Qur'an to newborn infants, to ferry souls in palliative care onward, and to wash and anoint the bodies of sisters who have passed. In moments of change or crisis, the veil between *shahadah* and *ghayb*, the seen and the unseen, thins out. I say we dwell in a *ghayborhood*—a realm of shared intuition, spiritual listening, and witnessing. Rather than bringing in a stranger officiant authorized in the world of form, we strive to culminate our intimate journeys in meaningful collaborative ceremonies, both traditional and newly inspired.

I led my first *janazah* (funeral prayer) for my friend Mehry who passed in her sixties of cancer. She was a nurse, a devotee of Mawlana Rumi, and the founder of a Sufi center she named Dell Khaneh—the Heart's Abode. When I first visited her in palliative care on the twelfth floor of St. Paul's, I admired the panoramic view and exclaimed, "Mehry Jan, *masha Allah*, they gave you the penthouse suite!" She laughed heartily, glanced heavenward, and responded, "Seemi Jan, for you it is the penthouse. For me, *al-hamdu lillah*, it is only the basement!" When Mehry ascended, her husband, Azim, asked that I lead the funeral prayer; he insisted, "She would want only you."

On that rainy Vancouver afternoon, two hundred of us gathered around her grave, a canopy of black umbrellas over us like the dome of a somber sanctuary. Evergreen sentinels in solemn watch. I called the *takbirs, Allah Akbar,* God is most Great, recited the *surahs,* offered greetings of peace, *salaam.* I signaled our dervish sister Linda to turn in *sema.* Her arms rose as Mehry's spirit flew, and we lowered her form into the earth.

Perhaps eighty Iranian men were in the congregation that day, and because Shi'i tradition calls for formal qualifications, such as years of study in a *hawza* (Shi'i seminary) in Qom, for one to lead communal prayers, I still find it notable that not one of them withdrew or objected. What had authorized me, a Sunni, a layperson, a woman, in their eyes? Was it Azim's trust in his most vulnerable moment? Was it my friendship with Mehry? Or was it my leadership of *dhikr* in the Dell Khaneh? Perhaps my alternative Sufi credentials transcended gender and approximated the Shi'i clerical requirement.

Perhaps once my alternative authority had been established, a Shi'i sense of protocol would have prevented an unauthorized "civilian" brother from intervening to lead prayer himself, as might easily have happened in my Sunni community where every bro is technically authorized. Perhaps I slid into the interstices between Sunni, Shi'i, and Sufi modes of authority as a child moves even unconsciously within the slippages between her parents' lines of discipline. In truth, my *imamat* that day felt as deep, natural, and inevitable as the land upon which we stood.

In the early 2000s, thoughtful couples of diverse backgrounds began asking me to perform *nikah* ceremonies that would harmonize their traditions and families. They wanted to invoke the Divine in ways that would be palpable for all wedding guests. I remember laughing and saying, "Well, I'm neither authorized by classical shari'ah nor by the government of Canada." I sent some of them to a Muslim notary public who could issue a legal marriage license. If anyone questioned the validity of a *nikah* performed by a woman, then, with two witnesses, the license also constituted *nikah* according to Islamic law. For some, the formality mattered; for others, a trusted voice, a ceremony reflecting the couple's deeper aspirations, mattered more.

The first khutbah here was my second *nikah* sermon. Arian was Iranian born and raised in Canada; Elena was Swiss, raised in the United States but completing a doctorate in Persian literature. I composed it the morning of the ceremony, sitting by the Pacific Ocean on sacred unceded Salish ground. I thought of Hafez and Goethe. The combined "easts" and "wests" of bride and groom reminded me of Surah al-Rahman, the Qur'an chapter of Divine Compassion. The words by Rilke they chose for their program evoked a beloved verse.

Other couples have called other references to mind. For my Gujarati Sufi friend Fazeela and her Cuban beloved, Andres, I spoke of the confluence of Muslim and Latin cultures in Andalus, of the Lord of the Ka'bah and Audre Lorde. I commissioned a Spanish translation of Rumi's poem in which the poet blesses his son's wedding. Andres's cousin taught me to read it in a Cuban accent during interludes at the rehearsal dinner. These subtle gestures sow the seeds of love between new families. In this way, as a *khatibah*, I strive to enact the Qur'an's imperative of *silat al-arham*, connecting the wombs with insight and compassion.

It is heartbreaking that for some Muslims, compassion fails. Ten years ago, I met my vibrant, vulnerable friend Maimoenah, in Cape Town. She lived with courage amid precarity, marginalized by her community, which she loved nonetheless. A year ago, she joyously asked me whether I would perform her *nikah* by Skype. As the date approached, I wondered why she hadn't been in touch with all the usual questions, favorite verses, and familial preferences. Finally, I got hold of her the night before the event and asked, "What should I say? How should this unfold?" She was puzzled and also lighthearted; "We want you to *marry us*, you know, with a *nikah*." As if all answers were henceforth self-evident. "Our families won't be there. It's just us." "Just them," I thought; "oh, my heart." "Well, how would you like to do the requesting and accepting? You want the vows in English, yes, not Arabic?" She paused, "Actually . . . *could* we have them in Arabic . . . you know *nakahtuki bi fulanin* (I have married you to so-and-so)?" And she began to recite the Arabic formula she knew from her witness of countless weddings in the same community that would not be present to witness hers.

I realized that while other couples wanted ceremonies tailored to their plural worlds, Maimoenah yearned simply to be married in the way of her people, to be dignified with the solemnity of *fiqh*, legal tradition, with a Cape Muslim resonance. In offering her the vitality of that liturgy, I regained an enduring appreciation of the wellspring of the tradition within me, flowing out to others.

In the dark morning I draped my head with a sparkling *dupatta;* Maimoenah and her beloved shimmered across cyber-time, cyber-space; five bars curving a *mihrab* niche signaled that the Wi-Fi *rabitah*, connection, was strong. I began reciting the blessings upon the Prophet Muhammad and his family. I offered an exegesis of the Qur'anic ode to spouses as mutual "garments" and a paean to the love of Muhammad (peace be upon him) and his noble Khadijah (may Allah be pleased with her). From the same world, and having learned the same litanies from the same sort of madrasah every day after school, these beloveds were as twins. The moment they heard the familiar *salawat*, tears streamed down their faces like the fountains watering the gardens of Surah al-Rahman after the verses of smoke and flame.

Earlier I spoke about an image of water, inspired by the beaches of Vancouver. The Qur'an offers a deeper aquifer, speaking of paradise as "a garden beneath which rivers flow." The feminine word *jannah*, garden, imbues this image with a delicate eros. There are fruit of every kind and elegant companions reclining on green silken divans. There is no *laghw*, or empty chatter, only the *shura* confluence of intimate connection. *There*, of course, is *here*. The garden is the world we create within and around us.

Women are so often the rivers that flow beneath the visible garden, nourishing that which is verdant and sweet. From my window in Vancouver I observe the glaciers receding. In August, wildfires bring us an acrid haze. The garden of this earth is burning. The hijab of her seven heavens is singed and unraveling, and her wellsprings are being poisoned. Increasingly, we live the verses of smoke and flame. In such times women too, women especially, are called to rise and speak. I pray that we can plant the saplings we hold within our hands.[124] May the rivers running within us emerge as fountains of our shared experience, arise glimmering, beyond gender, and soak this garden, our haven, in a healing rain.

꘏

Divine Love, Human Love:
Marriage as Heart-Cultivation
SA'DIYYA SHAIKH
(South Africa)

> Unless love is connected to God, unless it is connected to truth,
> to compassion, to justice, to grace, it is possible for it to break down.
> —Bawa Muhaiyaddeen, *A Book of God's Love*[125]

The great spiritual teacher Shaykh Muhammad Raheem Bawa Muhaiyaddeen distills the essential divine qualities that spouses are meant to cultivate in their intimate relationship with each other. Truth, compassion, justice, and grace are vital spiritual nutrients that nourish love and enable it to grow, endure, and become a source of mutual plenitude. In Islam, each of these attributes of God—truth, compassion, justice, and grace—integral to love, are also the attributes that humans are meant to cultivate in themselves and in their relationships with one another. Since these qualities capture some of the most significant spiritual dimensions of an intimate love relationship in marriage, I want to reflect on how we might embody these in everyday life.

Practically, the connection between love and truth translates into honesty and candor in one's relationship—being frank and unguarded with one's partner frees one to "feel comfortable in one's skin." However, this attitude requires the corresponding quality of compassion—the ability to genuinely extend oneself to another human being with sensitivity and gentleness, which provides deep comfort to that person. Compassion provides a necessary balance to the quality of honesty; when honesty has the potential to become brutal and hurt one's spouse, it is compassion that holds honesty together with tenderness in the relationship. Thus one may raise difficult issues without causing injury to the heart of one's partner.

Justice is essential to harmony and balance in a marriage—treating one's partner fairly and respectfully, even in times of conflict and disagreement, allows love to deepen. This is especially important when we are angry and feel justified in our anger—perhaps having brought up the same irritating behavior or quality in a partner a hundred times before. Justice insists that we recognize, even in intense moments, other aspects of the person that are good and admirable. Justice asks us to not myopically focus on the "bad" aspect in our spouse and to resist the impulse to constantly find fault or see the cup as half empty. Justice invites us to rise to the challenge of keeping the whole person in view, particularly remaining attentive to our partner's good qualities during difficult times. Such modes of perception enable a shift in negative patterns in our relationships.

Justice summons us to establish equality in our relationship, thereby fostering greater intimacy between partners. A spiritual component of equality urges each spouse to consciously rein in that persistent inner voice that asserts its self-importance, arrogance, that voice that "reasons": "I know better," "I am right." Equality is vital in cultivating genuinely mutual relationships, and mutuality is that most beautiful dimension of marriage that the Qur'an exquisitely captures:

Hunna libasun lakum wa antum libasun lahunna.

(Your spouses) are a garment for you, as you are a garment for them.
(Q. 2:187)

The profound symbolism of spouses being garments to one another invites deeper reflection. Garments sit right up against our skin, alluding to the deep intimacy and closeness that marriage can bring; garments protect our bodies against the withering influence of the elements; so, too, can marriage provide protection from the harshness life sometimes brings. In the same way that garments cover private parts and shield them from the public, spouses hold the sanctity and vulnerabilities of each other's innermost, private being— covering one another's weaknesses and faults from the public eye, all the while gently supporting each other to overcome these. Such is the trust of the marital covenant in the Qur'an. Significantly, a garment also beautifies the wearer; so, too, loving, compassionate partners accentuate one another's inner beauty.

Finally, love is sublimely connected to grace in the Qur'an:

> And among God's signs is that
> God created partners for you from among yourselves
> That you may find tranquility in them,
> And God puts between your hearts, love and compassion.
> Surely there are signs for people who reflect. (Q. 30:21)

Love, tranquility, and compassion between intimate partners are gifts from God to humanity, gifted not only to make us feel good but to present us with *ayaat* for our existential reflection, signs for perceiving the Divine Beloved. Marriage enriches our spiritual journeying when we approach it as a form of heart-cultivation.

So, Laila and Rob, I wish you a life filled with love and a love filled with the most beautiful divine qualities—truth, compassion, justice, and grace. God willing, yours will be a sustaining love weathering the storms of life and marriage; indeed, marriage is filled with both wonder and difficulty. My *du'a* for you as a couple:

Oh Allah, *Ya Wadud*, The Loving, *Ya Rahim*, The Gracious, shower this union with blessings unceasing.

Oh Allah, *Ya Wali*, The Protecting Friend, grant your loving friendship to this couple so that they each become sheltering and protective garments of the other.

Oh Allah, *Ya Nur*, The Radiance, fill this marriage with laughter and ease so that in their togetherness is the light and lightness of Your luminous being.

Oh Allah, *Ya Karim*, The Generous, bestow bounty in their labor so that they become a wellspring of your abundance and service for other lives.

Oh Allah, *Ya Sabur*, The Ever-Patient, *Ya Rahman*, The Compassionate, grant them endurance, gentleness, and perseverance in times of anger, struggle, and difficulty and when life's weariness overtakes them.

Oh Allah, grace these two hearts so that their love remains steadfastly connected to your most beautiful, sublime qualities, to your divine attributes of mercy, truthfulness, subtlety, integrity, compassion, and justice.

Amin

Not a *Nikah* Khutbah
FATIMA SEEDAT
(South Africa)

> The subject tonight is love,
> And for tomorrow night as well
> As a matter of fact I know of no better topic
> For us to discuss
> Until we all leave this earth.[126]

Beautiful words, by the wise Hafez: love is why we gather at wedding ceremonies, to honor a tradition that commits in our presence two people to a lifetime of loving each other.

At a regular wedding this poem would lead my *nikah* khutbah, and I would continue to speak about marriage in the vein of love, compassion, and mercy, the *muwaddah wa rahmah* of *nikah*, and marriage as *mithaqan ghalidhan*, which is how it is described in the Qur'an, a strong covenant or commitment. Now, however, I take the liberty of a coauthor of this book to share with you what would not be considered a *nikah* khutbah and offer instead a *nikah* khutbah as I wish I could present it.

I would begin frankly, reminding every young couple that marriage is not exactly *nikah* (Islamic marriage) and divorce is not exactly *talaq* (unilateral dissolution). The heady Hollywood-infused visions we have of both are not shared in the realities of *nikah* and *talaq*. Next, I would explain that the day of the wedding is not the marriage, but a portal entry into millennia of primordial human negotiation on sexuality, masculinity, femininity, family, property, ego, and ethics. It is a process of personal self-definition and collective community formation, where you will have to carve out your own realities of self and other.

If possible, before the wedding, I would insist on an open discussion about the marriage contract with young women who explain they have no time for it because of the hundred things still to prepare for the wedding day. I would explain that the discomfort of an ill-fitting dress lasts but a day—nothing compared with a poorly planned *nikah* contract, which could mean a lifetime of marital hardship. I'd tell them that the difficult, unromantic talk of property ownership, delegated *talaq* and deferred *mahr* (dower), marital and postmarriage maintenance, and guardianship of their children *must* be part of their wedding preparation.

I would require every couple to spend at least a month before "the big day" discussing the pragmatics of their future married life, about how to share work within and outside the home, and how and who will earn their income and care for their home, children, elderly parents, extended family, and community. Questions need to be considered about their future children's education, renting or buying a home and in whose name, living expenses and standards, and how they will take care of each other. What role will their extended families and community play in their new family lives?

As beautiful as their entry into marriage on their wedding day might be, I would insist that they envision together how they might exit their marriage someday in the future, whether through natural death or divorce.

Indeed, it has become a cliché that "in Islam marriage is a contract"; but we seldom complete the sentence to explain the nature and requirements of the *nikah* contract, traditionally related to concepts of *tamlik* (male ownership) and *tamkin* (pleasure). I would explain that *mahr,* or "bridal gift," as it is sometimes mischaracterized, is based on a contractual exchange for a wife's exclusive sexual availability to her husband, but not vice versa because the payment in fact ensures that he can simultaneously participate in three more *nikah* contracts with other women while still married to today's bride.

I would tell the young woman that even as she gives her consent entering her marriage, she will not simply be allowed to revoke it to exit her marriage. Also, without property or other wealth specifically signed in her name, she will not have ownership of or access to assets accumulated during the marriage, regardless of the many years she set aside her career to raise children.

I would alert her that the imam performing her wedding may also perform another in secret for her husband. Even without her consent, the imam, community, and her husband will consider this other marriage "valid." The imam may advise her husband how to pronounce *talaq* and terminate her marriage with one or three words, depending on the *madhhab* (school of law) he chooses. Yet when she requests termination, he will most likely respond with obstacles, citing *fiqh* she has never been taught but that could place her in a holding pattern for years without adjudication of her request.

Before performing a *nikah*, I would insist the couple enter into a marriage contract carefully discussing the terms of their marriage, including whether they might want a polygynous life, their responsibilities and assets, and how they may both exit the *nikah* in a mutually responsible way.

I would tell them that even when couples undertake such discussion with earnestness and integrity, this is never a guarantee because to complete the sentence "in Islam, marriage is a contract," we must add "the ultimate test of which lies in the ethics of the more powerful partner at the end of that contract." To realize the contractual nature of the relationship is also to know and teach our children how to disagree and leave relationships ethically and with dignity.

I would let them know that for most wives who want to end a *nikah*, their challenge is in a husband, imam, or judge who won't enact that termination with either a *talaq* or a *faskh* (judicial divorce). In response, we would look at the historical mechanism of *khula*, a legal counterbalance to the unilateral male "right" to *talaq* allowing wives to exit marriages they no longer consent to. We would take inspiration from the companions of Muhammad, specifically Jamila bint Abdullah and Al-Rubayyi bint Mu'awwadh, who performed *khula* during the time of the Prophet; based on Q. 2:229 we would learn how women may return their "bridal gift" and thereby formally terminate the *nikah* and release themselves from its obligations.[127]

Sometimes, the most loving action one can perform is leaving a bad relationship and returning to the ultimate Subject of our Love, Allah Most Sublime.

3. Conceptualizing a *Tafsir* of Experience

The khutbahs in this book stand as a form of spirited resistance to the exclusion that many Muslim women have been indoctrinated to accept in the name of a contested tradition. Patriarchal constructions of woman as "lack" have schooled us in incapacity; unsurprisingly, then, when invited to contribute to this book, some women wrestled with their possibilities for being a *khatibah*. Notwithstanding these struggles, the rich contributions that they offer stand as testimony to the undiminished potential within women, and they open possibilities that once seemed unimaginable.

We organized the khutbahs so that they traveled from the cosmological to the individual and the social. The first set of khutbahs concentrate on framing the origins of human-divine relations, and our ontological locations—in other words, the nature of our humanity in Islamic cosmology. The next group of khutbahs focus on subjectivity and virtuous self-formation in everyday relationships, critical for spiritual growth, and the practical realization of our ontological potential. Third, we presented khutbahs that focus on cultivating spirituality through respectful forms of engagement with "others." Finally, the last group of khutbahs analyze various forms of systemic violence and injustice, and respond with communal solidarities among the greater community of believers.

To conceptualize the theological implications of the khutbahs in this book, we explore the interweaving and far-reaching insights they provide on the integrity between the spiritual and the political realms. Below we offer an analysis of the wisdoms emerging from the khutbahs and elaborate what we have called a *"tafsir* of possibility." We present three Qur'anic models to guide newer visions of justice and beauty made possible as access to the minbar expands.

Feminist Ontologies: Rahmah *and* 'Adl

These khutbahs present a vision of humanity arising from a single, undifferentiated soul, *nafs al-wahida,* without duality and separation, reflecting the primordial human state. The origin of humanity in the genderless, unified self, emerging from the all-encompassing One, is the archetypal condition through which each person derives their mandate as moral agent in the world, *khalifah fi al-ard.* Justice and the equality of each life is thus grounded in our deepest spiritual moorings. Many of the khutbahs remind us that this universal model for humanity, imbued with the transformative spiritual insights of revelation, inspired early Muslim women in the prophetic community to engage in all spheres of public life. They aim at rekindling an approach to revelation that was pushed back by the unfortunate tide of patriarchal interpretation of scripture. Retrieving models of powerful women into our current time and space serves to reframe our modes of engagement with tradition, encourages dynamic forms of religious subjectivity, and responds to the contextual needs for greater social justice.

Grounding the human journey in an existential map, described as the four-arched portal of *rahmah* (divine love and mercy), provides a capacious guide for embodying inner spiritual illumination and outer social integrity. The Qur'anic teaching that God has inscribed *rahmah* upon God-self, defined as divine love and mercy, provides a foundational model for humanity. We too are invited to inscribe upon ourselves *rahmah* in all our ways of being, doing, and becoming, treading the path of the Prophet Muhammad, whom the Qur'an describes as a loving mercy to all the worlds, the *rahmatun lil 'alamin.*

While a single meaning cannot exhaust the logic of the Qur'an, an integrated mode of reading through *rahmah* locates justice (*'adl*) as the seed of ethical values for establishing social and spiritual balance (*mizan*). This translates into equity and fairness (*qist*), affording rights and dignity especially to those inhabiting the social margins. The God who inscribes mercy on the Divine Self is irreconcilable with patriarchy, which actively disables justice, balance, and *rahmah.* Patriarchy, premised on the Satanic logic of arrogance

and elemental superiority, results in a logic of domination among human beings and in our relationships to the earth. Such abusive modes of engagement
reflect the primordial sin of heedlessness to the Divine nature. It blinds us to
humanity's unitary origin, our agency in embodying virtue, and our ultimate
return to the One. This reading provides an organic spiritual critique of patriarchy as a Satanic, or *Iblisi*, model of power, to be resisted at all costs in
our earthly mandate.

Subjectivity and Consciousness: Ihsan

This group of khutbahs presents an exploration of the nature of the self
and subjectivity in relation to being in the world. Our existential capacity is
realized when we move beyond our biological birth to the fullness of our
conscious birth as spiritual, social, and intellectual beings. In doing so, we
potentially manifest goodness and virtue in order to bring the highest benefit
(*maslahah*) into the world. When a person unconditionally enacts goodness
in the world, their very presence becomes a gift to humanity; the ultimate embodiment of this subjectivity is the "complete human" (*al-insan al-kamil*),
the fulfillment of humanity's highest existential purpose.[1]

The cultivation of human subjectivity as a form of beautiful presence
(*ihsan*) happens in everyday forms of interaction and experiences, premised
on the clarity of intention (*niyyah*) and choice. Recognizing that human beings are a composite of their own stories, such cultivation circumvents a
checklist form of Islam. Instead, *ihsan* calls us to embark on an internal journey, receptive to the Divine in varied and unanticipated forms, cherishing the
unique spiritual gifts that others also embody. In relinquishing our fixed constructions of reality, we become open to new forms of knowledge and the
primordial *fitrah* of God's hidden treasure within the human heart. Such forms
of subjectivity draw on the Qur'an as an intimate companion on the journey
of spiritual unveiling. Self-refinement has profound implications for how we
engage the world and other lives—it is shaped through relations with other
people and bears fruit in the realms of sociality, public virtue, and communal
ethics. Indeed, the personal and spiritual are profoundly political.

Sociality and Difference: Maslahah

These khutbahs touch on the contours of the cosmological self and how it
takes form as the self in relationship. Humanity begins from Oneness, which

first experiences separation from the Divine and, subsequently, separation from others; this differentiation is contrapuntally designed to produce knowledge of the Creator and other human beings. Difference functions as a way of being and as a vector of encountering the Divine. Encountering difference in this way, the khutbahs guide us against the temptation for our various forms of difference to result in divergence, schism, and ultimately exclusion or othering.

The focus instead is on justice as an articulation of *rahmah* presented through the inclusion of the marginalized and vulnerable. The shari'ah is fashioned as spiritual and ethical guidance based on the interests of all humanity and not the exclusive interests of the powerful. Injustice represents the indulgence of human pride, which reproduces false hierarchies of gender, class, race, religion, and sexuality. Creating justice requires attention to the systemic and structural ways in which people are marginalized and rendered vulnerable.

Our social relations reflect our spiritual selves. Achieving social justice is an act of spiritual refinement aligned with our external public life, thus balancing the realms of the *zahir* (manifest) and the *batin* (hidden). When we exercise our social responsibility and spiritual knowledge to promote justice, we realize our sociospiritual selves. Guided by the collective interests of the community and the common public good (*maslahah*), we find ways to overcome difference and avoid social divisions. We become open to others' ways of being and respect multiplicity, remaining in relation even when our views differ.

Disagreement need not be considered disbelief; instead, we may fashion beautiful forms of argument and ways of differing that bring us increasingly closer to our ideals of justice as divine intent. Without critical disputation, the powerful, who presume themselves to be the obvious audience of the Qur'an, reserve its guidance for themselves and exclude subaltern communities from the revelation.

Resisting Injustice: Ummah *and* Ubuntu

This group of khutbahs moves us deeper into our relationalities with others to connect our spiritual and political lives by questioning the nature of the *ummah*, or community, and our understandings of violence. The khutbahs extend spiritual care beyond the individual into community for solidarity and support, recognizing that the individual and the collective are spiritually entwined, resonating the African philosophy of *ubuntu:* "I am because we are." A careful calibration between the self and the community is required to counter destructive communal prejudices that maintain patriarchal norms and marginalize nonconforming individuals.

The khutbahs show that violence is the rape of our bodies as well as the withholding of resources that deny our capacity to survive with dignity. Without food, health care, homes, and quality education for everyone, the body of the *ummah* is violated, weakened by the Satanic logic of exploitative hierarchies and individualism. The endemic nature of gender-based violence is the slow decay of our collective human spirit, producing social wounds that fracture our communities—and our inner selves. The khutbahs challenge us to establish nourishing forms of relationality, discarding prevailing varieties of toxic masculinity. In rendering visible the connection between external chaos and internal despair, we need instead to teach new masculinities that do not detach men from their higher selves.

These khutbahs guide our attention to youth, who trouble our peace with questions and protests that dislodge us from the comfort zones we retreat to with age; their agitations force us to envision a better, more just world. The intersection of oppressions, especially evident in the contemporary lives of impoverished Black Muslim women, emphasizes ideas of justice that have been erased from the history of the prophetic mission. Our task is to reclaim and give new voice to the egalitarian and compassionate visions of personal, familial, and social relationships to build healthy and supportive communities.

Marriage: Mawaddah *and* Mithaq

The final set of khutbahs recalibrate Muslim marriage in terms of equality and mutuality and return us to the principle of *rahmah* and its beautiful connection with compassion (*mawaddah*). Weaving this spirit through our understandings of intimacy and love, these khutbahs beckon us to ways of being in relationship that provide comfort and companionship, while deepening our inner growth and connection to the divine Beloved. Threading justice into the foundations of marriage as a *mithaq* (covenant) enables modes of intimacy within the family that feed healthier, more inclusive approaches to community. These khutbahs illuminate the profound connections and mutual effect between private, domestic realms and social, communal life.

We cannot ignore, however, the normativity of marriage as a model for negotiating sexual intimacy. Historically, Muslim society allowed for sexual intimacy only through contract—whether of enslavement or potentially polygynous marriage—and it needs no elaboration to appreciate the loss of the first option. However, in retaining potentially polygynous marriage as the preferred form of sexual intimacy, we have also privileged marriage as the exclusive legitimate location of sex, rendering other negotiations unacceptable. Moving forward, we might ask how our experiences of the exclusively marriage-based models of sexuality restrict the possibilities of other more inclusive understandings of intimacy.

A further challenge is in the modes of relationship underlying the model of *nikah* we have inherited, that is, a negotiated exchange of money and sexual access modeled upon a historical contract of sale, which we have yet to recognize and transform or abandon. While the popular contemporary view of marriage is of partnership, the prevailing legal contract of *nikah* is not; and too many couples understand this only at the point of divorce. As we reimagine the intimacy of a protected relationship, we need to ask what bold transformations are required to allow us sexual partnerships that do not rely on hierarchy and possession.

A Tafsir *of Possibility*

Having mapped the theological concerns raised by the collection of khutbahs, we now bring these into a creative conversation on approaches to knowledge and authority that are responsive to the needs of our time.

Epistemologically, the possibilities produced in these khutbahs allow different locations of knowledge to unfold. In grappling with the values, challenges, and lived realities of being women, these khutbahs accentuate our existential frameworks, deepening our knowledge about religion, spirituality, and society. Integrating experiences of marginalization and injustice, they source and reconstitute new forms of knowledge made available at the minbar, thus bringing forward new ways of being and becoming. The *khatibahs* expand our notions of a *tafsir* of praxis located in everyday life with a "*tafsir* of possibility" to illuminate the openings that become available when they enter into spaces of religious and political authority. The effect of these possibilities is that women are positioned not only for the authority of their experience, but equally for their experience of authority.

The vibrant existential vistas opened by our *khatibahs* are attentive to current political challenges, and engaged by their reflections on the Qur'an and the prophetic tradition, these women move toward an intimate relationship between the self and the collective destiny of creation. The *khatibahs* boldly enter spaces of unknowing, birthing new approaches and understandings about the self, others, the world we live in, our approaches to justice, and the Divine.

A *tafsir* of possibility is an approach to the text and tradition that is both receptive and productive. It requires a posture of openness that seeks out fresh and expanded, as well as ever-expansive, modes of justice and inclusivity. It turns on the possibility of incorporating new ways of knowing, allowing hitherto unknown modes of being to flourish. Being receptive to surprise and the unpredictable, it makes room for the unthought to someday become thinkable, indeed possible.

We suggest that the *khatibahs* in this book are following in the powerful lineage of our Qur'anic ancestors, allowing for openings not considered possible before they took to the minbar. They are our Hajars, our Khawlahs, and our Maryams—models that inspire and enable different trajectories of personhood to blossom. We suggest that Hajar, Khawlah, and Maryam offer Qur'anic archetypes open to the unexpected. Through them, suffering and pain are made purposive, and our consciences are urged toward the solidarities required for systemic transformation and prompted toward action to produce change. These Qur'anic ancestors present us with creative paths for religious self-formation and ways to engage the Divine and the community in ever-expanding circles of justice.

The Hajar Model: Plenitude from the Margins

The starting point of the Hajar model is the radical recognition that the Muslim tradition was born in the material realities of an enslaved, exiled, and unmarried Black woman whose struggle and perseverance have been erased even as they form the axis of our faith. We rotate about the Ka'bah, her last resting place, without recognizing her centrality to the very origin of the community of Muslims. As noted by amina wadud, Muslims focus on Hajar's struggles in hajj rituals while simultaneously rendering her challenges invisible for the purposes of law, ethics, and community.[2] Instead of tracing our lineage to Hajar, we identify as a people of Abraham. Yet it is Hajar's fate that cultivates the emptiness of the desert into the thriving economic and cultural center of Muhammad's mission and the physical and spiritual birthplace of the Muslim tradition. Hajar's abandonment and her consequent struggle have not been the starting point of our theologies; rather, we either repress or uncomfortably pass over the cruel circumstance of a young mother left alone with a newborn in the desert.[3]

Muslim feminists have given renewed attention to Hajar in creative and insightful ways.[4] Drawing on the traces of Hajar's experiences, Jerusha Lamptey presents the concept of "transformative *taqwa*," God-conscious action that is alert to systemic inequality and directed at the inclusion of people in the social margins.[5] We draw on this to ask a number of ethical questions: What might happen if we pivot all the contemporary Hajars into the center of our communities? What if we respond to those who reside in the margins of our communities with genuine interest and care? What if we put at the center of our ethical gaze the concerns and lives of the poor; of women, queer, and trans individuals; of differently abled and Black people?

A model drawing on Hajar demands that we attend to such questions carefully and with an ethical and moral mapping that is dynamic. There will always be margins that we have not yet encountered, imagined, or even conceived of; as the center grows bigger with each inclusion, the margins shift to incorporate areas we have yet to contemplate. These widening ripples of inclusion hold transformative potential for deepening forms of loving and just community.

Lamptey also points our attention to the critical space between the real conditions of a community and its aspirational ideal (*khayr ummah*).[6] Recognition of this gap keeps us conscious of the distinctions between where we are and where we wish to be as an ethical community. Conscious action within this space requires wrestling with new and responsive praxis toward a better society; our challenge is not to diminish or obscure these struggles but to recognize and enable them. The desert of Hajar's abandonment is not the *khayr ummah* of the prophetic community. Hajar is an active agent despite her abandonment and her pain. She represents an agency that combines physical and spiritual action. Hajar is abandoned and so "Hajar runs," but she also speaks: she runs looking for water *as* she implores her Creator. Between the material and the metaphysical, her *taqwa* transforms the desert into an oasis that gushes—at first, water to quench the thirst of her infant son, and then the waters that establish the community of the Ka'bah and eventually an oil-rich nation that even today sadly denies citizenship to nonnatives.

The model of Hajar as a *tafsir* of possibility shows what can happen when we bring the intersecting experiences of injustice to the center of our ethical gaze, compelling ourselves to learn from and be guided by the interstices of the subaltern experience. In Hajar, whose courage, tenacity, and wisdom constitute that fountain birthing our very community, we witness the potential of those residing in the social margins to reveal the oppressions produced in the heart of the community; the degree to which we are willing to recognize and acknowledge these oppressions is the degree to which the margins can also enable radical change for an entire community. Her model demands that we expand our focus to include the realities of marginalized groups as equal subjects for whom the community and living tradition must be fully available.

The Model of Khawlah, the Mujadila: Fierce Integrity

In Khawlah, we are presented with a powerful Qur'anic model of fierce integrity and spirited contestation. Discontent with the flagrant injustice of normative gender practice, she rejects the Prophet's complicity with unfair Arab customs. Bypassing the Prophet, she directs her complaint to God, and revelation responds in her favor. An entire Qur'anic chapter (Q. 58) is named after her mode of engaging the Prophet, revelation, and God: Surah al-Mujadila, "She Who Disputes." This requires pause and restatement: a Qur'anic chapter is *named* after a woman who contests the unjust gender and sexual customs of the day and who refuses to accept even the authority of the Prophet himself in her quest for dignity. *And*, despite such seeming audacity, God responds affirmatively to her disputations.

What powerful lessons are there to be learned from this story? Mohja Kahf astutely points to the ways in which God presents the bold, fearless Khawlah to teach a lesson to all readers of the Qur'an: as a community of revelation, we are not meant to submit to unjust traditions, even if these are socially approved and widely unquestioned. "The *mujadila* method," Kahf observes, is that dynamic "yank and tug, against custom and against established religious authority, until a way is opened for what is more just." She asks: "What sexual issues and what gender role issues have produced new dilemmas in which justice is not being achieved by long-embedded traditions? Are we stuck around women imaming prayer? Are we stuck around human rights for lesbian, gay, transgendered, and queer folk? How can we use the way of Khawlah to open a way forward to greater justice?"[7]

What further questions might we ask that destabilize our zones of comfort, enabling us to sculpt more expansive forms of justice? How might we weave more refined garments of human dignity? The model of Khawlah enlivens a critical apparatus that demands our social categories and norms of "the good" result in tangible and actual goodness in our lived experiences, insisting on integrity between our ideals and realities.

There are resonances of fierce integrity between Khawlah and other early Muslim women, including Umm Salamah and A'ishah, who each produce their own forms of critique. Umm Salamah also resists male-centeredness, this time interrogating the gendered language of Qur'anic address. In seeking clarity about who the Qur'an is addressed to, her intervention invites a divine response which explicitly clarifies that women are essential in the audience of the Qur'an—an inclusion that happens specifically, grammatically, and comprehensively (Q. 33:35).

A'ishah, on two accounts, questions the Prophet's judgment. First, when she is unintentionally left behind by her caravan and later returns to the group with an unrelated man as her guide, some troublemakers cast doubt on her sexual propriety. In the ensuing scandal, even the Prophet became doubtful and distanced himself from her, as did her father. A'ishah prayed for guidance, and ten Qur'anic verses descended exonerating her and limiting the possibilities for future scandals (Q. 24:11–20). When instructed by her mother to thank the Prophet, A'ishah refused, and since it was only God who proved her innocent, she said, "By Allah, I will not go to him and will not thank but Allah."[8] Second, we recall also how A'ishah wittily expressed dissatisfaction with revelation that grants the Prophet polygamous rights beyond those granted to his followers with the acerbic comment, "seems to me that your Lord hastens to satisfy your desire."[9] In both incidents we see an A'ishah who vocally criticizes imbalanced or unjust gender relations that diminish women's dignity.

A'ishah, Umm Salamah, and Khawlah each contested the gendered norms of their time, norms that militated against their personal experiences of justice or fairness. In this, a *tafsir* of possibility pushes us to consider what benefits may result from challenges that at first might seem unreasonable, improper, cheeky, or impossible. The model of Khawlah teaches us that dissent, questioning, and inquiry, even against the highest forms of authority, can act as purifying filters against established forms of unjust power. The story of the *mujadila* offers Qur'anic readers an instruction on disputation—the spirited women who contest, argue, and wrestle with God and the Messenger remind us that challenging human suffering enables more refined understandings of revelation for a whole community.

The Maryam Model: Divine Provisions

In the model of Maryam we witness the possibilities evident when women are recognized for their full spiritual and social potential. Maryam is a prophet and the mother of a prophet. She begins as a young woman embroiled in the "scandal" of so many women who have children without male partners. Maryam maintains her spiritual convictions, claims divine guidance, and alone in the *mihrab*, the innermost sanctum of worship, the holiest of holies of the Israelites, God speaks with her and provides nourishment for her. She receives winter fruits in summer and summer fruits in winter. Alone under a date palm, experiencing the excruciating pangs of childbirth, she cries out for death, and again divine sustenance and succor are provided. Maryam challenges our seasons and our categories—she is not only a prophet's mother, but Prophet as Mother.

In Maryam, the Qur'an presents the community of believers with divine provisioning through a powerful counternarrative to exclusively male claims of prophecy and leadership. Maryam exemplifies women's spiritual wholeness, the capacity to receive revelation and to take on the mantle of prophecy; Maryam is prophetic not only through the child she carries in her womb, but also through her engaged surrender. Through her receiving provisions from the Divine for her spiritual formation, the niche of Maryam's seclusion also becomes the niche that births salvation and guidance for humanity. The detailed Qur'anic depictions of childbirth and mothering present the centrality of women's reproductive labor for the perpetuation of human society.

Qur'anic depictions of Maryam simultaneously recognize her universal human capacities and her specifically female reproductive power. Through this young, unwed mother, who is the recipient of revelation and nourished in the *mihrab* with unseasonal fruit, prevailing social norms are destabilized. As Kecia Ali argues, Qur'anic narratives of Maryam collectively disrupt binaries and trouble normative, patriarchal family structures.[10]

Maryam as a prophetic model presents a *tafsir* of possibility that allows us to ask the following: What unexpected blessings might be realized when we think beyond binary models for human beings? How might we be receptive to those who seem out of place in normative gender and sexual cartographies? What are the summer fruits that each of us needs to recognize in times that we experience as heavy winter? Potentially, these questions direct us to aspects of *insaniyya,* or the human condition beyond our comfortable constructions of gender difference or sameness, opening up forms of religious subjectivity unconstrained by available categories. In embodying the model of Maryam, we not only bring the margins to the center and embrace the unexpected, we also embrace these *as* generous forms of divine provisioning for the entire community.

Conclusion

The *khatibahs* in this book tread brave pathways opened by powerful women in Muslim history. The Qur'anic archetypes of resistance found in Hajar, Khawlah, and Maryam recall an emancipatory prophetic legacy. Returning women to the minbar is a project of both retrieval and future possibilities, representing our aspirations for continuously expanding understandings of the human condition. The khutbahs presented here instruct us in the ways of those who love and argue with God and the Prophet to align their ideals and realities of justice and goodness; they show us the radically transformative potential of *taqwa* at the margins; and they teach us to identify the means of our spiritual refinement from unexpected sources in unconventional ways.

Our Hajars, our Khawlahs, and our Maryams, past and present, do not allow us to become complacent with fixed notions of justice or goodness as they are at any moment. In the pursuit of new possibilities, they make us ever impatient for more justice, more goodness, more expansive manifestations of the Merciful, so that the ripples of *rahmah* that radiated out from the minbar of Umm Waraqa continue to find newer, deeper, and more inclusive manifestations of the Divine on earth.[11]

They encourage us to be unafraid of unknowing, to discard arrogance, to embrace humility and openness, so that we may empty ourselves and be continually receptive to the Divine, who is the ultimate teacher of that which we do not yet know.

4. A Practical Guide to Writing Khutbahs

Drawing on the khutbahs in this book and the expertise of the authors and our book project manager, Roshila Nair, we have created three templates or practical guides for khutbah writing. The first guide emerged from our reflections on the exemplary khutbah by Omaima Abou Bakr, which displays knowledge and the authorial voice of personal experience.

The second emerged with amina wadud's visit to South Africa marking twenty-five years since her first khutbah, for which we organized celebratory and commemorative events. On the prompting of Roshila, we also hosted the first Khutbah Writing Workshop for women at the University of Cape Town in August 2019. Facilitated by us and headlined by amina wadud, it was attended by twenty-five women from across South Africa. Drawing on our animated discussions on spiritual and gendered knowledge, as well as Roshila's expertise as a writing coach, editor, and Black feminist thinker, Roshila developed a further template for preparing khutbahs.

The third draws on the traditional *Khutbah al-Hajah* template, a selection of Qur'an verses and *du'as* the Prophet taught his companions, which is commonly used to open Friday khutbahs.

Omaima's Khutbah Planning Guide

1. The khutbah should state clearly at the beginning its focus and themes as they pertain in Islam. Together with your title, this will immediately help to orientate your reader toward understanding your presentation.

2. The khutbah should engage with its chosen theme(s) via metaphors, images, and stories that might be drawn from Muslim tradition, everyday experiences, and shared communal narratives. Choose one or two key sources of inspiration—too many images/stories/quotations create clutter and thus disperse the focus of the khutbah.

3. Central to its unfolding, the khutbah must present its key Qur'anic or hadith inspiration, discussing *your* interpretation of it.

4. The khutbah, as it gathers force in its contemplation of spiritual and social concerns, should clearly show the integration and application of your ideas in the contemporary world for Muslims. Rather than presenting the teachings in abstract or theoretical ways only, animate or enliven your spiritual sources to make the khutbah immediate and relevant to current social and ethical issues of faith.

5. As you draw to the khutbah's end, review its key ideas to reinforce the initial points; that is, powerfully reiterate the khutbah's central spiritual thread.

6. Finally, the khutbah should clearly articulate the questions and concerns it is raising for Muslims attending to their faith and appropriate action in their daily lives.

Roshila's Khutbah Planning Guide

When I plan my khutbah, I draw on the following:

- My own spiritual knowledge from my religious observance and practices
- My body, my form, my experiences, my knowledge, my skills, and my expertise as a woman
- My voice and my presence before God, the Compassionate

KHUTBAH ELEMENTS

Planning My Khutbah

Logic and focus	Build authority in my voice through my words.
	• I must think carefully to decide the focus for my khutbah.
	• The first step to achieving authority is a khutbah with well-chosen, clearly thought-through elements that set the pace for the writing and delivery.

Themes	Ask: What themes/ideas/issues do I want to cover?
	• Too many/too few?
	• Main and secondary ideas?
Goals	Ask: What message do I want to convey?
	• Knowledge I want to share
	• Teachings I want to highlight
Self-knowledge	Ask: What do I personally want to achieve through this khutbah?
Qur'an	Ask: Which Qur'anic verses do I want to invoke and reflect on?
	• Why?
	• What do they mean?
Hadith	Ask: Which hadith do I want to invoke and reflect on?
	• Why?
	• What do they mean?
Other sources	Ask: What other sources might I work with—poetry, stories, sayings, information, life examples?
	• Which?
	• Why?

Writing My Khutbah

Main idea	Flesh out the idea clearly.
	• I want the audience to reflect and learn about this . . .
Key points	Identify two or three points I want to make.
	• Identify a sequence.
	• Ensure they link with the key idea, even as subthemes.
Write the draft	Decisions for content: Are these the best decisions for
	• Each aspect of the writing?
	• The writing as a whole?
	Structure, argument, flow. Is the writing
	• Structured logically, well-argued (not shallow or convoluted), flowing?
	• Understandable?
	• Coherent/holding together?
	• Solid (no confusing gaps)?

	Tone
	• What tone am I aiming for (didactic/strong/ philosophic)?
	• What do I want my audience to hear (gentleness/ empathy/power/strength/humor)?
	• How do I want my audience to feel (joyous/happy/ thoughtful/chastised)?
	Tone
	• What is my tone (conversational/informal/ academic/reverent)?
Checklist: Rewrite and rewrite again	Critique the draft. Have I • Stated my main idea/theme clearly? • Made my two or three points well? • Sequenced them well? • Discussed well the scriptural evocations (Qur'an and hadith)? • Given my interpretations? • Illustrated my meaning with practical examples from life?
Edit	Check language: • Sentence structure • Grammar and spelling • Sentence length (not too long or too short) • Paragraphing (not too long or too short) • Punctuation (such as commas and full stops, to help with flow of your verbal presentation)

Presenting My Khutbah

How does my khutbah sound when I read it out loud?	Presentation begins with the words I choose, so if my draft is good, I'm good to go. How does my voice sound and my presence feel in the words? Do I sound • Centered/grounded or all over the place? • Logical, authoritative, compelling?

- Knowledgeable/convincing/inspiring?
- Like I deeply understand what I am saying and not winging it or parroting someone else?

Am I there?
- My body
- My being
- My voice
- My knowledge
- My spiritual knowledge
- Myself in the presence of Allah

The Traditional Friday Khutbah al-Hajah Guide

- Begin with your personal intention to give a khutbah and give *salam* (a greeting of peace) to your congregation.
- Begin with the following opening statement and subsequent verses.

إِنَّ الْحَمْدَ لِلَّهِ نَحْمَدُهُ و نَسْتَعِينُهُ و نَسْتَغْفِرُهُ وَنَعُوذُ بِاللهِ مِنْ شُرُورِ أَنْفُسِنَا وَمِنْ سَيِّئَاتِ أَعْمَالِنَا مَنْ يَهْدِهِ اللهُ فَلاَ مُضِلَّ لَهُ ومن يَضْلِلْ فَلاَ هَادِيَ لَهُ و أَشْهَدُ أَنْ لاَ إِلَهَ إلا اللهُ وَحْدَهُ لا شَرِيكَ لَهُ و أَنَّ مُحَمَّدًا عَبْدُهُ وَرَسُوْلُهُ.

Inna al-hamda lillahi nahmaduhu wa nasta'inuhu wa nastaghfiruhu, wa na'udhu billahi min shururi an fusina wa min sayyi-ati a'malina. Man yahdihillahu fala mudillalah wa mayudlilhu fala hadiya lah. Ashhadu an la ilaha illa Allah. Wahdahu la sharika lahu, wa anna Muhammadan abduhu wa rasuluh.

Praise belongs to Allah, we praise Allah, and ask Allah for help and forgiveness. We seek refuge and protection in Allah from the malice within our own souls, and the evil of our actions. Whoever Allah guides, no one can lead astray, and whoever Allah misguides, no one can guide to the Truth. I bear witness that there is none worthy of worship but Allah, the One without partners or equals, and indeed that Muhammad is the servant and messenger of Allah.

يَا أَيُّهَا الَّذِينَ آمَنُوا اتَّقُوا اللَّهَ حَقَّ تُقَاتِهِ وَلَا تَمُوتُنَّ إِلَّا وَأَنْتُمْ مُسْلِمُونَ

Ya ayyuha alladhina amanu ittaqu Allaha haqqa tuqatihi wa la tamutunna illa wa antum muslimun.

O you who believe! Be conscious of Allah, in a way that you should be conscious, and die not except in a state of submission. (Q. 3:102)

يَا أَيُّهَا النَّاسُ اتَّقُوا رَبَّكُمُ الَّذِي خَلَقَكُمْ مِنْ نَفْسٍ وَاحِدَةٍ وَخَلَقَ مِنْهَا زَوْجَهَا وَبَثَّ مِنْهُمَا رِجَالاً كَثِيراً وَنِسَاءً وَاتَّقُوا اللَّهَ الَّذِي تَسَاءَلُونَ بِهِ وَالأَرْحَامَ إِنَّ اللَّهَ كَانَ عَلَيْكُمْ رَقِيباً

Ya ayyuha al-nas ittaqu rabbakum alladhi khalaqakum min nafsin wahidatin wakhalaqa minha zawjaha wabatha minhuma rijalan kathiran wanisa'an wattaqu Allaha alladhi tasa'aluna bihi wa al-arham inna Allaha kana alaykum raqiba.

O humankind! Be dutiful to your Lord, who created you from a single soul, and from her, the partner, and from them both Allah created men and women. Be conscious of Allah through whom you claim your mutual rights, and toward the wombs (that bore you). Surely, Allah ever watches over you. (Q. 4:1)

يَا أَيُّهَا الَّذِينَ آمَنُوا اتَّقُوا اللَّهَ وَقُولُوا قَوْلاً سَدِيداً يُصْلِحْ لَكُمْ أَعْمَالَكُمْ وَيَغْفِرْ لَكُمْ ذُنُوبَكُمْ وَمَنْ يُطِعِ اللَّهَ وَرَسُولَهُ فَقَدْ فَازَ فَوْزاً عَظِيماً

Ya ayyuha alladhina amanu ittaqu Allaha, waqulu qawlan sadidan. Yuslih lakum a'malakum wayaghfir lakum dhunubakum wa man yuti'i Allaha warasulahu faqad faza fawzan 'azima.

Oh you who believe! Be conscious of Allah, and always speak the truth. Allah directs you to do righteous deeds and forgives your sins. And whosoever observes Allah and the Messenger has indeed achieved a great achievement. (Q. 33:70–71)

- You can now continue with your substantive khutbah talk.
- You can pause in the middle of your khutbah, and say this before you pause:

أَقُولُ قَوْلِي هَذَا وَأَسْتَغْفِرُوا اللهَ لِي وَلَكُمْ وَ لِسَائِرِ الْمُسْلِمِينَ فَاسْتَغْفِرُوهُ إِنَّهُ هُوَ الْغَفُورُ الرَّحِيمُ

Aqulu qawli hadha, wastagfiru Allaha li wa lakum wa lisa-ir al-muslimin. Fastaghfiruhu innahu huwa al-Ghafur al-Rahim.

I say this, and I seek forgiveness from Allah for me and for you and for the rest of the Muslims. So ask Allah for forgiveness. Allah is surely the One who forgives, the most Merciful.

- You can now pause, sit, and make a silent *du'a*.
- After the pause you can stand again and say:

بِسْمِ اللهِ وَالحَمْدُ لِلّٰه وَالصّلاةُ وَالسَّلامُ عَلَى رَسُوْلِ اللهِ صَلَّى اللهُ عَلَيهِ وَسَلَّمَ

Bismillahi, wa al-hamdu lillahi, wassalatu wassalamu ala rasulillahi sallallahu alayhi wasallam.

I begin in the name of Allah, and all praises are for Allah. May Allah's peace and blessings be on the Messenger.

- You can continue with the second part of your prepared khutbah.
- You can finally conclude your khutbah with the following:

عِبَادَ الله إِنَّ اللّٰهَ يَأْمُرُ بِالْعَدْلِ وَالإِحْسَانِ وَإِيتَاىِٕ ذِى ٱلْقُرْبَىٰ وَيَنْهَىٰ عَنِ ٱلْفَحْشَاءِ وَٱلْمُنكَرِ وَٱلْبَغْىِ يَعِظُكُمْ لَعَلَّكُمْ تَذَكَّرُونَ ٱذْكُرُوا اللّٰهَ يَذْكُرْكُم وَاشْكُرُوه يَزِدْكُم وَاتَّقُوهُ يَجعَلْ لَكُم مَخْرَجاً وَأَقِم الصّلاةَ

Ibad Allah. Inna Allaha ya'muru bil 'adli wal-ihsani wa ita-i dhi'l qurba, wa yanha 'anil fahsha-i wal munkari wal baghyi. Ya 'izhukum la'allaqum tadhak-karun. Udhkuru Allaha yadhkuru-kum, washkuruhu yazidkum wattaquhu yaj'al lakum makhrajan. Wa aqimis salah.

Servants of Allah! Allah commands justice, goodness, and giving to kinsfolk; Allah forbids indecency, injustice, and transgression. Allah instructs you, that you may remember (Q. 16:90). Remember Allah, and Allah will remember you. Be thankful to Allah, and Allah will increase your bounty. Be conscious of Allah, and Allah will make a path out of your hardships. Establish the prayer.

- You have concluded the khutbah and may now begin the *salah*.

Glossary of Arabic Terms

adab	etiquette, refinement, good manners
'adl	justice
Amin	Amen, or "Accept oh Lord"
ayah/ayaat (pl.)	verse(s) of the Qur'an
baghy	insolence, trespassing, rebellion
basmalah	see *bismillah al-Rahman al-Rahim*
bismillah al-Rahman al-Rahim	in the name of Allah, the Most Loving, the Most Kind
dargah	shrine over the grave of a religious figure
da'wah	teaching, invitation to Islam
dhikr	remembrance of God
din	religion
du'a	prayer of supplication
al-dunya	the temporal world
Eid al-Adha	celebration marking the conclusion of the hajj
Eid al-Fitr	celebration marking the conclusion of Ramadan
Eidgah	open-air Eid prayers (South Africa)
fatwa	a ruling on a point of Islamic law
fiqh	Islamic jurisprudence
fitrah	primordial disposition, innate human nature
hadith	record of the words, actions, and the silent approval of the Prophet Muhammad
hadith qudsi	special category of hadith, attributed to God
hajj	pilgrimage to Mecca
al-hamdu lillah	all praises be to God

haram	sanctified space (referring to the precincts of the Ka'bah)
hijab	head, face, or body covering
hijrah	migration of Muhammad from Mecca to Madinah
Hira	Meccan cave where Muhammad received revelation
ibadah	worship
Iblis	Satan
iddah	women's waiting period after a spouse's death or divorce
ihsan	excellence, beautiful presence
ikhtiyarat	choices
imam(ah)	male (female) leader of congregational worship
iman	belief
insan	human being
isra wa'l mi'raj	two parts of Muhammad's Night Journey through the heavens
jahili	pre-Islamic, ignorant
Jumu'ah (yawm al-Jumu'ah)	Friday (lit.: day of gathering/Friday), often used to refer to the Friday prayer
Jumu'ah khutbah	Friday sermon
Ka'bah	holy mosque in Mecca
Kahf	a cave mentioned in the Holy Qur'an
khatib(ah)	male (female) person who delivers the khutbah
khutbah	sermon
Khutbah al-Hajah	the traditional Arabic Friday sermon template
madhahib	schools of Islamic law
madrasah	Islamic center of learning
maghrib	one of the five daily prayers
mahr	marriage payment
majlis al-ta'lim	study group (South Africa)
ma'ruf (adj., *ma'rufan*)	goodness, appropriate action
ma sha' Allah	as Allah wills
masjid	mosque
maslahah	public interest

mawaddah	love, affection
mawlana	honorific term, religious leader
mawlid al-nabi	celebration of the birth of the Prophet Muhammad
mihrab	mosque prayer niche indicating the direction of prayer
minbar	mosque location from which the khutbah is delivered
mithaq	covenant, commitment, agreement
mizan	scale, balance
muadhin	person who calls to prayer
Muharram	first month of the Islamic calendar
murshid(ah)	male (female) spiritual guide
musallah	general prayer space
nafs	self, soul
nikah	marriage, marriage contract
nur	divine light
qalbun salim	sound, unimpaired heart
qist	equity in relationships
qiwamah	male authority over women
Rabb	God the Sustainer
al-Rahim	God the Most Compassionate
rahmah	compassion, mercy, love
al-Rahman	God the Most Merciful
Ramadan	ninth month of the Islamic calendar, observed by fasting
Rasulullah	messenger of God
salah	daily obligatory prayers
salawat	salutations of peace on Muhammad
shari'ah	Islamic law, or more broadly defined, a divinely revealed ethical code of conduct
shaykh(ah)	honorific designating male (female) leader
shaytan	devil
shifa	cure, healing
Shi'i	adjective of Shi'ah, a denomination of Islam
shura	consensus, consultation
subhanahu wa ta'ala	(God) Glorified and Elevated
sufi	mystic

sunnah	exemplary custom, particularly the practices based on Muhammad's deeds and words
Sunni	denomination of Islam
surah	chapter of the Qur'an
tadabbur	reflection, contemplation
tafsir	exegesis, usually of the Qur'an
talaq	termination of marriage by husband (male pronouncement)
taqwa	God-consciousness
tarawih	additional ritual prayers performed during Ramadan
tariqah	Sufi order
tawaf	circumambulation of the Ka'bah
tawhid	monotheism in Islam
ulama	religious scholars
ummah	Muslim community
wilayah	authority
wudu	ritual ablution for prayer
zakah	alms-giving
Zam-Zam	sacred well in Masjid al-Haram in Mecca
zawj(ah)	male (female) spouse
zulm	oppression, injustice

Notes

Introduction

1. Ahmad Abd al-Rahman Al-Banna, *Al-Fath al-Rabbani li Tartib Musnad al-Imam Ahmad ibn Hanbal al-Shaybani ma'a Sharhihi Bulugh al-Amani*, vol. 5, no. 3 (Beirut: Dar Ihya'al-Turath al-Arabi), 1375, available at Sunnah.com, https://sunnah.com/abudawud/2/201.

2. Hadith cited in Abd al-Halim Abu-Shuqah, *Tahrir al-mar'ah fi 'asr al-risalah*, vol. 5 (Kuwait: Dar al-qalam, 1995), 230.

3. Sa'diyya Shaikh, "A *Tafsir* of Praxis: Gender, Marital Violence, and Resistance in a South African Muslim Community," in *Violence against Women in Contemporary World Religions: Roots and Cures,* ed. Dan Maguire and Sa'diyya Shaikh (Cleveland: Pilgrim Press, 2007), 66–89.

4. Abd al-Malik ibn Hisham, 'Abd al-Salam Muhammad Harun, and Inas Amin Farid, *Sirat Ibn Hisham: Biography of the Prophet* (Cairo: al-Falah Foundation, 2000).

1. From the Musallah to the Minbar

1. Leila Ahmed, *Women and Gender in Islam* (New Haven: Yale University Press, 1992).

2. Nevin Reda, "Women in the Mosque: Historical Perspectives on Segregation," *American Journal of Islamic Social Science* 21, no. 2 (2004): 77–96.

3. See Fatima Mernissi, *The Veil and the Male Elite: A Feminist Interpretation of Women's Rights in Islam* (Reading, MA: Addison Wesley, 1991).

4. Reda, "Women in the Mosque," 77–96.

5. Translations from the Qur'an are the *khatibahs'* own unless otherwise noted.

6. Reda (ibid., 83–85), provides an incisive reading of Qur'anic verses on Maryam.

7. Grammatically in Arabic the masculine plural refers to both exclusively male collectives or gender-mixed collectives; if she had been in an exclu-

sively female congregation, the feminine plural would have been used instead.

8. For a reflection on this incident and gendered Qur'anic language, see Asma Barlas, *Believing Women in Islam: Unreading Patriarchal Interpretations of the Qur'an* (Austin: University of Texas Press, 2002), 20–22; some classical exegetes attribute the occasion of the revelation of this verse to a question raised by Asma' bint 'Umays rather than Umm Salamah.

9. This phrase was coined by Omid Safi, *Memories of Muhammad* (New York: HarperOne, 2009), 97–101.

10. Ahmed, *Women and Gender*, 60–61.

11. Asma Sayeed, "Early Sunni Discourse on Women's Mosque Attendance," *ISIM Newsletter* 7 (2001): 10.

12. Muhammad Bukhari, *Sahih al-Bukhari*, "Call to Prayers (Adhaan)," Book 10, Hadith 260, Sunnah.com, https://sunnah.com/bukhari/10/260.

13. Benham Sadeghi, *The Logic of Law Making in Islam: Women and Prayer in the Legal Tradition* (Cambridge: Cambridge University Press, 2013), 50–53.

14. Bukhari, *Sahih*, "Menstrual Periods," Sunnah.com, Book 6, Hadith 29, https://sunnah.com/bukhari/6/29.

15. Sadeghi, *Logic*, 106; Marion Katz, "Corruption of the Times and the Mutability of Sharia," *Cardozo Law Review* 8, no. 1 (2006): 171–85.

16. Sadeghi, *Logic*, 135.

17. Ibid., 105.

18. Marion Holmes Katz, *Women in the Mosque: A History of Legal Thought and Social Practice* (New York: Columbia University Press, 2014), 116.

19. Ibid., 24–26.

20. Ibid., 29.

21. Cited in ibid., 108–9.

22. Ibid., 103–4.

23. Ibid., 98.

24. Ibid., 37; ironically, the Maliki school also does not recognize women-led prayer among women, which means that only male-led prayer in a mosque is considered as public prayer.

25. Ibid., 40.

26. Ibid., 208.

27. Ibid., 254–57.

28. Rochona Majumdar, "Review: Processes That Rendered Muslim Women Invisible," *Economic and Political Weekly* 44, no. 28 (2009): 31.

29. See ch. 4 in Katz, *Women in the Mosque*.

30. Ibid., 261.

31. South African Islam at the time was impacted by the early gains of the Iranian revolution, which transformed the narrative of Muslim women's rights globally. Later there was an increasing Arabization of mosques and, with the influence of Salafi ideology, a rise in conservatism within the community.

32. amina wadud, *Inside the Gender Jihad: Women's Reform in Islam* (Oxford: Oneworld, 2006), 177–81.

33. Later, seeking a broader social impact, some members of this community joined a new congregation at Masjidul Islam in Brixton, Johannesburg, which provided a gender-inclusive minbar for women to give the English *khutbah* but did not retain the more comprehensive gender-inclusive *imamat* of their earlier congregation.

34. For an in-depth treatment of the debates of this period, see Juliane Hammer, *American Muslim Women, Religious Authority, and Activism: More Than a Prayer* (Austin: University of Texas Press, 2012).

2. *A* Tafsir *of Experience*

1. For a more detailed account, see amina wadud, *Inside the Gender Jihad: Women's Reform in Islam* (Oxford: Oneworld, 2006), 163–74.

2. Years later, a Muslim nurse told me that this sermon was used to prepare women in her community for labor and delivery.

3. Arabic text from Ibn Qayyim al-Jawziyya, *Mukhtasar Zad Al-Ma'ad*, vol. 1, ed. Abdul Wahab Tamimi (Riyadh: Darussalam, 2008), 374. This is the author's translation.

4. Muhsin Khan and Muhammad Taqi ud-Din Hilali, trans., *The Noble Quran*, Legacy.quran.com, https://legacy.quran.com/24. Translation modified by the author.

5. Ibn 'Arabi, *al-Futuhat al-Makkiyya*, vol. 3. (Cairo: n.p., 1911), 89.

6. Author's translation. The original Arabic version of the hadith is found in Muhammad al-Bukhari, *Al-Adab Al-Mufrad*, "Mercy," Book 20, Hadith 373, Sunnah.com, http://sunnah.com/adab/20/2.

7. Cited in Susan Sachs, "Conference Confronts the Difficulties of Being Muslim and Gay," *New York Times*, May 30, 1999, https://www.nytimes.com/1999/05/30/nyregion/conference-confronts-the-difficulties-of-being-muslim-and-gay.html.

8. Abu Abd Allah al-Razi, *Al-Tafsir al-Kabir*, vol. 20 (Beirut: Dar Ihya' al-Turath, 1420/1999), 26.

9. Abu al-Qasim Al-Zamakhshari, *Al-Kashshaf*, vol. 2 (Beirut: Dar al-Kitab al-Arabi, 1407/1986), 629.

10. Abd al-Halim Abu-Shuqah, *Tahrir al-mar'ah fi 'asr al-risalah*, vol. 5 (Kuwait: Dar al-qalam, 1995), 230.

11. Ali bin Ahmed al-Wahidi, *Asbab al-nuzul* (Beirut: 'Alam al-kutub, n.d.), 268.

12. Muhammad bin Jarir Al-Tabari, *Jami' al-bayan 'an ta'wil 'ay al-qur'an*, vol. 22, ed. Ahmad Muhammad Shakir (N.p.: Mu'assasat al-Risalah, 2000), 179.

13. Al-Zamakhshari, *Al-Kashshaf*, vol. 3, 295.

14. Muhammad Asad, trans., *The Message of the Qur'an* (2008), 1266, http://www.muhammad-asad.com/Message-of-Qur'an.pdf.

15. Muhammad al-Bukhari, "Oneness Uniqueness of Allah," Book 97, Hadith 34, Sunnah.com, https://sunnah.com/bukhari:7405.

16. Muhammad Ahmad Rassoul, *The Approximate Meaning of the Qur'an* (Cologne: Verlag Islamische Bibliothek, 1996), 57.

17. Kerem Adıgüzel, *The Key to Understanding the Quran* (Romanshorn, Switzerland: Al-Rahman, 2015), 81.

18. Abdullah Yusuf Ali, trans., *The Holy Quran*, Quranyusufali.com, https://quranyusufali.com/99/. Capitalization is normalized to usual usage.

19. Ibid., https://quranyusufali.com/31/, slightly modified.

20. Ibid., https://quranyusufali.com/6/.

21. Ibid., https://quranyusufali.com/17/, with normalized capitalization.

22. Muhammad Asad, trans., *The Message of the Quran*, Islamicity, https://www.islamicity.org/quransearch/?q=chapter:22.

23. Sa'id bin Ali bin Wahf Al-Qahtan, *Hisn al-Muslim*, "Fortress of the Muslim," Sunnah.com, https://sunnah.com/hisn/74.

24. Abu Zakriya Yahya al-Nawawi, "Forty Hadith of an-Nawawi," Sunnah.com, https://sunnah.com/nawawi40/27.

25. Saheeh International, *The Qur'an: English Meanings and Notes* (Jeddah: Al-Muntada Al-Islami, 2012), 504.

26. Ibid., 401.

27. Imam Khatib at-Tabrizi, *Mishkat al-Masabih*, "Offices of the Commander and Qadi," Book 18, Hadith 36, Sunnah.com, https://sunnah.com/mishkat:3696.

28. Saheeh International, *The Qur'an*, 416.

29. Ibid., 641.

30. Abu Hamid Al-Ghazali, *Ihya ulum al-Din* (Cairo: Matba'at al-'Amirat al-Sharafiyya, 1909), 12.

31. Shabbir Banoobhai, *Seeing Perfection: Meditations for Living in Peace* (Cape Town: Mega Digital, 2013), 69.

32. Bawa Muhaiyaddeen, born in Sri Lanka, arrived in Philadelphia in 1971, establishing the Bawa Muhaiyaddeen Fellowship. He died in 1987.

33. The Arabic words and phrases here and below draw on the Khutbah al-Hajah found in Chapter 4.

34. Muhammad Muhsin Khan, *Sahih Al-Bukhari*, vol. 2 (New Delhi: Kitab Bavan, 1987), 136.

35. William Chittick, *The Sufi Path of Knowledge* (Albany: State University of New York Press, 1989), 396.

36. Kabir Helminski, *The Knowing Heart: A Sufi Path of Transformation* (Boston: Shambhala Publications, 2000), 20.

37. Khan, *Sahih Al-Bukhari*, 253.

38. Original Arabic found in Muhammad al-Bukhari, *Sahih al-Bukhari*, "Good Manners and Form (Al-Adab)," Book 78, Hadith 205, Sunnah.com, https://sunnah.com/bukhari/78/205.

39. Ibid., "Fasting," Book 30, Hadith 12, Sunnah.com, https://sunnah.com/bukhari/30/12.

40. Abu 'Isa Muhammad al-Tirmidhi, *Jami al-Tirmidhi*, "The Book on Fasting," Book 8, Hadith 126, Sunnah.com, https://sunnah.com/tirmidhi/8/126.

41. Abu Zakariyah Yahya Al-Nawawi, *Riyad as-Salihin*, "The Book of Miscellany," Sunnah.com, https://sunnah.com/riyadussalihin/introduction/405.

42. Prophet Muhammad, "The Prophet's (S.A.W.) Ramadan Sermon," Ahadith.co.uk, https://ahadith.co.uk/resources/prophet-muhammads-ramadan-sermon.php.

43. A term used in Greek philosophy to refer to matter or substance.

44. Fariha al-Jerrahi, *Letter to the Dervishes of the Nur Ashki Jerrahi Sufi Order* (New York: Unpublished, Ramadan 2019); reproduced by permission.

45. Cited in Abu Bakr al-Sarraj, *Kitab al-luma' fi al-tasawwuf*, ed. Kamil Mustafa al-Hindawi (Beirut: Dar al-Kutub al-Ilmiyya, 2001), 152–53.

46. Bukhari, *Sahih*, "Dress," Book 77, Hadith 142, Sunnah.com, https://sunnah.com/bukhari:5927.

47. Quoted in Lex Hixon, *Atom from the Sun of Knowledge* (New York: Pir Press, 1993), 232.

48. Muzaffer Ozak, *Irshad: Wisdom of a Sufi Master* (New York: Amity House, 1988), 544.

49. Ibid., 252.

50. Jalal al-Din Rumi, *The Essential Rumi*, trans. Coleman Barks (New York: HarperCollins, 2004), 151.

51. Quoted in Najm Al-Din Razi, *The Path of God's Bondsmen from Origin to Return*, trans. Hamid Algar (North Haledon, NJ: Islamic Publications International, 1980), 49.

52. Sohaira Siddiqui, "Jadal and Qiyas in the Fifth/Eleventh Century: Two Debates between al-Juwayni and al-Shirazi," *Journal of the American Oriental Society* 139, no. 4 (October–December 2019): 925. Also see Walter Edward Young, *The Dialectical Forge: Juridical Disputation and the Evolution of Islamic Law* (Cham: Springer, 2017).

53. Mohja Kahf, "She Who Argues: A Homily on Justice and Renewal," *Muslim World* 103 (July 2013): 296.

54. Ibid.

55. Ebrahim Moosa and Ali Altaf Mian, "Islam," in *Encyclopedia of Applied Ethics,* ed. Ruth Chadwick (San Diego: Academic Press, 2012), 769.

56. Taqi ad-Deen Ahmad Ibn Taymiyya, *Majmoo'al-fatawa* (Cairo: Maktabat Ibn Taymiyyah), 30, 80.

57. Seyyed Hossein Nasr, Caner K. Dagli, Maria Massi Dakake, Joseph E. B. Lumbard, and Mohammed Rustom, eds., *The Study Quran: A New Translation and Commentary* (New York: HarperOne, 2015), 988–89.

58. Ibid., 206.

59. For an excellent summary of Fazlur Rahman's approach on this verse and other gender-related verses, see Ziba Mir-Hosseini, "Muslim Legal Tradition and the Challenge of Gender Equality," in *Men in Charge?*, ed. Ziba Mir-Hosseini, Mulki Al-Sharmani, and Jana Rumminger (London: Oneworld, 2015), 24–28.

60. Ibid., 33. This is Abu Zayd's translation of the verse cited in Mir-Hosseini's text.

61. Ibid.

62. Mahmoud Mohammed Taha, *The Second Message of Islam*, trans. Abdullahi An-Naim (New York: Syracuse University Press, 1987).

63. Nasr et al., *Study Quran*, 281.

64. Ibid., 280.

65. Mir-Hosseini, Al-Sharmani, and Rumminger, *Men in Charge?*, vii.

66. Sa'diyya Shaikh, "Islamic Law, Sufism and Gender," in Mir-Hosseini, Al-Sharmani, and Rumminger, *Men in Charge?*, 110.

67. Kecia Ali, *Sexual Ethics and Islam* (London: Oneworld, 2016), 1–27.

68. Mir-Hosseini, Al-Sharmani, and Rumminger, *Men in Charge?*, 31.

69. Sa'diyya Shaikh, "Islamic Law, Sufism and Gender," in Mir-Hosseini, Al-Sharmani, and Rumminger, *Men in Charge?*, 110.

70. Nasr et al., *Study Quran*, 681.

71. Ibid., 682; the discussion in this section presenting views of both Razi and Nasr are drawn from this source.

72. Ibid., 988.

73. Ibid.

74. Translation from "Justice in the Quran," Understand the Quran, Quran Explorer, posted June 11, 2017, https://www.quranexplorer.com/blog /Understand-the-Quran/justice-in-the-quran.

75. Mustafa Khattab, trans., *The Clear Quran*, IslamAwakened, https://www .islamawakened.com/quran/4/135/.

76. I draw on the commentary from Nasr et al., *Study Quran*, 253.

77. Lynn Welchman, "A Husband's Authority: Emerging Formulations in Muslim Family Laws," *International Journal of Law, Policy and the Family* 25, no. 1 (2011): 1–23.

78. Al-Haddad quoted in Roanak Husni and Daniel Newman, eds., *Muslim Women in Law and Society* (London: Routledge, 2007), 36.

79. Hashim Kamali, "The Shari'a: Law as the Way of God," in *Voices of Islam*, vol. 2, *Voices of the Spirit*, ed. Vincent Cornell (London: Praeger, 2006), 152.

80. Abdullah Yusuf Ali, trans., *The Holy Quran*, https://quranyusufali.com /4/.

81. Other Qur'anic verses on marital conflict and divorce are Q. 4:35 and Q. 4:128.

82. This khutbah reflects my own views; I acknowledge the work of scholars amina wadud and Farid Esack, and my social justice activism with the Inclusive Mosque Initiative (IMI).

83. Abdullah Yusuf Ali, trans., *The Holy Quran*, https://quranyusufali.com /2/.

84. "Meaning of Justice in Islam," *Arab News*, last updated September 22, 2012, https://www.arabnews.com/meaning-justice-islam.

85. Sahih Muslim, "The Book of Virtue, Enjoining Good Manners, and Joining of the Ties of Kinship," Sunnah.com, https://sunnah.com/muslim /45/70.

86. Saheeh International, *The Qur'an*, 128.

87. For South Africans, June 16 marks the day in 1976 when Black school students in Soweto rose against the racist education of the apartheid government, including the introduction of Afrikaans as a medium of instruction. A peaceful march by unarmed students was met by the South African police with teargas and live ammunition, resulting in severe injuries and killings of students. Mass student protests spread across the country.

88. Aimé Césaire cited in Steve Biko, *I Write What I Like* (Johannesburg: Heinemann, 1987), 61.

89. Mashinini's popular rallying call "My people first!" is part of South Africans' collective oral memory of June 16, 1976.

90. Annemarie Schimmel, *And Muhammad Is His Messenger: The Veneration of the Prophet in Islamic Piety* (Chapel Hill: University of North Carolina Press, 1985), 85.

91. Ali Khangela Hlongwane, *Historical Development of the Commemoration of the June 16, 1976 Soweto Students' Uprisings: A Study of Re-representation, Commemoration and Collective Memory*, PhD diss., University of the Witwatersrand, 2015, 81.

92. Ibid., 85.

93. The statue of Cecil John Rhodes was removed from UCT's campus on April 9, 2015, following protests by Black students, workers, and academics.

94. "Remember September 3 1984: Grave Fees Must Fall Campaign—Asinamali!," anarkismo.net, https://www.anarkismo.net/article/29584.

95. Jane Battersby-Lennard, "Why #ThePriceOfBreadMustFall Matters," GroundUp, October 22, 2015, https://www.groundup.org.za/article/why -thepriceofbreadmustfall-matters_3421/.

96. Bantu Stephen Biko, "The Definition of Black Consciousness," paper produced for South African Students Organisation (SASO) Leadership Training Course, December 1971, Chimurenga, September 11, 2017, https://chimurengachronic.co.za/the-definition-of-black-consciousness-by -bantu-stephen-biko/.

97. As translated by Abdul Rashied Omar, "Human Dignity: The Foundation of Human Rights," March 21, 2011, Contending Modernities, University of Notre Dame, https://contendingmodernities.nd.edu/theorizing -modernities/human-dignity-the-foundation-of-human-rights/.

98. Mohammad-Baqer Al-Majlesi, *Bihar al-Anwar al-Jami'ah li-Durar Akhbar al-A'immah al-Athar*, vol. 19, Hadith 31 (Beirut: Dar Ihya Turath al-Arabi, 2000), 182.

99. Quoted at #BlackMuslimWisdom, https://twitter.com/BlkMuslimWisdom /status/832728433977200641.

100. Angela Davis quoted in the motion picture *The Black Power Mixtape 1967– 1975*, Anika Rogell (producer) and Göran Olsson (director) (Sweden: IFC Films), 2011.

101. See Mogobe Bertrand Ramose, "Towards a Post-Conquest South Africa: Beyond the Constitution of 1996," *South African Journal on Human Rights* 34, no. 3 (2018): 326–41.

102. As translated on the Muslim Youth Movement home page, "Welcome to the Muslim Youth Movement," http://mym.za.org/index.php/78-content /90-welcome-to-the-muslim-youth-movement.html.

103. University of Cape Town Muslim Youth Movement, "The UCT MYM's Position on the Rhodes Statue Protest," Facebook, March 13, 2015, https://web.facebook.com/UCTMYM/photos/a.1571210753118309 /1585917448314306/.

104. "Born-free" refers to the generation born after 1994 and South Africa's first democratic elections.

105. "Muslims' *Koeksuster* Culture Mentality," *Muslim Views* (March): 1990; a *koeksuster* is a popular Cape Malay donutlike spiced cake.

106. UN Special Representative of the Secretary-General on Violence Against Children, "Data Report on Girls," https://violenceagainstchildren.un.org /content/girls.

107. The facts and figures presented here are from the following sources: CrimeStats, South Africa, statistics for Western Cape Province, https:// www.crimestatssa.com/province.php?ShowProvince=Western+Cape; Sabbir Mir, "Nusrat Jahan Rafi: Burnt to Death for Reporting Sexual Harassment," BBC News, April 18, 2019, https://www.bbc.com/news/world -asia-47947117; "Facts and Figures: Ending Violence against Women," UN Women, last updated November 2019, http://www.unwomen.org/en /what-we-do/ending-violence-against-women/facts-and-figures; "We'll Show You You're a Woman: Violence and Discrimination against Black Lesbians and Transgender Men in South Africa," Human Rights Watch, December 2011, https://www.hrw.org/reports/southafrica1211ForUpload _0.pdf.

108. Aisha Bewley and Abdullah Bewley, *The Noble Qur'an: A New Rendering of Its Meaning in English*, IslamAwakened, https://www.islamawakened .com/quran/4/st6.htm.

109. Ibid.

110. Ibid., https://www.islamawakened.com/quran/2/st6.htm.

111. Maulana Wahidudin Khan, trans., *The Quran*, IslamAwakened, https:// www.islamawakened.com/quran/2/231/.

112. Bewley and Bewley, *Noble Quran*, https://www.islamawakened.com /quran/65/printview6.html.

113. Ibid., https://www.islamawakened.com/quran/4/st6.htm.

114. Translation is the author's own; see also Bukhari, *Sahih*, "Oneness, Uniqueness of Allah (Tawheed)," Book 97, Hadith 34, Sunnah.com, https://sunnah .com/bukhari/97/34.

115. Nawawi, *Riyad as-Salihin*, "The Book of Miscellany," Sunnah.com, https://sunnah.com/riyadussalihin/introduction/224.

116. Bewley and Bewley, *Noble Quran*, https://www.islamawakened.com/quran/3/st6.htm.

117. Shehnaaz Shaikh and Kauser Katri, *The Glorious Qur'an: Word for Word Translation*, IslamAwakened, https://www.islamawakened.com/quran/33/st78.htm. Translation slightly adjusted by the editors.

118. Ibid., https://www.islamawakened.com/quran/4/st78.htm.

119. Ibid., https://www.islamawakened.com/quran/30/st78.htm.

120. Ibid., https://www.islamawakened.com/quran/3/st31.htm. Slightly modified.

121. Ibid., https://www.islamawakened.com/quran/9/st31.htm.

122. Quoted in Najm Al-Din Razi, *The Path of God's Bondsmen from Origin to Return*, trans. Hamid Algar (North Haledon, NJ: Islamic Publications International, 1980), 49.

123. Rainer Maria Rilke, *Rilke on Love and Other Difficulties: Translations and Considerations*, trans. John L. Mood (New York: Norton, 1975), 34.

124. In Hadith 12837, Anas ibn Malik reported that the Messenger of Allah said, "If the resurrection were established for one of you while he holds a sapling within his hand, then let him plant it"; see Ahmad Ibn Hanbal, *Musnad Ahmad*, vol. 11 (Al-Qahirah: Dar al-Hadith, 1995), 34.

125. M. R. Bawa Muhaiyaddeen, *A Book of God's Love* (Philadelphia: The Fellowship Press, 1981), 2.

126. A poem by Hafiz from Daniel Ladinsky, *The Subject Tonight Is Love: 60 Wild and Sweet Poems of Hafiz* (New York: Penguin Compass, 2003), 47.

127. Bukhari, *Sahih*, "Divorce," Sunnah.com, https://sunnah.com/bukhari/68/22.

3. Conceptualizing a Tafsir of Experience

1. For a detailed discussion of *al-insan al-kamil* in the Sufi tradition, see Sa'diyya Shaikh, *Sufi Narratives of Intimacy: Ibn 'Arabi, Gender and Sexuality* (Chapel Hill: University of North Carolina Press, 2012), 71–73.

2. amina wadud, *Inside the Gender Jihad: Women's Reform in Islam* (Oxford: Oneworld, 2006), 148.

3. amina wadud, "Hajar: Of the Desert by amina wadud," Feminism and Religion, October 17, 2013, https://feminismandreligion.com/2013/10/17/hajar-of-the-desert-by-amina-wadud/.

4. See wadud, *Inside the Gender Jihad*, 120–47; Hibba Abugideiri, "Hagar: A

Historical Model for 'Gender Jihad,'" in *Daughters of Abraham: Feminist Thought in Judaism, Christianity, and Islam,* ed. John Esposito and Yvonne Haddad (Gainesville: University Press of Florida, 2001), 81–107; Jerusha Lamptey, *Divine Words, Female Voices: Muslima Explorations in Comparative Feminist Theology* (New York: Oxford University Press, 2018), 156–89; Mohja Kahf, *Hagar Poems* (Fayetteville: University of Arkansas Press, 2016).

5. Lamptey, *Divine Words,* 188.

6. Lamptey, *Divine Words,* 221.

7. Mohja Kahf, "She Who Argues: A Homily on Justice and Renewal," *Muslim World* 103 (July 2013): 295–304, quotations at 298.

8. Muhammad Bukhari, *Sahih al-Bukhari,* "Witnesses," Sunnah.com, https:// sunnah.com/bukhari:2661.

9. Leila Ahmed, *Women and Gender in Islam* (New Haven: Yale University Press, 1992), 51–52.

10. Kecia Ali reads the Qur'anic narratives of Maryam through a queer lens in "Destabilizing Gender, Reproducing Maternity: Mary in the Qur'an," *Journal of the International Qur'anic Studies Association* 2 (2017): 90–108.

11. Zahra Ayubi provides an incisive critique of gendered ethics in Islamic philosophy and a powerful set of tools to reconstitute an inclusive moral subject. See her *Gendered Morality: Classical Islamic Ethics of the Self, Family, and Society* (New York: Columbia University Press, 2019).

Acknowledgments

This book is born from sisterly solidarities and vibrant communities. It builds upon a legacy of Islamic feminism among women who have endured despite inhospitable terrain. Without their work, this book would not be possible.

We are enormously grateful to the *khatibahs* who have contributed their extraordinary sermons to a project of Muslim feminist theology. Their wisdom offers foundations for reviving contemporary Muslim thought through an *adab* of presence in the contemporary world.

We acknowledge our online and in-person communities that gifted us with the space to live out the creative theologies that emerged through the writing of the book.

We are especially grateful to Roshila Nair, our project manager, for keen feminist insights, for her thoughtful and thorough feedback as part our editorial team, and for her innovative khutbah template. Waseema Abduraouf was generous with her time and skills in helping us with images for the Arabic text.

We thank Jennifer Banks for embracing our vision for this book and trusting us to open new pathways. We also are grateful to the excellent editorial team at Yale University Press for their thorough and careful editorial work.

We cherish the love of family and friends, who tirelessly cheered us on in the long, joyful, and sometimes arduous process of birthing this book.

Sa'diyya is thankful for her family, Ashraf, Nuriyya, and Ismael, for making home a space of incessant laughter, robust conversations, and loving growth. Also, she acknowledges the Stellenbosch Institute for Advanced Studies for a four-month fellowship that allowed her time and space to focus on final editing work.

Fatima is grateful to her Mum and late Dad, Reyhana and Mando, and her nieces, Imaan, Malaika, and Talia, the two ends of our family, who make this work possible and necessary. Also, she acknowledges the resources provided by the National Research Foundation Thuthuka Grant for the Legal Experience Project, which allowed a focus on religious authority.

General Index

Abdullah, Jamila bint, 200
Abdullah, Shifa bint, 33
Abou Bakr, Omaima, 213; background of,
    50–52; on justice, goodness, and
    generosity, 5, 46–47, 51–52; khutbah
    planning guide by, 213–14; and Sufi
    poetry, 51
Abu Bakr, 95
Abu Bakr, 'Ai'sha bint, 107
Abu Zayd, Nasr Hamid, 112, 113
Adawiyya, Shaykha Rabia, 79, 80
Adigüzel, Kerem, 56
'adl. See justice
Advaita Vedanta tradition, 101
A'ishah, 8, 11, 14, 125, 210; as khatibah, 32
al-Azhar University (Cairo): women-led
    prayers at, 125
Ali, Kecia, 114, 211
Ali, Yusuf, 59, 60, 64, 121
Ali ibn Abi Talib, 186, 190
Allah: as Divine Light, 34–35, 36, 92; human
    beings as Allah's representatives on
    earth, 61; our relationship with, 51,
    70, 75, 88–89, 107, 127, 164, 172
Ansari, Taner, 142
Anwar, Ghazala, 5; background of, 44–46;
    on compassion (rahmah) for queer
    strangers, 5, 38–44; faith journey of,
    45
Anwar, Zainah, 177; background of, 169–71;
    on justice and gender equality, 6,
    165–71
Arabi, Ibn, 35, 124
Asad, Muhammad, 50
Aseshananda, Swami, 101
Auws, 106–7

awliya. See friends/allies
Ayaz, 98–99
Ayubi, Zahra, 235

Baharudin, Sheena: background of, 85–87;
    on presenting her khutbah, 81–82, 85,
    87; spoken word poem by, 5, 82–85,
    86–87
Bawa Muhaiyaddeen, Shaykh Muhammad
    Raheem, 77, 79, 116–17; on marriage,
    195
Bawa Muhaiyaddeen fellowship, 45, 46
Beata Maria, Sister, 141–42
Biko, Stephen, 109, 137, 145
Black consciousness, 6; and activism in
    South Africa, 149–50; Blackness, 109,
    145–46; and intersectionality, 145–46;
    and the Soweto uprising, 137–40; and
    the spirit of Ramadan, 137–40
Black Muslim women (as single mothers):
    Islamic law as applied to, 158; so-
    ciety's obligation to, 157–64, 205
Buddhism, 45, 101

Center for Islamic Women's Studies (Co-
    logne), 58
Césaire, Aimé, 137
childbirth, 211; as engaged surrender, 20–21,
    25–26
China: women-led mosques in, 3, 15
Claremont Main Road Mosque (Cape Town),
    17, 19, 24, 25, 80, 110, 118, 148–50;
    segregation of men and women at,
    149
common good (maslahah), 5–6, 203–4
community-building, 174–75

compassion/mercy (*rahmah*), 5, 202; as em-
    bodied by women, 33; God as, 21; in
    marriage, 23, 182, 183, 196, 197; as
    portal to acceptance of queers and
    strangers, 38–42
Crenshaw, Kimberlé, 145

daily prayers (*salah*): led by women, 15, 17,
    32, 43–44. *See also* Friday prayers
David, Prophet: as human and imperfect,
    126–28
Davids, Imam, 150
Davis, Angela, 147
dhikr. See remembrance of God
disagreement (on personal, social, spiritual,
    and political levels): language as a
    means toward resolution of, 173–75;
    meeting the challenge of, 171–75, 204
discrimination: laws allowing for, 53; against
    Muslims, 128–30; against women, 50,
    117–18, 121. *See also* gender equality
Divine Light: Allah as, 34–35, 36; within
    human beings, 75–76, 77, 78
divorce: women's right to, 122–23, 200
du'a. See prayer of supplication
duality: of male and female, 35–36, 38

earth, the: as addressed in the Qur'an, 59–63
Effendi, Sefer, 101
Effendi, Shaykh Muzaffer Ozak, 95–96, 99,
    100, 101
Egypt: women's mosque presence in, 15
Eid, festivals of the: women's presence at,
    11–12, 110–11. *See also* Ramadan
Eid al-Adha, 26
Eid al-Fitr, 137
Eidgahs, 110–11, 142
embodied ethics, 24–25, 27–28
#End Outsourcing, 144
engaged surrender, 20–24, 26; childbirth as,
    20–21; marriage as, 22–24
environment. *See* earth, the
equality: as aspect of *tawhid*, 181, 184; and
    justice, 128–29. *See also* gender
    equality; social justice
expectations of others: relinquishing, 76–77

faith (*iman*), 90
Fallists, 144

Fariha, Shaykha, 37, 38, 101
fasting: Jesus on, 97; during Ramadan, 96–97
fatwas, 16, 108
Fees Must Fall (FMF) movement, 143–44,
    147
feminism. *See* Islamic feminism
feminist ontologies, 5, 202–3
Field of Dreams (film), 93
forgiveness: asking for, 23, 87–88; as given to
    Prophet David, 127–28
freedom: as aspect of *tawhid*, 181–82, 184
Friday prayers (*Jumu'ah salah*), 17, 18, 34,
    63; led by Ghazala Anwar, 45; led
    by Amira Quraishi, 92–94; led by
    Sa'diyya Shaikh, 80; led by amina
    wadud, 27, 118; at the Mariam Mosque,
    124; violence against Muslims at, 130
friends/allies (*awliya*): men and women as, 9
Fu-ad, Umm, 1

Gabriel (Jibril), 90; and Ramadan, 95; reve-
    lation brought by, 31
gender-based and sexual violence, 150–55,
    205; and male entitlement, 154–55;
    statistics on, 153, 157; women believed
    to be responsible for, 153–54
gendered subjectivity, 4
gender equality: as addressed in the Qur'an,
    10, 48–50, 54–57, 111–16, 121–22,
    167–68, 170–71; Ibn Arabi on, 35;
    argument surrounding, 165–66; con-
    sequences of, 55; historical context of,
    in Muslim culture, 113–14; in marriage,
    183, 184; in Muslim culture, 5, 6, 16,
    17, 25, 52–57, 141–43, 165–71; Nur
    Rofiah on, 73–74; as subject of poetry,
    86–87; root causes of of the lack of,
    175–76. *See also* gender-based and
    sexual violence; patriarchy
generosity: as essential virtue, 46–47
Ghazi, Abidullah, 191
Ghazi, Seemi: background of, 191–95; on
    marriage, 6; as student of Sufism,
    192; on wedding khutbahs, 187–95
Ghazi, Tasneema, 191
ghuraba. See queers and strangers
Gibran, Khalil, 100
Glassman, Roshi Tetsugen Bernard, 101
Goethe, Johann Wolfgang von, 188, 193

goodness/kindness (*ihsan*), 5, 46, 90
Graham, Edlín Ortiz. *See* Jerrahi, Shayka
 Amina Teslima al-
Great Mosque of Djenné (Mali), 43
Guadalupe, Virgin of, 101
Gueye, Shaykha Oumou Malik, 5; back-
 ground of, 36–38; on female figures
 in Islam, 31–36

Habiba, Umme, 175
Haddad, Tahir al-, 116
Haeri, Shaykh Fadhlalla, 77
Hafez, 188, 193, 198
Hajar, 8, 158; as model for Muslim women,
 207–9, 212
Halveti Jerrahi Order, 99, 100
haram (sanctified space in the Ka'bah), 8;
 women banned from, 14–15
Haron, Imam, 149
Harris, Rabia Terri: background of, 63–65;
 on the earth and the environment, 5,
 59–63; as *khatibah*, 64–65
Hazm, Ibn, 14
Hinduism, 45
Hixon, Lex. *See* Nur, Shaykh
homosexuality: and Islam, 45. *See also*
 LGBTQI+; queers and strangers
Hudaybiyyah, Treaty of, 32, 138
human and Divine: separation of, 105–6
human beings: as Allah's representatives on
 earth, 61; divine light within, 75–76,
 77; four births of, 69–72; uniqueness
 of, 76
humanity: gender-free unity of, 32, 35–36, 38
human rights: and gender equality, 165, 168,
 184; and Islamic law, 119; and religion,
 165–66. *See also* justice; social justice
Human Rights Watch, 153

Iblis, 52–53
idolatry: prohibition against, 182
ihsan. See goodness/kindness
imamahs (woman leading congregational
 prayer), 1–2, 17–18, 28; inner being
 of, 43–44; in the present day, 124–26;
 resistance to, 117–18; in the time
 of Muhammad, 124, 125. *See also*
 women's mosque presence
iman. See faith

Inclusive Mosque Initiative (IMI), 131–32, 133
Indonesia: as Muslim society, 73
inheritance, laws of: as addressed in the
 Qur'an, 160
Inner Circle, the, 169
Institute for Interreligious Pedagogy and
 Didactics, 57
Institute of Qur'anic Sciences (Indonesia), 73
Interfaith Council of religious leaders
 (Mexico), 101
intersectionality: and Black consciousness,
 145–46
Iqbal, Allama Muhammad, 175
Islam: as "engaged surrender," 20, 26; five
 pillars of, 90; and homosexuality, 45;
 and social justice, 117, 126, 128–29,
 131–32, 137, 143–50; as surrender, 46.
 See also Qur'an; women's mosque
 presence; *and names of contributors
 to this volume*
Islamic feminism, 4, 80, 165–68. *See also*
 gender equality
Islamic law (shari'ah), 6; as applied to Black
 single Muslim women, 158, 159–62;
 as applied to gender equality, 113, 117;
 as a code of ethics, 119–20, 121–22;
 disputation within, 106–8, 209–10;
 historical debates on women in
 mosques, 10–18; and interfaith
 marriage, 122–23; negative perceptions of, 119, 120–21; the Qur'an as
 source for, 119, 120, 121–22, 160–61;
 schools of, 107–8; on wealth and
 property, 160–61
Islamophobia: and social justice, 128–31
Isma'il, Prophet, 8

Jerrahi, Fariha Fatima al-, 101
Jerrahi, Pir Nureddin al-, 100, 101
Jerrahi, Shayka Amina Teslima al-: on
 Ramadan, 5, 94–99; spiritual journey
 of, 99–102
Jesus ('Isa), 97
Jilani, Abdul-Qadr, 79
jinns: as devils, 53
Jumu'ah salah. See Friday prayers
Junayd, 63
justice (*'adl*): as addressed in the Qur'an,
 57–58, 113–16, 143, 145–48, 204; as

justice (*'adl*) (*continued*)
    applied to Muslim women, 47–50, 52,
        56–57; and equality, 6, 128; as essential
        virtue, 46–47, 78, 80, 202; in marriage,
        196–97. *See also* Black consciousness;
        gender equality; social justice

Ka'bah (holy mosque in Mecca), 8, 14, 43, 49,
    191, 207–8
Kamali, Hashim, 120
Kardec, Allan, 100
Katz, Marion, 13, 16
Khadijah, 32, 190, 194
Khan, Leila: spiritual journey of, 148–50; on
    struggles for social justice in South
    Africa, 6, 24, 143–48
Khan, Nusrat Fatah Ali, 175
Khankan, Sherin: background of, 124–26;
    as *imamah*, 125; on Islamic law
    (shari'ah), 6, 119–23
khatibahs (women who deliver the khutbah),
    3–4, 17, 19, 27–28, 64–65, 133, 194,
    212. *See also names of contributors to
    this volume*
Khawlah: as model for Muslim women,
    106–7, 207, 209–10, 212
Khays, Fatima bint, 33
Khutbah al-Hajah, 17; as template for writing
    khutbahs, 213, 217–19
khutbahs: early history of, 5; guide to writ-
    ing, 213–19; on marriage, 184–85,
    187–95, 198–200, 205–6; by men, 26;
    theological and practical insights
    provided by, 201–6; by women, 3–6,
    17–18, 26–27, 176–77, 201–12. See
    also *khatibahs; and names of contrib-
    utors to this volume*
King, Martin Luther, Jr., 24
Kipling, Rudyard, 188
Krausen, Halima, 126
Krishnamurti, Jiddu, 100

Lamptey, Jerusha, 208
Last Day, the, 60, 63
leaders of worship. See *imamahs; khatibahs;*
    women's mosque presence
LGBTQI+: choose being either Muslim
    or gay, or lesbian, or bisexual, or
    transsexual, or queer, 167; inclusive

mosque initiative, 27; for the love of
    queer strangers, 38, 45, 46; narratives
    of Maryam through a queer lens, 235;
    perceived as threat to Islamic way of
    life, 86; queer Muslims, 86; sexual
    minorities in Malaysia, 86; stuck
    around human rights for lesbian, gay,
    transgendered, and queer folk, 209;
    trans and other nonheteronormative
    individuals, 145; and trans antagonism
    and misogyny 146; women, queer, and
    trans individuals, 208
light. *See* Divine Light
Lorde, Audre, 194

Madinah: Muslim community in, 8
Mahalakshmi, 45
Mahmud of Ghazna, Sultan, 98–99
Malaysia: Islam in, 166
Mandela, Nelson, 16, 24, 64
Mariam an-Nur, 101
Mariam Mosque, 120, 121, 122, 123, 124,
    125–26
marriage (*nikah*), 6; as addressed in the
    Qur'an, 182–84; attributes to culti-
    vate in, 195–98; as a contract, 183,
    198–200; as engaged surrender,
    22–24; equality in, 183, 196; and
    grace, 197; guiding principles for,
    183–84; as heart cultivation, 195–98;
    interfaith, 122–23; khutbahs for,
    184–85, 187–95, 198–200, 205–6;
    monogamy in, 184; and mutuality,
    183–84, 196; truth in, 196
Maryam, 101; in the *mihrab*, 9–10; as model
    for Muslim women, 207, 211–12
Mashinini, Tsietsi, 137
Masibi, Tshegofatso: as *khatibah*, 142–43;
    on Ramadan and Black consciousness,
    6, 137–40; on the spiritual and the
    political, 137–40; spiritual journey
    of, 141–43
masjid. *See* mosques; women's mosque
    presence
maslahah. See common good
Maxwele, Chumani, 149
Meer, Ayesha, 109
Mian, Aziz, 175
mihrab. See prayer niche

minbar. *See* women's mosque presence; *and names of contributors to this volume*

Mir-Hosseini, Ziba, 112–13, 114

monogamy, 184

monotheism in Islam. See *tawhid*

mosques: aesthetics of, 42–43; and connection to nature, 43; segregation of men and women in, 149, 169. *See also* women's mosque presence

Mu'awwadh, Al-Rubayyi bint, 200

Muhammad, Prophet, 3; asked a woman to lead prayer,125; and marital discord, 112; as Rasulullah, 106–7, 108, 148; revelations received by, 10, 31, 32, 58, 83, 137; as source of *rahmah*, 35–40, 72; on women's presence in the mosque, 7, 8, 10, 11, 32–33

mujadila. See woman who argues

Mulia, Musdah: on marriage, 6, 181–84

Müller, Rabeya: background of, 57–59; on gender equality, 5, 52–57; as *imamah*, 58; as teacher, 57–58; on the Satanic Principle, 52–54, 57

Mumin Foundation, 37

Musa, Prophet, 82, 130; supplication of, 172–74

musallah. See prayer space

Muslim community (*ummah*): and Islamophobia, 128–31; social transformation in, 186; violence against, 129–30, 204–5. *See also* Qur'an; Sufi Muslims; women's mosque presence

Muslim Women's Freedom Tour, 118

Muslim Youth Movement, 149

Muthana, Shaykha Fatima bint, 35

mutuality: as aspect of *tawhid*, 181, 184

Nair, Roshila, 213; khutbah planning guide by, 214–17

New Zealand: violence against Muslims in, 130

Ngaji KGI (Keadilan Gender Islam), 74

Ngubane, Sindile Amina: background of, 162–64; on single Black mothers, 6, 157–64

nikah. See marriage

Nur, Shaykh (Lex Hixon), 100; on fasting, 97; on Ramadan, 98; as spiritual teacher, 100, 101

Omar, Imam Rashied, 25, 148

Parveen, Abida, 175

Patel, Nafisa: background of, 155–57; on gender-based violence, 6, 150–57

patriarchy: based on interpretation of the Qur'an, 5, 6, 49–50, 56–58, 111–16; changing gender norms as challenge to, 27, 52, 53–54, 126; as injustice, 57–59, 80, 114, 170, 202–3; and Islamic law, 12

peace: and social justice, 126–31

Perguruan Tinggi Ilmu al-Qur'an (PTIQ/Indonesia), 73

poetry: as part of a wedding ceremony, 188–89

poets: social responsibility of, 86–87

polygyny, 74, 123

prayer niche (*mihrab*), 9–10

prayer of supplication (*du'a*), 24, 92, 94

prayer space (*musallah*), 2, 7, 17

Progressive Muslim Union, 118

Qadri Rifai Ansari *tariqah*, 142

queers and strangers (*ghuraba*): compassion extended to, 38–42; khutbah for, 38–44

Qur'an: aesthetic power of, 51; critical interpretations of, 4; feminist readings of, 4, 167–68, 170–71; gendered Muslim practice as spelled out in, 9; gender equality as addressed in, 10, 48–50, 54–57, 111–16, 121–22, 167–68, 170–71; gender-fluid language as used in, 40–42; as guidance for a just and moral life, 46–50; as guidance for a spiritual journey, 88–90; justice as addressed in, 57–58, 113–16, 143, 145–48; marriage as addressed in, 182–84; patriarchal exegesis of, 5, 6, 111–16, 170; as source for Islamic law, 119, 120, 121–22, 160–61; vices forbidden by, 47

Quraishi, Amira: background of, 92–94; as Muslim chaplain, 93; on unknowing and the spiritual journey, 5, 87–92

Qutb, Sayyid, 151

race, 137, 146, 182, 204

racial inequality. *See* Black consciousness; South Africa

racism; and colonialism, 149; empowering to
resist, 129; fighting against, 141–42;
intersecting with sexism, 79; and
intersectionality, 145–46. *See also*
Black consciousness

rahmah. See compassion/mercy

Rahman, Fazlur, 112

Ramadan: and Black consciousness, 6,
137–40; fasting during, 96–97; as
sacred time, 94–99; Shaykha Amina
al-Jerrahi on, 5, 94–99; Shaykha
Fariha al-Jerrahi on, 96; Shaykh Nur
on, 98; as time for reflection, 138–40

rape. *See* gender-based and sexual violence

Razi, Fakhr al–Din, 47, 115

receptivity: importance of, 32, 75

Reda, Nevin, 9–10

remembrance of God (*dhikr*), 21, 45, 93, 157,
192, 193

Rhodes Must Fall (RMF) movement, 143–44,
147, 150; removal of statue of, 144,
149

Rida, Rashid, 16

Rilke, Rainer Maria, 189, 193

ritual purification (*wudu*), 11

Rofiah, Nur: background of, 72–74; on the
four human births, 5, 69–72; as lecturer in Qur'anic *tafsir*, 73–74

Rumi, Mawlana, 91, 99, 192, 194

Rumminger, Jana, 114

Rushd, Ibn, 125

Saad, Ibn, 124

Sabri brothers, 175

Sadeghi, Benham, 12

salah. See daily prayers

Satanic Principle, 52–54, 57

Sayeed, Asma, 11

secular Muslims, 120

Seedat, Fatima, 5–6, 80; background of,
109–11; on dealing with difference,
105–8; on marriage and the marriage
contract, 198–200

sexual violence. *See* gender-based and sexual
violence

Shah, Baba Buleh, 175

Shaikh, Sa'diyya, 4, 5, 6; background of,
79–80; on divine love and marriage,

195–98; on the patriarchal interpretation of the Qur'an, 114; on spirituality
and everyday experience, 74–78; on
tafsir of praxis, 4, 206, 225

Shaikh, Shamima, 149

shari'ah. *See* Islamic law

Sharmani, Mulki Al-, 114

Simmons, Gwendolyn Zoharah: on
patriarchal exegesis of the Qur'an, 6,
111–16; spiritual journey of, 116–19

slavery: abolition of, 116

social justice, 6, 204; and Black consciousness, 137–40, 143–48; and Islam, 117,
126, 128–29, 131–32, 137, 143–50; in
Islamophobic environments, 128–31;
and jihad, 146; and spiritual peace,
126–31

soul: as genderless and unified, 31, 32, 35, 54,
112, 202; arriving into being, 105;
being soft on, 173; cleansed, 96;
created, 189; as feminine, 112; in the
Qur'an, 128, 161, 218

South Africa: anti-apartheid struggle in,
16–17; Black consciousness movement in, 137–40, 143–48; khutbah by
women in, 5, 18, 19, 25–27, 64, 80,
110, 124, 137–40, 143–48, 157–62;
social justice in, 6, 24. 143–48; student
protests in, 143–50; amina wadud in,
24, 25, 110, 111, 124; women's mosque
presence in, 16–17, 79–80, 109–11

Soweto Action Committee, 139

Soweto Students League, 139

Soweto uprising (1976), 137

subjectivity: cultivation of, 201, 203; the
nature of, 5, 70, 90, 203

Sufi Muslims, 36–37, 51, 76, 77–78, 79, 100,
116–17, 192

Sufism: and the unified soul, 32

sunnah (traditions and practices of Muhammad): as applied to vulnerable
members of the community, 162;
following, 93; women in, 32–33

Surah al-An'am, 39

Surah al-Baqarah, 91

Surah al-Infitar, 154

Surah al-Inshirah, 21–22

Surah al-Maidah, 130

Surah al-Mujadila, 106–7, 209
Surah al-Mulk, 90
Surah al-Nisa, 121, 184
Surah al-Rahman, 51, 188, 193, 195
Surah al-Shura, 130
Surah al-Takwir, 150–51, 155, 157
Surah al-Zalzalah: interpretations of, 59–62, 65
Surah Taha, 81, 172

Tabari, al-, 49, 125
tafsir (critical interpretation of the Qur'an), 4; of experience, 19; of possibility 4, 206–11; of praxis, 4, 206, 225; reflections on, 201–6; of women's experiences, 19. *See also names of contributors to this volume*
Taha, Mahmoud Mohammed, 113
Ta'if, city of, 138
Takata, Roshi Ejo, 101
Taking Islam to the People (TIP), 17, 111, 142
Tauqir, Tamsila: as *khatibah*, 133; as social justice activist, 131–33; on social justice and spiritual peace, 6, 126–31
tawhid (unity of God in Islam), 70; as applied to marriage, 181–84
Taymiyya, Ibn, 13
Tha'laba, Khawlah bint, 106–7, 209–10
Tijani Sufi *tariqah* (order), 36–37
truth: in marriage, 195–96

Umar, Caliph, 58, 159; and debate surrounding women's mosque presence, 10–11
Umays, Asma bint, 33, 48
ummah. See Muslim community
Umm Salamah, 2, 10, 32, 48, 125, 210
Umm Waraqa, 125
Universal Declaration of Human Rights, 165
University of Cape Town (UCT): struggle for social justice at, 144

violence: against Muslim communities, 129–30, 204–5; and resistance to

oppression, 147–48. *See also* gender-based and sexual violence

wadud, amina, 5, 17, 18, 80, 118, 146, 207, 213; background of, 24–25; on embodied ethics, 24–25, 27; on engaged surrender, 20–24; in South Africa, 24, 25, 26–27, 110, 124, 148
wedding khutbahs, 184–85, 187–95
Welchman, Lynn, 116
woman who argues (*mujadila*), 6, 106–7, 209–10
women: as authority figures in the present day, 3–4, 38, 80; as authority figures in the time of Muhammad, 32–33; discrimination against, 50, 117–18, 121, 175–76; as equal to men, 35–36, 48–50; legal rights of, 159–61; as potential threat, 11; violence against, 150–55. *See also* Black Muslim women; gender equality; Hajar; Khawlah; Islamic feminism; leaders of worship; Maryam
women's mosque presence: in China, 3, 15, 33; conditions applied to, 13; debate surrounding, 7–18; defense of, 14; in Egypt, 15; expansion of, 18; hadith relating to, 9, 11–12, 13, 14; inequities relating to, 49–50; in Iran, 33; Muslim law relating to, 11–15; return of, 15–16; opposition to, 10–11, 13–14; revelation relating to, 10; in South Africa, 16–17, 148–49; in the time of Muhammad, 7, 8, 10, 32–33. See also *imamah*s; *khatibahs;* women; *and names of contributors to this volume*
wudu. *See* ritual purification

Zafar, Wahid, 175
Zahra, Fatima, 33
Zamakhshari, 47, 49
Zeb, Farah, 169; background of, 175–77; on gender inequality, 175–77; on opening the heart, 6, 171–75

Index of Qur'anic Verses

Q. 2:30	35	Q. 7:29	9
Q. 2:31	105	Q. 7:31	9
Q. 2:85	48	Q. 7:52	119
Q. 2:114	9	Q. 9:71	9, 48, 167, 171
Q. 2:115	87	Q. 11:85	47
Q. 2:152	162	Q. 13:28	92
Q. 2:156	105	Q. 15:91	48
Q. 2:186	75	Q. 16:61	60
Q. 2:187	167, 183, 196	Q. 16:90	46, 114, 115, 219
Q. 2:229	200	Q. 17:35	50
Q. 2:231	161	Q. 17:44	61, 62
Q. 2:241	160	Q. 17:70	146
Q. 2:255	62	Q. 17:82	39, 42
Q. 2:286	128	Q. 17:110	33
Q. 3:18	55	Q. 20:2	81
Q. 3:37	9	Q. 20:8	41
Q. 3:43	9	Q. 20:25–28	82, 172–73
Q. 3:102	217	Q. 20:29–33	174
Q. 3:103	164, 190,	Q. 20:44	130
Q. 3:104	149	Q. 20:120–21	54
Q. 3:195	42, 48, 167, 171	Q. 21:37	89
Q. 4:1	54, 112, 184, 218	Q. 21:47	47
Q. 4:3	170, 184	Q. 21:107	31, 39, 72
Q. 4:11	160	Q. 22:5	167
Q. 4:19	123, 183	Q. 22:25	9
Q. 4:21	183	Q. 22:65	62
Q. 4:32	160	Q. 24:11–20	210
Q. 4:34	55, 56, 112, 116, 121	Q. 24:35	34, 92
Q. 4:35	56	Q. 25:73	49
Q. 4:43	9	Q. 26:88–89	42
Q. 4:124	41	Q. 26:182	50
Q. 4:135	80, 115, 143, 146, 148	Q. 30:21	23, 111, 115, 171, 183,
Q. 5:8	57, 113, 130	Q. 30:31–32	108
Q. 6:12	39	Q. 31:14	69
Q. 6:38	60	Q. 31:27	60
Q. 6:115	131	Q. 33:35	10, 48, 165, 167, 210
Q. 7:11–12	52	Q. 33:70–71	88, 218

Q. 33:72	70	Q. 58	106–7, 209
Q. 36:36	167,	Q. 59:18	41
Q. 38:24–26	127	Q. 59:21	91
Q. 42:17	47	Q. 65:1	161
Q. 42:40	130	Q. 67:28–29	90
Q. 46:15	69	Q. 78:8	167
Q. 47:24	48	Q. 81:8	151
Q. 49:10	181	Q. 81:17	155
Q. 49:13	105, 122, 189	Q. 81:18	92, 155
Q. 50:7	167	Q. 81:26	94
Q. 51:49	167	Q. 81:28	155
Q. 51:56	182	Q. 82:6	154
Q. 53:45	167	Q. 83:1–3	50
Q. 55:1–3	31, 187	Q. 87:1	174
Q. 55:5–9	43, 187	Q. 89:27–30	42
Q. 55:17–20	188	Q. 94:1–8	21
Q. 55:60	51, 90	Q. 95:4–6	71
Q. 57:4	93	Q. 96.1	31, 33
Q. 57:25	115	Q. 99:1–8	59

Index of Hadiths

It is reported that a companion said to
    the Prophet, "Ya Rasul Allah, I
    was about to slaughter a sheep
    but was overcome by *rahmah.*"
    The Prophet replied, "Since you
    took *rahmah* on the sheep, Allah
    will take *rahmah* on you
    twicefold."   40

The first involves Umm Salamah, a wife
    of the Prophet, who once heard
    him calling from the minbar
    "O people!" and prepared to
    respond to the call, only to be
    cautioned by her maid who said,
    "He called upon the men, not
    the women." Umm Salamah
    sharply replied, "Verily, I *am*
    from the *people.*"   48

The second account also involves Umm
    Salamah, who inquired of the
    Prophet whether the reward for
    the *hijrah* is bestowed only upon
    men. . . . This was the occasion
    of the revelation where God
    states: "I will not let the work of
    any male or female be in vain /
    Each of you is like, and from,
    the other." (Q. 3:195)   48

The third occasion of revelation
    involves Asma' bint 'Umays,
    who, having returned from
    Habasha (Ethiopia), asked the
    Prophet's wives, "Did a reve-
lation descend concerning us?"
    to which they said no, so she
    went to the Prophet and
    exclaimed, "O God's Prophet,
    women are in such failure and
    loss because they are not men-
    tioned in righteousness as the
    men are mentioned." And thus
    verse Q. 33:35 was revealed.   48

"I am as My servant thinks I am. I am
    with him when he makes men-
    tion of Me." (*Hadith Qudsi*)   50

"The heavens and earth do not contain
    Me, but the heart of my faithful
    servant contains Me." (*Hadith
    Qudsi*)   75

"Who of my servants are calling to me?
    I will respond to them." (*Hadith
    Qudsi*)   88

"When you know yourself, you know
    Allah."   88

In a hadith, the Prophet Muhammad
    responds to the angel Jibril
    (Gabriel), questioning him about
    the meanings of *islam, iman,*
    and *ihsan.* The five pillars are
    the cornerstones of Islam. . . .
    Iman is faith in Allah, the angels,
    the books, the prophets, and the
    Last Day. . . . *Ihsan* [is] "beauti-
    ful presence."   90

"The children of Adam misunderstand Me when they complain against Time, for I am Time . . . I alone cause the day of knowledge to follow the night of ignorance." (*Hadith Qudsi*)   95

"Whoever provides the food for a fasting person to break his fast with, then for him is the same reward as is (the fasting person's), without anything being diminished from the reward of the fasting person."   95

"I was a hidden Treasure, and desired to be known; thus I brought forth creation, that I may be known." (*Hadith Qudsi*)   105, 172

"O My servants, I have forbidden oppression [*al-ẓulm*] for Myself and have made it forbidden amongst you, so do not oppress one another." (*Hadith Qudsi*)   128

The hadith tradition tells us that on the day of judgment, when all people will try to save their own individual souls, saying "*nafsi, nafsi*" (myself, myself), our Prophet's call to God for Mercy will be for his community: "*ummati, ummati*" (my community, my community).   138

"Take one step toward Me, I will take ten steps toward you. Walk toward Me, I will run toward you." (*Hadith Qudsi*)   163

"The believers in their mutual kindness, compassion and sympathy are just like one body. When one of the limbs suffers, the whole body responds to it with wakefulness and fever."   163